AWESOME ALMANAC™

INDIANA

SEAL OF THE STATE OF INDIANA 1816

**Created by
Jean F. Blashfield**

**Compiled and Written by
Nancy Jacobson**

B&B Publis

B & B Publishing, Inc.
P. O. Box 393
Fontana, Wisconsin 53125

Editor – **Jean B. Black**
Photo Researcher – **Margie Benson**
Computer Design and Production Manager – **Dave Conant**
Computer Specialist and Indexer – **Marilyn Magowen**
Cover Design – **Gary Hurst**

Publisher's Cataloging in Publication

Blashfield, Jean F.
    Awesome almanac—Indiana / Jean F. Blashfield.
    p. cm.
    Includes index.
    Preassigned LCCN: 92-074708
    ISBN 1-880190-04-4

1. Indiana—Miscellanea. 2. Indiana—History. 3. Almanacs,
American—Indiana. I. Title.

F524.B53 1993

                    977.2'003
                    QBI92-20125

Printed in the United States of America

93 94 95 96 97   5 4 3 2 1

AWESOME ALMANAC is a trademark of B&B Publishing, Inc.

ATTENTION SCHOOLS AND BUSINESSES:
    This book is available at quantity discounts with bulk purchases for educational, business, or sales promotional use. For information, please write to B&B Publishing, Inc., P.O. Box 393, Fontana, WI 53125

DISTRIBUTOR TO THE BOOK TRADE:
    Publishers Distribution Service, 6893 Sullivan Road, Grawn, MI 49637

TABLE OF CONTENTS

Indiana, the Hoosier State.................5
   It's an Indiana Fact
   Indiana's Government
   How Many Hoosiers?
   Indiana: Land of Plenty
   Hoosier Counties

Natural Heritage 15
   In the Beginning
   Indiana Dunes
   Going Underground
   Endangered Species
   Lakes and Rivers
   The Environment
   Hoosier Parks
   Wildlife Preservation
   Hoosier Flora
   Natural Disasters

Old Indianny 29
   Indiana Indians
   The French Invasion
   Indiana Territory
   Heads of State
   The Presidents
   The Political Arena
   Historical Firsts
   Women in History
   The Battlefield
   Underground Railroad

Hoosier Hamlets..................49
   Under Construction
   Indianapolis: The City
   Claims to Fame
   R & R Hoosier Style
   What's in a Name?
   Disastrous Events

In the Spotlight..................61
   Actors and Actresses
   Awards and Honors
   Indiana in the Movies
   Behind the Camera
   Comics, Clowns & Circuses

   Singers, Musicians & Their Songs
   Indiana on TV

Making It in Indiana 73
   Birth of the Automobile
   Industrial Stronghold
   With Heads in the Clouds
   Indiana Farming
   Inventions, Firsts & Great Ideas
   Made in Indiana
   Hoosier Communicators
   Riding the Rails

The Sporting Life..................87
   Hoosier Hysteria
   Go! Zebras! Go!
   Knight Time in Indiana
   Great Indiana Cagers
   Indiana Pro Basketball
   Basketball Hall of Famers
   The Indianapolis 500
   Take Me Out to the Ball Game
   Baseball Hall of Famers
   Indiana's Football
   Hoosiers in Sports

Creative Indiana 107
   A Verse and a Rhyme
   Pen and Ink
   Hoosier Winners
   On the Lighter Side
   On Stage
   Top Designers
   With Brush and Canvas

Indiana Encore..................119
   Famous Hoosiers
   Nobel Recipients
   Infamous Hoosiers
   Indiana's Higher Education
   Lifestyles

Indiana Day by Day..................131

Index 140

Union Station in Indianapolis

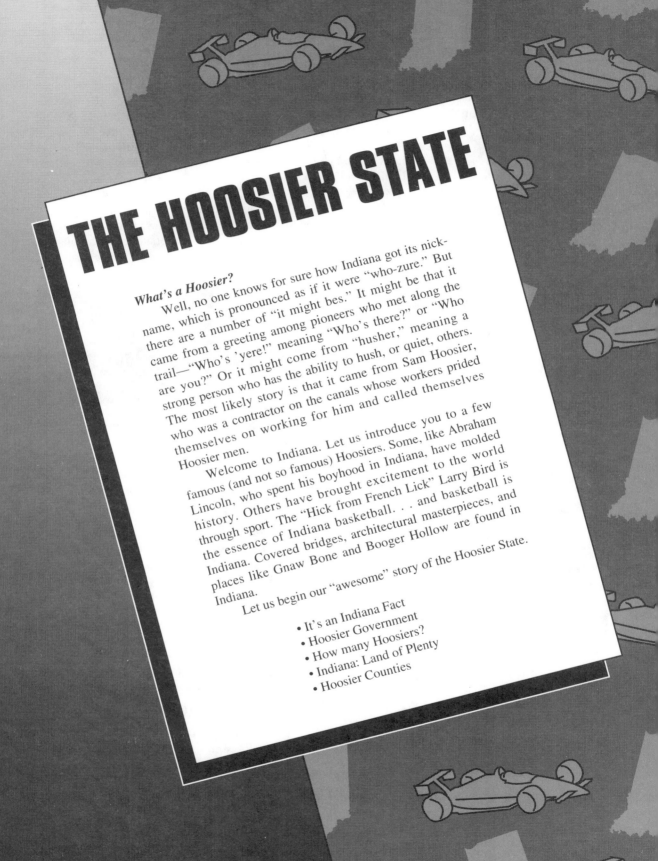

THE HOOSIER STATE

What's a Hoosier?

Well, no one knows for sure how Indiana got its nickname, which is pronounced as if it were "who-zure." But there are a number of "it might bes." It might be that it came from a greeting among pioneers who met along the trail—"Who's 'yere!" meaning "Who's there?" or "Who are you?" Or it might come from "husher," meaning a strong person who has the ability to hush, or quiet, others. The most likely story is that it came from Sam Hoosier, who was a contractor on the canals whose workers prided themselves on working for him and called themselves Hoosier men.

Welcome to Indiana. Let us introduce you to a few famous (and not so famous) Hoosiers. Some, like Abraham Lincoln, who spent his boyhood in Indiana, have molded history. Others have brought excitement to the world through sport. The "Hick from French Lick" Larry Bird is the essence of Indiana basketball. . . and basketball is Indiana. Covered bridges, architectural masterpieces, and places like Gnaw Bone and Booger Hollow are found in Indiana.

Let us begin our "awesome" story of the Hoosier State.

- It's an Indiana Fact
- Hoosier Government
- How many Hoosiers?
- Indiana: Land of Plenty
- Hoosier Counties

IT'S AN INDIANA FACT

Why Indiana?

The "Land of the Indians" is the Latin meaning of Indiana. Miami, Wyandot, Shawnee, Ottawa, Chippewa, Piankashaw, Wea, and Kickapoo all found refuge on Indiana soils in the 18th and early 19th centuries after being pushed by white settlers in the East. It was a land of Indians. (see p. 30)

American crossroads

"Crossroads of America" was adopted as Indiana's motto in 1937. The state was the population center of the U.S. at the time of the motto's adoption. Today, it remains an appropriate motto because of the highways intersecting Indiana. It has more than any other state.

Indiana statehood and its flag

On December 11, 1816, Indiana becomes the 19th state admitted to the Union. Its flag was adopted in 1917. Nineteen gold stars and a gold torch are found on the blue field. The rays reaching toward the stars represent the far-reaching influence of liberty and enlightenment which is represented by the torch. The stars in the outer circle are the thirteen original states. The inner circle stars represent the next five states admitted to the Union. The largest star stand for Indiana.

Indiana's make up
- Average altitude: 700 feet
- Highest point: Franklin Township in Wayne County—1,257 feet
- Lowest point: Ohio River, Posey County—320 feet
- Largest lake: Lake Wawasee, Kosciusko County
- Most important rivers: White and Wabash rivers
- Geographical center: Boone, 14 miles north-northwest of Indianapolis
- Largest body of water: Monroe Reservoir
- Three regions: Lake country (north) contains watershed area for two huge waterways, the St. Lawrence and the Mississippi; agricultural plain (center); hills and lowlands area (southern)

How big is Indiana?
Except for Hawaii, Indiana is the smallest state west of the Appalachian Mountains. Indiana is 265 miles long (north to south) and 140 miles wide (east to west). Its area is 35,932 square miles. Its water is 253 square miles.

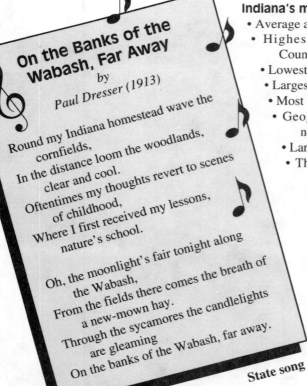

On the Banks of the Wabash, Far Away
by
Paul Dresser (1913)

Round my Indiana homestead wave the cornfields,
In the distance loom the woodlands, clear and cool.
Oftentimes my thoughts revert to scenes of childhood,
Where I first received my lessons, nature's school.

Oh, the moonlight's fair tonight along the Wabash,
From the fields there comes the breath of a new-mown hay.
Through the sycamores the candlelights are gleaming
On the banks of the Wabash, far away.

State song

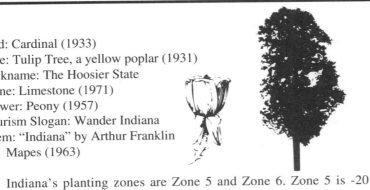

Bird: Cardinal (1933)
Tree: Tulip Tree, a yellow poplar (1931)
Nickname: The Hoosier State
Stone: Limestone (1971)
Flower: Peony (1957)
Tourism Slogan: Wander Indiana
Poem: "Indiana" by Arthur Franklin
　　　Mapes (1963)

Indiana symbols

**Planting time
in Indiana**

Indiana's planting zones are Zone 5 and Zone 6. Zone 5 is -20 degrees to -10 degrees and covers the upper two-thirds of the state, spring is April 15 to June 15. Fall is September 1 through October 15. Zone 6 is -10 degrees to 0 degrees. The southern-most third of the state is in this zone. Spring is March 15 to May 15 and fall is September 15 to November 1.

The Old National Road

Indiana can quite logically be divided in two parts, the northern and southern. The Old National Road, which was first surveyed in 1832, is the dividing line. The road crosses Indiana from Richmond through Indianapolis to Terre Haute. The name Old National Road has given way to a less than interesting title of Interstate 70. The Interstate marks a definite distinction between the two parts. North of the Interstate, Indiana is fairly flat and fertile. South of the highway, the state starts to get hilly and the number of rivers increases. The southern limit of the last glacier to spread from the Arctic down over North America approximately matches this dividing line.

HOOSIER GOVERNMENT

Who's in charge

The leader of the pack is Indiana's governor. The legislative power goes to the General Assembly which consists of a 50-member Senate and a 100-member House of Representatives. The governor is elected for a term of four years and can only serve eight out of every twelve years. The Senate is elected for a term of four years and the House of Representative for two years.

The Judicial Branch of Indiana has a five-justice Supreme Court, a twelve-judge Court of Appeals, and circuit courts. The General Assembly also has the power to create other courts. Supreme Court justices are appointed by the governor for an initial two-year term. At the completion of the two years and, after a yes-no retention ballot decides if they are retained, the justices serve a ten-year term. The Court of Appeals selection and term are the same as the Supreme Court. The circuit courts consist of judges elected by the voters for six-year terms.

First Capital: Corydon

General William Henry Harrison originally owned Corydon, naming it after a shepherd in his favorite song, "Pastoral Elegy." The town was later sold by Harrison to Henry Heth who made it the seat of Harrison County in 1808. A courthouse was built there in 1811. On May 1, 1813, the Indiana territorial seat was moved from Vincennes to Corydon. The courthouse became the first State Capitol building when 44 delegates to the Indiana Constitutional Convention named the city as the Indiana capital in June of 1816. It remained the capital until 1825 when the government was moved to Indianapolis.

The Corydon State Capitol is not among the most stately of buildings, but it has endured. Built of rough blue limestone from a nearby quarry, it is now a Hoosier historical landmark.

Today's capital

In January 1820, the legislature at Corydon chose the site of Fall Creek as the new state capital because of its central location. The General Assembly approved the location in 1821 and named it Indianapolis. Albert Ralston who had helped lay out Washington, D.C., completed the task of surveying Indianapolis. "Indianapolis" is the Latin word for Indian (*Indiana*) and the Greek name for city (*polis*). Indiana's state records and treasury were transported from Corydon to Indianapolis in 1824. The journey took 10 days to carry Indiana's most precious possessions. First State Capitol building construction, which began in 1832, was finally completed in 1835.

First governor

Indiana's first governor was Jonathan Jennings. Among the governor's accomplishments was sending commissioners to St. Mary's in Ohio to negotiate with the Indians in 1818. The outcome of the meeting left the middle third of Indiana, south of the Wabash River, free of Indian titles, opening up the land for settlement.

Heads of state

Governor: Birch Evans Bayh III, Democrat (to Jan. 1 1997)
Lt. Governor: Frank O'Bannon, Democrat (to Jan 1997)
Sec. of State: Joseph H. Hogsett, Democrat (to Dec 1994)
Treas. Majorie H. O'Laughlin, Republican (to Feb 1995)
Atty. General Pam Carter, Democrat (to Jan 1997)
Auditor: Ann G. Devore, Republican (to Dec 1994)

HOW MANY HOOSIERS?

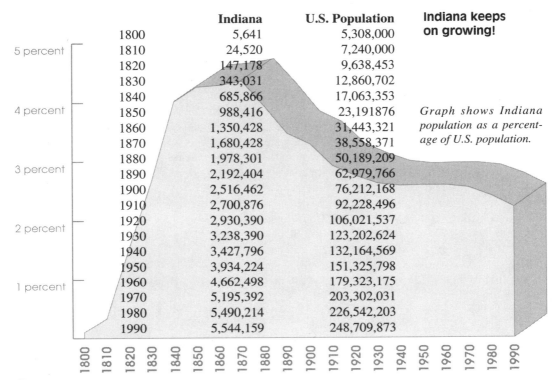

	Indiana	U.S. Population
1800	5,641	5,308,000
1810	24,520	7,240,000
1820	147,178	9,638,453
1830	343,031	12,860,702
1840	685,866	17,063,353
1850	988,416	23,191876
1860	1,350,428	31,443,321
1870	1,680,428	38,558,371
1880	1,978,301	50,189,209
1890	2,192,404	62,979,766
1900	2,516,462	76,212,168
1910	2,700,876	92,228,496
1920	2,930,390	106,021,537
1930	3,238,390	123,202,624
1940	3,427,796	132,164,569
1950	3,934,224	151,325,798
1960	4,662,498	179,323,175
1970	5,195,392	203,302,031
1980	5,490,214	226,542,203
1990	5,544,159	248,709,873

Indiana keeps on growing!

Graph shows Indiana population as a percentage of U.S. population.

The 1990 census shows how diverse Indiana has become in its population. The breakdown of the 1990 census shows 2,688,181 males and 2,855,978 females living in the Hoosier State. A further breakdown includes 5,020,700 Caucasians which is 90.6 percent of the population. African Americans are 7.8 percent (432,092), American Indians, Eskimos, and Aleutians are 0.2 percent (12,720), Asians or Pacific Islanders 0.7 percent (37,617), and Hispanics are 1.8 percent (98,788) of the population. The median age of all Hoosiers is 32.8.

Diversity in today's population

INDIANA'S 10 LARGEST CITIES

1. Indianapolis - 731,327
2. Fort Wayne - 173,072
3. Evansville - 126,272
4. Gary - 116,646
5. South Bend - 105, 511
6. Hammond - 84,236
7. Muncie - 71,035
8. Bloomington - 60,633
9. Anderson - 59,459
10. Terre Haute - 57,483

INDIANA: LAND OF PLENTY

A microcosm of the United States

Indiana has a balance between agriculture and industry. It lies right on the heaviest east-west traffic route, and has many topographical variations which make it not your typical corn-belt state. It is known as a microcosm of the United States. One could even call it a "Jack-of-all-trades."

Indiana's industry

Indiana's principal industries are manufacturing, wholesale and retail trade, government, services, and agriculture. The state's primary manufactured goods are steel, transportation equipment, electrical and electronic equipment, non-electrical machinery, plastics, chemical products, pharmaceuticals, and foods. It is a leader in musical instrument production (see p. 81).

Percent of U.S. manufacturing employment:
1972 - 3.70 percent
1977 - 3.60 percent
1982 - 3.06 percent
1987 - 3.18 percent
1988 - 3.20 percent
1989 - 3.29 percent
1990 - 3.27 percent

East Chicago Harbor and Inland Steel

Any port in the harbor

Indiana's 41-mile Lake Michigan waterfront is one of world's greatest industrial centers. Chief ports are Burns Harbor, Portage; Southwind Maritime, Mt. Vernon; Clark Maritime, Jeffersonville.

Although Indiana ranks 38th in the nation for land area, agriculture is a major industry in the state. Corn production tops the list. Hogs, dairy products, and soybeans also rank high. Other home-grown products are rye, oats, winter wheat, tomatoes for processing, apples, popcorn, spearmint, peppermint, and tobacco.

Agriculturally speaking

At the turn of the century, round barns became a fad and Fulton County, Indiana, was full of them. There are only nine still standing. The purpose of a round barn was to make feeding livestock more efficient. The farmer only had to bring feed into one central station. But round barns were hard to heat and light. Soon the idea lost popularity among farmers. Construction of the barns ended in 1924. Today, the round barn is a favorite subject for artists and photo buffs.

The round barn

Indiana coal ranks 10th in the nation. Its coal reserves (bituminous) are primarily in the southwestern part of the state. In 1991 it produced a total of 31,284 tons. Its highest production in history occurred in 1984 (37,540 tons).

Petroleum and natural gas reserves are located in the central part of the state, while limestone comes mainly from the south-central part.

Mother Earth's contribution

A tree that bears shoes?

Trees usually bear fruit, nuts, or cones. But a large white oak bearing 150 pairs of shoes is definitely unusual. Five miles south of Milltown in Crawford County stands a shoe-bearing oak. Conjecture from local people has it that someone probably didn't want to throw away a good and "loyal" pair of old shoes and so chose to hang them on the tree. Others followed. No one knows how long the custom has existed, but the living shoe tree has been a landmark for at least 25 years.

INDIANA COUNTIES

Brown County is considered one of Indiana's most beautiful. Billboards are a definite "no-no." Air pollution is nonexistent. It is the home of Brown County State Park, Yellowwood State Forest, and a portion of Hoosier National Forest.

Most unusual names have been given to the towns and villages scattered throughout the county—try Booger Holler, Slippery Elm Chute Road, Gnaw Bone, Scarce O'Fat Ridge, Milk-Sick Bottoms, Bear Wallow Hill, and Bean Blossom. When the fall season hits, around 100,000 people visit Nashville (the county seat) on weekends.

A natural beauty

Indiana has no counties among the 50 largest in the U.S., according to the 1990 census. The largest county in the state is Marion with 797,159 residents. The first county created was Knox on June 20, 1790. The last was Tipton on January 15, 1844. The following table tells the story of Indiana's counties:

County	Population	County Seat	Sq. Mi.	Created	Named After
Adams	31,095	Decatur	340	2/7/1835	John Quincy Adams
Allen	300,836	Fort Wayne	659	12/17/1823	Col. John Allen
Bartholomew	63,657	Columbus	409	1/8/1821	Gen. Joseph Bartholomew (Battle of Tippecanoe)
Benton	9,441	Fowler	407	2/18/1840	Thomas H. Benton (Senator of Missouri)
Blackford	14,067	Hartford City	166	2/15/1838	Isaac Newton Blackford (Judge)
Boone	38,147	Lebanon	423	1/29/1830	Daniel Boone
Brown	14,080	Nashville	312	2/4/1836	Gen. Jacob Brown
Carroll	18,809	Delphi	372	1/7/1828	Charles Carroll (Signed Declaration of Independence)
Cass	38,413	Logansport	414	12/18/1828	Lewis Cass (Michigan Territorial Governor)
Clark	87,777	Jeffersonville	376	2/3/1801	Gen. George Rogers Clark
Clay	24,705	Brazil	360	2/12/1825	Kentucky Senator Henry Clay
Clinton	30,974	Frankfort	405	1/29/1830	New York Gov. DeWitt Clinton
Crawford	9,914	English	307	1/29/1818	Wm. Harris Crawford (Secretary of War)
Daviess	27,533	Washington	432	12/24/1816	Joseph Hamilton Daviess
Dearborn	38,835	Lawrenceburg	307	3/7/1803	Maj. Gen. Henry Dearborn
Decatur	23,645	Greensburg	373	12/31/1821	Naval hero Stephen Decatur
De Kalb	35,324	Auburn	364	2/7/1835	French Gen. Johann De Kalb
Delaware	119,659	Muncie	392	1/26/1827	Delaware Indians
Dubois	36,616	Jasper	429	12/20/1817	Toussaint Dubois (French immigrant)
Elkhart	156,198	Goshen	466	1/29/1830	Elkhart Indian tribe
Fayette	26,015	Connersville	215	12/28/1818	Gen. Marquis de Lafayette
Floyd	64,404	New Albany	150	1/2/1819	Virginia Gov. John Floyd
Fountain	17,808	Covington	398	12/20/1825	Maj. James Fontaine
Franklin	19,580	Brookville	385	11/27/1810	Benjamin Franklin
Fulton	18,840	Rochester	369	2/7/1835	Inventor Robert Fulton
Gibson	31,913	Princeton	490	3/9/1813	Gen. John Gibson
Grant	74,169	Marion	415	2/10/1831	Indian fighters Moses and Samuel Grant

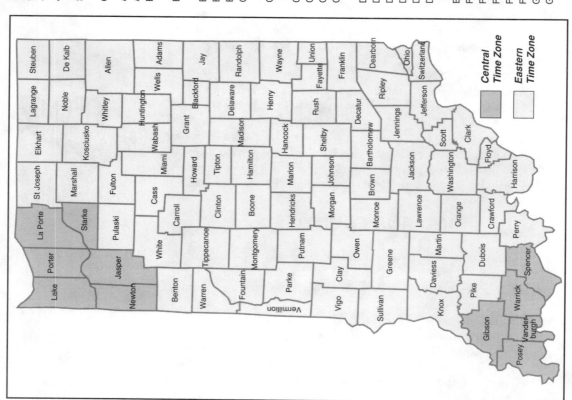

Central Time Zone

Eastern Time Zone

County	Population	County Seat	No.	Date	Date	Named for
Greene	30,410	Bloomfield	546		1/5/1821	Gen. Nathanael Greene
Hamilton	108,936	Noblesville	398		1/8/1823	Alexander Hamilton
Hancock	45,527	Greenfield	307		1/26/1827	John Hancock (Signed Declaration of Independence)
Harrison	29,890	Corydon	486		10/11/1808	Pres. William Henry Harrison
Hendricks	75,717	Danville	409		12/20/1823	Gov., Sen. William Hendricks
Henry	48,139	New Castle	394		12/31/1821	Patrick Henry
Howard	80,827	Kokomo	293		1/15/1844	Rep. Tilghman Ashurst Howard
Huntington	35,427	Huntington	366		2/2/1832	Samuel Huntington (Member of first Continental Congress)
Jackson	37,730	Brownstown	513		12/18/1815	President Andrew Jackson
Jasper	24,960	Rensselaer	561		2/7/1835	William Jasper (Revolutionary soldier of South Carolina)
Jay	21,512	Portland	384		2/7/1835	Chief Justice John Jay (U.S. Supreme Court)
Jefferson	29,797	Madison	363		11/23/1810	President Thomas Jefferson
Jennings	23,661	Vernon	378		12/27/1816	Jonathan Jennings (First governor of Indiana)
Johnson	88,109	Franklin	321		12/31/1822	Judge John Johnson (Indiana Supreme Court)
Knox	39,884	Vincennes	520		6/20/1790	Henry Knox (Secretary of War)
Kosciusko	65,294	Warsaw	540		2/7/1835	Thadeus Kosciusko (Polish patriot)
Lagrange	29,477	Lagrange	380		2/2/1832	Gen. Lafayette's home
Lake	475,594	Crown Point	501		1/28/1836	Lake Michigan
LaPorte	107,066	LaPorte	600		1/9/1832	French for the port or the door
Lawrence	42,836	Bedford	452		1/7/1818	Captain James Lawrence
Madison	130,669	Anderson	453		1/4/1823	President James Madison
Marion	797,159	Indianapolis	396		12/31/1821	General Francis Marion, the "Swamp Fox"
Marshall	42,182	Plymouth	444		2/7/1835	Justice John Marshall
Martin	10,369	Shoals	339		1/17/1820	John P. Martin
Miami	36,897	Peru	369		2/2/1832	Miami Indians
Monroe	108,978	Bloomington	385		1/14/1818	President James Monroe
Montgomery	34,436	Crawfordsville	505		12/21/1822	Gen. Richard Montgomery (Continental Army)
Morgan	55,920	Martinsville	409		12/31/1821	Daniel Morgan, Indian fighter
Newton	13,551	Kentland	401		2/7/1835	Sgt. John Newton
Noble	37,877	Albion	413		2/7/1835	Senator James Noble
Ohio	5,315	Rising Sun	87		1/4/1844	River and state from Indian word "beautiful river"
Orange	18,409	Paoli	408		12/26/1815	Prince William IV of Orange

County	Population	County Seat	No.	Date	Named for
Owen	17,281	Spencer	386	12/21/1818	Col. Abraham Owen (Battle of Tippecanoe)
Parke	15,410	Rockville	444	1/9/1821	Judge Benjamin Parke
Perry	19,107	Cannelton	382	9/7/1814	Naval hero Oliver H. Perry
Pike	12,509	Petersburg	341	12/21/1816	Explorer Zebulon Pike
Porter	128,932	Valparaiso	418	2/7/1835	Naval Commander David Porter
Posey	25,968	Mount Vernon	409	9/7/1814	Brig. Gen. Thomas Posey
Pulaski	12,643	Winamac	435	2/7/1835	Casimir Pulaski (Polish nobleman)
Putnam	30,315	Greencastle	482	12/31/1821	Indian fighter Israel Putnam
Randolph	27,148	Winchester	454	1/10/1818	Thomas Randolph and Randolph Co., North Carolina
Ripley	24,616	Versailles	447	12/27/1816	Eleazar Wheelock Ripley (General and politician)
Rush	18,129	Rushville	408	12/31/1821	Dr. Benjamin Rush (Signed Declaration of Independence)
St. Joseph	247,052	South Bend	459	1/29/1830	Joseph, husband of Virgin Mary
Scott	20,991	Scottsburg	191	1/12/1820	Kentucky Gov. Charles Scott
Shelby	40,307	Shelbyville	413	12/31/1821	Kentucky Gov. Isaac Shelby
Spencer	19,490	Rockport	400	1/18/1818	Capt. Spear Spencer
Starke	22,747	Knox	309	2/7/1835	General John Stark (French and Indian War)
Steuben	27,446	Angola	308	2/7/1835	Baron Friedrich von Steuben
Sullivan	18,993	Sullivan	452	12/30/1816	Indian fighter Daniel Sullivan
Switzerland	7,738	Vevay	223	9/7/1814	Country of Switzerland
Tippecanoe	130,598	Lafayette	502	1/20/1826	Battle of Tippecanoe and Tippecanoe River
Tipton	16,119	Tipton	260	1/15/1844	Senator John Tipton
Union	6,976	Liberty	162	1/5/1821	Union of American states
Vanderburgh	165,058	Evansville	236	1/7/1818	Judge Henry Vanderburgh
Vermillion	16,773	Newport	260	1/2/1824	Vermillion River
Vigo	106,107	Terre Haute	405	1/21/1818	French fur trader Francis Vigo
Wabash	35,069	Wabash	398	2/2/1832	Wabash River (Indian word for white water)
Warren	8,176	Williamsport	366	1/19/1827	Dr. Joseph Warren
Warrick	44,920	Boonville	391	3/9/1813	Captain Jacob Warrick
Washington	23,717	Salem	516	12/21/1813	President George Washington
Wayne	71,951	Richmond	404	1/24/1803	Gen. "Mad Anthony" Wayne
Wells	25,948	Bluffton	370	2/1/1835	Indian agent William Wells
White	23,265	Monticello	506	2/1/1834	Col. Isaac White
Whitley	27,651	Columbia City	336	2/7/1835	Indian fighter William Whitley

In another time zone

Indiana is unusual in that time zones change from Eastern to Central within the state, so each county was given the choice of which to be. The six counties closest to Chicago — Jasper, Lake, LaPorte, Porter, Newton, and Starke — are on Central Time, as are five counties in the southwest — Gibson, Posey, Spencer, Vanderburgh, and Warrick (see map on page 12). All other counties are on Eastern Time. Unlike most places, however, they stay on standard time all year round, instead of switching to Daylight Savings Time during the summer.

Have you ever shunpiked?

Martin County is known for its many back roads with beautiful rugged hills, woodlands, sandstone cliffs, and wildflowers. What does this county have to do with being shunpiked? Everything. It's the perfect spot to shunpike. Shunpiking means driving back roads.

Longest viaduct

The Greene County viaduct was completed in 1906. Part of the Illinois Central Railroad, it is 180 feet high and 2,295 feet long, making it the longest in the U.S. The longest viaduct in the world is located in Cantal, France.

Covered bridges

Parke County has the reputation of being the "Covered Bridge Capital of the World." And rightly so. Thirty-three covered bridges are scattered throughout the county. Its next door neighbor, Putnam County, has nine. One of the oldest bridges, the Jackson Bridge built in 1861, has the longest span (207 feet) still in use. It crosses Sugar Creek, north of Annapolis.

The 84-foot Sim Smith Bridge, built in 1883 near Armiesburg, has the reputation of being haunted. The longest bridge in Parke County is the West Union double spanning 315 feet across the Sugar Creek. All the bridges are in the National Register of Historical Sites. There were 50 covered bridges in existence before the preservation effort was begun in 1978. Fire and deterioration has lowered that number.

Parke County holds an annual covered bridge festival in early October. It has five routes to drive, covering 39 bridges in all.

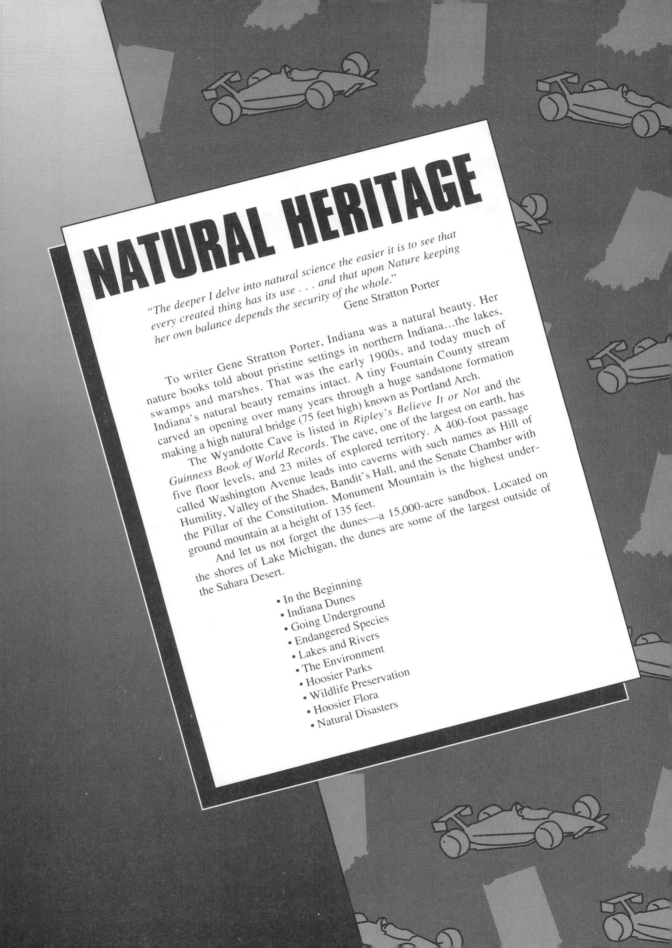

NATURAL HERITAGE

"The deeper I delve into natural science the easier it is to see that every created thing has its use . . . and that upon Nature keeping her own balance depends the security of the whole."

Gene Stratton Porter

To writer Gene Stratton Porter, Indiana was a natural beauty. Her nature books told about pristine settings in northern Indiana...the lakes, swamps and marshes. That was the early 1900s, and today much of Indiana's natural beauty remains intact. A tiny Fountain County stream carved an opening over many years through a huge sandstone formation making a high natural bridge (75 feet high) known as Portland Arch.

The Wyandotte Cave is listed in *Ripley's Believe It or Not* and the *Guinness Book of World Records*. The cave, one of the largest on earth, has five floor levels, and 23 miles of explored territory. A 400-foot passage called Washington Avenue leads into caverns with such names as Hill of Humility, Valley of the Shades, Bandit's Hall, and the Senate Chamber with the Pillar of the Constitution. Monument Mountain is the highest underground mountain at a height of 135 feet.

And let us not forget the dunes—a 15,000-acre sandbox. Located on the shores of Lake Michigan, the dunes are some of the largest outside of the Sahara Desert.

- In the Beginning
- Indiana Dunes
- Going Underground
- Endangered Species
- Lakes and Rivers
- The Environment
- Hoosier Parks
- Wildlife Preservation
- Hoosier Flora
- Natural Disasters

IN THE BEGINNING

350-year-old fossils

The world's largest exposed coral reef (fossil bed) is located in Indiana along the banks of the Ohio River near Clarksville. The fossil bed is 350 million years old. Once the coral reef was covered by the Falls of the Ohio—a two-mile stretch below Louisville that dropped 22 feet over limestone ledges. The damming of the Ohio has left the reef high and dry, opening up a treasure for research and discovery by archeologists. The fossil bed is now a part of the Falls of the Ohio State Park and National Wildlife Conservation Area.

Geographic make-up

Indiana is divided into three distinct geographic areas. Northern Indiana is full of lakes and moraines—hills of dirt and rocks dragged by huge glaciers. The central area is a low plain interrupted by small rivers and an occasional hill. The southern third of Indiana is its most beautiful area—instead of flat terrain, it's full of valleys and hills.

Indiana's lost natural areas

Land	Presettlement	1992
Prairie	2 million acres	600 acres
Forest	20 million acres	4 million acres
Wetlands	1.5 million acres	300,000 acres (estimate)

The Oolitic belt

The "Limestone Belt" between Bloomington and the Ohio River is known for its caves, streams that disappear, sinkholes, and mineral springs. Bedford, Bloomington, and Spencer are the major towns in this region. Indiana limestone is called oolitic because of its granular composition which looks like a mass of fish eggs. For over 100 years, many famous public buildings (see p. 83) have been constructed with Indiana limestone.

United they stand

The Marriage Tree near Baillytown can still be seen. On their wedding days, pioneer brides and grooms each planted a tree. Couples believed that if the trees grew, thrived, and endured, so would their marriages. Joseph Bailly's daughter and her husband each planted a tree on their wedding day in 1840. The oak and elm were planted so close together that the trunk and limbs intertwined until they looked like one tree with elm and oak leaves.

Hovey Lake looks like a swamp in the deep South with huge bald cypress trees, southern red oak, mistletoe, holly, and wild pecans growing. The lake, shaped like an oxbow, is an old channel of the Ohio River that was formed at least 400 years ago. It is now part of Hovey Lake State Fish and Wildlife Area (4,300 acres). The lake provides a home for cormorants, pileated woodpeckers, American egrets, and great blue herons. Osprey nest here, and bald eagles, hawks, owls, and white ibis are seen at times. In fall, approximately 500,000 ducks and geese move in for winter residency here.

Ancient wetlands

INDIANA DUNES

When you think of sand dunes, you picture a granular wasteland, but that isn't quite so. The 14,000 acres of Indiana Dunes National Lakeshore along Lake Michigan have sandy beaches, bogs, marshes, dense forests, and grassy hills. There are dead or stationary dunes covered with vegetation and live or traveling ones similar to the desert dunes with no vegetation. Dunes are products of habit—they mainly travel south or southeast.

Remarkably, the lakeshore and its dunes have survived even though they are located in one of the most heavily industrialized areas in the world—full of pollution, industry, and huge urban populations.

National Lakeshore

The continual motion of wind and water prevents Mount Baldy from settling in one spot long enough to grow a five-o'clock shadow. Mount Baldy, located in Indiana Dunes National Lakeshore, is aptly named because no plants grows on the big 135-foot dune.

A bald sand dune?

The rarest shrub in Indiana is the trailing arbutus. It is found only in the dune region and in Monroe County.

The rarest shrub

Indiana Dunes State Park

The Indiana Dunes State Park surrounds the National Lakeshore. Its 2,182 acres are simply a microcosm of the larger national park. Here the highest sand dune, Mount Tom, is located. It is 190 feet tall and covers 100 acres. The state park contains more species of trees than any other comparable area in the Midwest. Many rare flowers and ferns give the park a subtropical rain-forest impression.

Living in harmony

In the northern Indiana dunes area, a variety of desert and "jungle" plants thrive in close proximity. Northern plant species, such as white pines, oaks, and arctic lichen moss, grow near such southern species as sour gum, pawpaw, tulip, and sassafras. Contrasts are seen often. For example, the prickly pear cactus grows next to irises and orchids.

GOING UNDERGROUND

Fire and brimstone from Pulpit Rock

Marengo Cave, located north of Wyandotte Cave, was discovered in 1883 by a brother and sister who were exploring a sinkhole. The cave gained worldwide recognition for its beauty. Its underground rooms with a constant temperature of 54 degrees Fahrenheit are hot spots for weddings and concerts. (Acoustics are fantastic.) Fire and brimstone emanated from Pulpit Rock deep in the cave when an evangelist preached a sermon on the rock. A square dance is still held each year in July in the Music Hall Chamber.

Once upon a hidden treasure

McBride's Bluffs, near Shoals, is an area of rocky cliffs with numerous small caves and springs. According to legend, McBride's Bluffs was the headquarters of the Choctaw Indians for 100 years and the site of a treasure. Absalom Fields, an early settler, is said to have been taken by the Indians, blindfolded, to a cave they used for shelter in winter. They removed the blindfold and showed him their treasure, a huge amount of silver molded into crude blocks. They blindfolded him again and returned him to his home. The Indians left the area shortly after Fields was released. He spent the remainder of his life unsuccessfully looking for the treasure. Several bars of silver similar to those described by Fields have been found in the area aboveground but the whereabouts of the treasure remains a mystery.

Daniel Boone was here

Daniel Boone was always adventurous. In 1790, he shared an escapade with his brother, Squire. The two discovered a cavern near Corydon, but its only entrance was a bit tricky. It was blocked by a steady rush of water, which prevented extensive exploration of the cave. Daniel's brother chose to settle in the area. Squire, who died in 1815, was buried in the cave at his own request.

The Squire Boone Caverns, named after Daniel's brother, contain a mix of stalactites, stalagmites, underground streams, stone pillars, and the world's largest travertine dam formed by mineral deposits. In 1973, additional entrances and bridges were built to provide access to the caverns for tours. (Be prepared for a workout. The tour includes a 73-step spiral staircase.) The caverns also hold a variety of living creatures. Blind crayfish, isopods, amphipods, and some bats make the Squire Boone Caverns their home.

Boone left his mark

In the midst of big-city life lies a 1,300-acre reservoir and 3,500 acres of land. Eagle Creek Park in Indianapolis is one of the largest city parks in the country. Daniel Boone's initials are carved in a beech tree found in a 50-acre arboretum with 800 types of trees and plant.

Indiana bat

The Indiana bat was first discovered in 1928 at Wyandotte Cave in Crawford County. It is a small bat, ranging from 1.5 to 2 inches long, and weighing about 1/4 ounce. In 1967, the bat became one of the first species to make the Federal Endangered Species list. The population has declined nearly 60 percent in the past 30 years. Of the seven caves in the United States where 85 percent of the total population hibernate, two are located in Indiana. Human disturbance is the major cause of the bat population decline. If aroused during hibernation, the bat is forced to expend energy at a higher rate, leaving less for the remainder of the hibernation period. Attempts are being made to protect these caves.

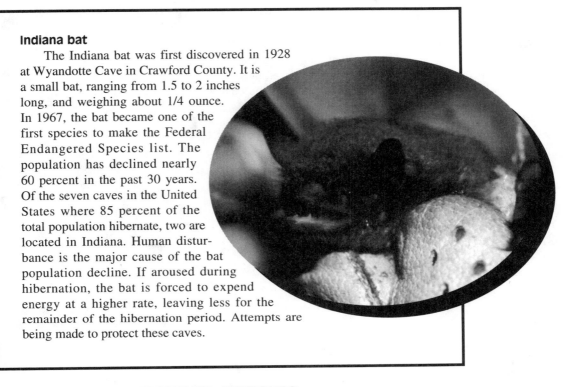

ENDANGERED SPECIES

Saving the bald eagle

The Indiana Non-game and Endangered Wildlife Program released 73 bald eaglets at Lake Monroe in a five-year project developed to restore the bald eagle in the state. The eaglets came from Wisconsin and Alaska. The project, which began in 1985, recorded 11 known dead; five were shot and killed. The goal was to have five nesting pairs by the year 2000. In 1989 a nesting attempt was made at the lake; however, only one egg was laid and hatched, which was a first in the state, but it had a tragic ending. The chick fell from the nest in a storm.

Indiana's loss

Species that roamed free through the Indiana countryside are disappearing, victims of progress. As settlers moved in and cleared lands, such species as the elk, bison, and red wolf were forced to leave. The following is a list of species that can no longer be seen in Indiana.

Species	Last Seen	Species	Last Seen
Elk	1830	Wolverine	1852
Bison	1830	Fisher	1859
Lynx	1832	Gray Wolf	1908
Red Wolf	1832	Porcupine	1918
Black Rat	1845	Eastern Spotted Skunk	1920
Black Bear	1850	River Otter	1942
Mountain Lion	1851	Greater Prairie Chicken	1972

The Endangered

There are many animals and plants that are disappearing from Indiana. The following list of species shows those animals that are endangered in the state. Those with an asterisk (*) by the name are on the 1992 federal list of animals protected by the Endangered Species Act.

Mammals
Southeastern bat
*Gray bat
*Indiana bat
Evening bat
Swamp rabbit
Bobcat

Birds
American bittern
Great egret
Black-crowned night heron
Yellow-crowned night heron
Osprey
*Bald eagle
Northern harrier
*Peregrine falcon
King rail
Sandhill crane
*Piping plover
Upland sandpiper
*Interior least tern
Black tern
Barn owl
Short-eared owl
Bewick's wren
Loggerhead shrike
Golden-winged warbler
*Kirtland's warbler
Backman's sparrow
Yellow-headed blackbird

Reptiles
Hieroglyphic turtle

Amphibians
Hellbender
Northern red salamander

Fish
Lake sturgeon
Redside dace
Popeye shiner
Northern cave fish
Southern cave fish
Bluebreast darter
Spotted darter
Spottail darter
Tippecanoe darter
Variegate darter
Gilt darter

Mollusks
Long-solid mollusk
*White wartyback
*Orange-foot pimpleback
Sheepnose
Clubshell
*Rough pigtoe
Pyramid pigtoe
Rabbitsfoot
Eastern fanshell pearly mussel
*White cat's paw pearly mussel
Northern riffleshell

*Tubercled-blossom mollusk
Snuffbox
*Pink mucket
*Fat pocketbook pearly mussel

Butterflies
Persius duskywing
Ottoe skipper
Karner blue
Mitchell's marsh satyr

Plants
There are at least 225 plants endangered or threatened in Indiana. However, only three of them have been added to the federal list and thus are likely to get some help in recovery. They are:

Mead's milkweed
Pitcher's thistle
Running buffalo clover

In an attempt to replenish the endangered peregrine falcon, Department of Natural Resources biologists released 15 falcon fledglings from the roof of the Blue Cross-Blue Shield building in Indianapolis. Twelve survived to migrate south.

Urban falcons

LAKES AND RIVERS

Named for an Indian chief whose nickname was Old Flat Belly, Lake Wawasee is the largest lake in Indiana, with 18 miles of shoreline. The lake is 4.09 square miles and has a maximum depth of 68 feet.

Old Flat Belly

The spring-fed Blue River winds its way through Crawford County. An ideal stream for canoeing, it offers quiet waters and challenging rapids. Blue River was Indiana's first river to be designated "natural and scenic."

The scenic Blue River

The mighty Ohio River along Indiana's southern border

On the southern edge of Orangeville, an underground river comes to the surface as an artesian spring. Called the Orangeville Rise of the Lost River, it flows from a cave into a 220-foot-wide pit at the bottom of a limestone cliff.

Flowing down under

THE ENVIRONMENT

Indiana tried to keep other people's trash out of its borders. But in 1991, U.S. District Judge John D. Tinder ruled that some key provisions of the Indiana law regulating out-of-state trash were unlawful because they inhibit commerce among states.

Unlawful trash

The facts

Energy use in Indiana in 1991 was residential (18%), commercial (11%), industrial (47%) and transportation (24%. The major sources of fuel are coal (50%) and oil (35%). Indiana generates 4.5 million tons of solid waste and its landfills have about 5 to 10 years before they are filled to the maximum. The state had 35 hazardous waste sites in 1991.

The state's environmental policies are not doing well. Policies on solid waste management, drinking water protection, and food safety programs are rated among the worst in the nation. Resource, energy, and pesticide policies are only slightly better.

How Indiana ranks

In toxic release of cancer-causing chemicals, Posey County ranks seventh in the nation, Marion County ranks eleventh, and Lake County ranks twenty-third. The Hoosier State places sixth among the states in per capita energy consumption and eighth in toxic emissions. It comes in 33rd for states with the most waste generated per capita. Little is spent on the environment. The state's budgeted expenditures on environmental protection has Indiana ranking 49.

Home developer thinks green

There are 148 "green" homes on a 70-acre development in Lake Forest, Indiana. The developer saved the woodlands and made them an arboretum with a nature trail. Since most of the site was farmland, over 200 trees were planted and numerous trees in the path of construction were transplanted to other areas. Underbrush and scrub trees were used as wood chips for the nature trails. Cedar trim left over from home construction was not tossed in the trash. Instead it was used for flower boxes, birdhouses, and other useful products.

Recycling oil

Safety-Kleen Corporation, an Elgin, Illinois, based recycler of industrial wastes, opened a new oil-recycling facility in East Chicago, Indiana. It doubled North America's capacity for oil recycling. It will process 75 million gallons of used automotive and industrial oils per year when it reaches full capacity. The oil will be converted into 43 million gallons of high-quality lubricating oil.

16.8 million-gallon leak

The residents of Whiting, Indiana, are not happy campers. During most of the 102-year history of the nearby Amoco oil refinery (page 77), its petroleum products have been leaking into Whiting's ground water. In 1991, the company acknowledged that more than 16.8 million gallons of petroleum products have leaked. The results from monitoring 150 ground-water wells, constructed on the refinery's land, showed four to eighteen inches of contamination. The company offered free testing to residents and would relocate them if there was an immediate health or safety hazard. Luckily, residents in the area do not drink ground water. They drink Lake Michigan water.

SUPERFUND SITES

The U.S. has earmarked funds to clean up certain hazaradous waste sites in the nation. Only 64 of these 1,200 Superfund sites, as they are called, listed in 1991 have had clean-up completed since 1981. Indiana has 32 sites plus one proposed. Three sites were deleted in 1991 because no further response was needed. They were International Minerals and Chemical Corporation East Plant in Terre Haute, Poer Farm in Hancock County, and Wedzeb Enterprises Inc, Lebanon.

1. American Chemical Service, Inc.
2. Bennett Stone Quarry
3. Carter Lee Lumber Co.
4. Columbus Old Municipal Landfill #1
5. Conrail Rail Yard
6. Continental Steel Corp.
7. Douglass Road/Uniroyal Inc. Landfill
8. Envirochem Corp.
9. Galen Mayers Dump/Drum Salvage
10. Himco Dump
11. Lake Sandy Jo (M&M Landfill)
12. Lakeland Disposal Service Inc.
13. Lemon Lane Landfill
14. Marion (Bragg) Dump
15. MIDCO I
16. MIDCO II
17. Neal's Dump
18. Neal's Landfill
19. Ninth Avenue Dump
20. Northside Sanitary Landfill, Inc
21. Prestolite Battery Division
22. Reilly Tar & Chemical Corp (Indianapolis Plant)
23. Seymour Recycling Corp.
24. Southside Sanitary Landfill
25. Tippecanoe Sanitary Landfill, Inc.
26. Tri-State Plating
27. U.S. Smelter and Lead Refinery, Inc.
28. Waste, Inc. Landfill
29. Wayne Waste Oil
30. Whiteford Sales & Service Inc./National Lease

HOOSIER PARKS

Only national forest

Hoosier National Forest has visible signs of heavy clear-cutting in its 187,812 acres; however, certain areas were saved from the sharp blade of the lumberjack's saw. One of the survivors is the Pioneer Mothers' Memorial Forest. Approximately 80 acres of virgin wood was patented by Joseph Cox in 1818 to protect it. In 1940, his patent was put to the test. To settle the Cox estate, the land was sold to a lumber company. The Indiana Pioneer Mothers' Association and other groups gave financial help to the state forest service to save the virgin forest. Within its boundaries a stand of black walnut trees, justly named Walnut Cathedral, ranging from 150 to 600 years old reign majestically.

Many other natural wonders can be found in the forest. Hemlock Cliffs adorned with—you guessed it—hemlocks is a region of bluffs, overhangs, and caves. Arrowhead Arch excavated by Indiana University is a large sandstone arch which is privately owned.

The shades of death

When early settlers first saw this lush area of forests and deep gorges along Sugar Creek near Waveland, they referred to it as "the Shades of Death." Dark, heavy shadows cast by the thick trees gave it a threatening look, as if shades were dropped over it. Still called that today, the land remains untouched. Shades State Park is 3,000 acres of a major natural landmark in the state. Within the park is the Pine Hills State Nature Preserve, the state's first dedicated nature preserve. Four 75- to 100-foot-tall narrow ridges surround its 470 acres.

Saving Turkey Run

At a time when the lumber industry was quickly destroying natural forests, journalist Juliet Strauss of Rockville decided that her childhood paradise, Turkey Run, originally called Bloomingdale Glen, was not going to fall prey to big business. In 1915, she asked Gov. Samuel Ralston to save her beloved paradise. Her request resulted in her appointment to a commission to save the area and create a park. Today, 2,182 acres including stands of virgin wood and 14 miles of hiking trails are preserved. In 1922, the Women's Press Club of Indiana had a fountain sculpted by Myra Reynolds in memory of Strauss. Turkey Run's protector began her career in Rockville and moved on to an Indianapolis newspaper. Strauss edited the "Ideas of a Plain Country Woman" department of the *Ladies Home Journal* in the early 1900s.

Founder of Indiana park system

Col. Richard Lieber of Indianapolis was the founder of Indiana's state park system. Among his first acquisitions were McCormick's Creek and Turkey Run. He was appointed to the first White House Conference on Conservation in 1908 and later held his own National Conference on Conservation in Indianapolis. Lieber was the first director of the Department of Conservation created in 1920. The German immigrant also co-founded the National Conference on State Parks held in Des Moines, Iowa, in 1921.

Big Clifty Falls

🦋 Big Clifty Falls drops 70 feet. It is found in Clifty Canyon State Nature Preserve in New Madison. The huge canyon, strewn with boulders, is so deep that the sun shines into the bottom of the canyon only at high noon.

🦋 Indiana's newest state park is still in its infancy. Prophetstown State Park is located about five miles north of Lafayette. The 1991 Indiana General Assembly appropriated $900,000 for the project for land appraisals and acquisition and planning. The master plan includes the restoration of the area's wetlands (the park will be laid out along the Wabash River), a proposed lake of nearly 70 acres, reforestation, and management of grassland. The 2,770-acre park will include a living history farm, campgrounds, and an Indian village. The famous Tippecanoe Battlefield Monument is located nearby (see p. 44).

Newest state park

🦋 Preserving Indiana's natural settings and its wildlife is a major concern of the state's Department of Natural Resources. In 1990 and 1991, 12 nature preserves were dedicated. The new preserves protect over 2,600 acres of Indiana's best nature areas. They are as follows:

Preserving Indiana

- Armstrong Glade in Perry County
- Fawn River Fen in LaGrange County
- Art Hammer Wetlands in Noble County
- Hornbeam Addition in Union County
- Charles McClue in Steuben County
- Mengerson in Allen County
- Rocky Hollow in Falls Canyon addition in Parke County
- Stoutsburg Savanna in Jasper County
- Spring Creek Seeps in Montgomery County
- Ziegler Woods in Henry County
- Eagles Crest Addition in Marion County
- Griffey Woods in Monroe County

Horse patrol

About 2 million people visit Brown County State Park each year. The park is the largest park in Indiana, nearly 16,000 acres. It is here the first horse patrol was initiated by the Indiana Department of Natural Resources in 1984. They control traffic, assist in emergencies, patrol undesignated trails, and watch for campground violations.

First environmental license plate

The bald eagle is coming back to Indiana in the form of an automotive license plate. The Indiana Heritage Trust, a program passed in the 1992 State General Assembly, calls for an environmental license plate. The plate will cost $35 with $25 going as a donation to the Trust and a $10 administration fee to the Bureau of Motor Vehicles. The license plates will help acquire more parkland in the state for nature, recreation, and to protect the environment. The plates display a soaring eagle.

INDIANA · 94
HT 4832
ENVIRONMENT

WILDLIFE PRESERVATION

Waterfowl refuge

Muscatatuck National Wildlife Refuge, east of Seymour, is an artist's dream come true. The 7,700-acre refuge offers a sanctuary for colorful wood ducks. Each spring and fall migrating waterfowl seek a respite from their journey in Indiana's only national wildlife refuge.

A crane convention

Ever hear of a bird convention? Jasper Pulaski State Fish and Wildlife Area has one during the last week of October and the first week of November every year. The area is literally covered with about 12,000 sandhill cranes taking a break from their migratory journey south. They aren't too rowdy, just a bit noisy at times.

Leader of the pack

Wolf Park in Tippecanoe County is a research and education facility where each wolf is named and rank ordered in the pack. The park displays a unique interaction between wolf and man, as well as between predator and prey. Visitors to weekly shows observe a wolf placed with bison to show that healthy animals have nothing to fear from wolves.

60-year-old blue heron rookery

Deep ravines, limestone rock protruding from the soil, and the great blue heron are found in Indiana's Big Walnut Valley Natural Area northeast of Bainbridge. For more than 60 years it has been a great blue heron rookery. The great horned owl and at least 120 other species of birds make their home in Big Walnut Valley.

Cageless zoo

The Indianapolis Zoo opened in 1988. Over 2,000 animals live in the 64-acre cageless zoo. The Whale and Dolphin Pavilion is one of the world's largest totally enclosed, environmentally controlled facilities of its kind.

A white-throated capuchin monkey named Bobo was donated to the Mesker Park Zoo in Evansville on January 1, 1935. He lived there happily until 1981 when the zoo was closed. Then he was moved to a Lederle Laboratories research center in Pearl River, New York. He died in 1988, at the age of 53, which is reported by the *Guinness Book of World Records* to be the longest known lifespan for a monkey.

Monkey lives 53 years

HOOSIER FLORA

The northwest corner of Lake County used to be a beautiful grassland. In fact, grass was so high that a rider on horseback couldn't be seen above it. Indiana grasslands have fallen prey to progress, but one area, the German Methodist Cemetery Prairie, remains intact. The one-acre plot, with 80 rare and vanishing plants growing in it, is the most "botanically diverse" acre in Indiana.

Vanishing plants

Rare ferns grow on the cliffs of a sharp curve of the East Fork of the White River known as Beaver Bend. The ferns are located west of Shoals. Farther northwest of the city is a unique boulder of sandstone sculpted by nature. The Jug Rock (which gave the Shoal High School its nickname; see p. 90) is 60 feet high and 15 feet wide.

Where the rare fern grows

Knobstone Trailblazers

Volunteers in southern Indiana have earned the name "Knobstone Trailblazers" for their dedication to the Knobstone Trail. They have helped develop Indiana's longest footpath. The path winds through 58 miles of forest in Clark, Scott, and Washington counties. The Trailblazers range from 19 to 72 years old.

NATURAL DISASTERS

Jennings County was in the path of the longest known continuous tornado on May 26, 1917. It began in Louisiana, working its way through Missouri and into Indiana, traveling 293 miles. In Konts, a mansion was literally picked up from its foundation and moved a full block without disturbing its contents. During the two days of tornadoes, 249 people were killed with damage of $5.5 million.

Miles of destruction

A huge tornado left a swath of death and destruction through Indiana, Missouri, Kentucky, Tennessee, and Illinois. Although it lasted only five hours, 689 people were killed, and damage amounted to over $500 million in 1925. Princeton was left in total destruction. A barber's chair which had been bolted down to the floor was found sitting upright two miles away in a field. Underwear from a women's shop clung to trees. The number of deaths were of those found; many people never were located.

1925 death storm

Tornado takes 130 Hoosier lives

○ On April 11, 1965, 35 tornadoes and approximately 50 thunderstorms struck what was known as Tornado Alley. Of the 271 people killed, 130 came from Elkhart, Goshen, Fort Wayne, Dunlap, Marion, Kokomo, and Lebanon. Clusters of tornadoes dropped down on these towns leaving devastation in their track.

The Ohio Flood of 1937

○ The residents of Evansville and other cities along the Ohio River were helpless to stop the swirling and raging flood waters in 1937. In Evansville alone the flood level reached 53.74 feet on January 30. Forty-six percent of the Evansville area was under water. The town of Leavenworth, located on a bend in the river, was devastated. As a result, citizens moved the town up a hill and out of harm's way. Due to the vast area the flood affected the number of casualties is unknown. Thousands of people were left homeless and property damage was in the millions of dollars.

NATURE'S MOST VIOLENT OUTBREAK

The average speed of a tornado can be about 100 miles per hour. That is an awesome fact, but think of being hit by 148 of these deadly tornadoes. It happened on April 3 and 4, 1974, and Indiana was in the middle (map at right). From midnight to 7 a.m., 315 people died and damages cost over $600 million.

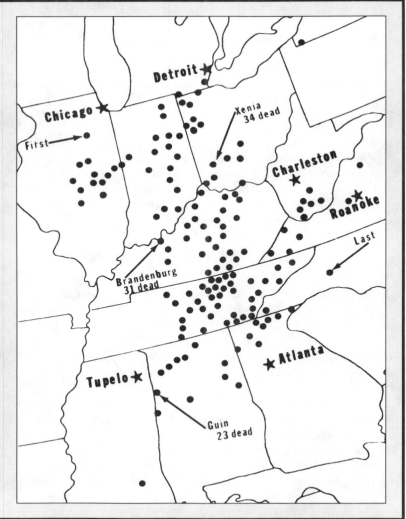

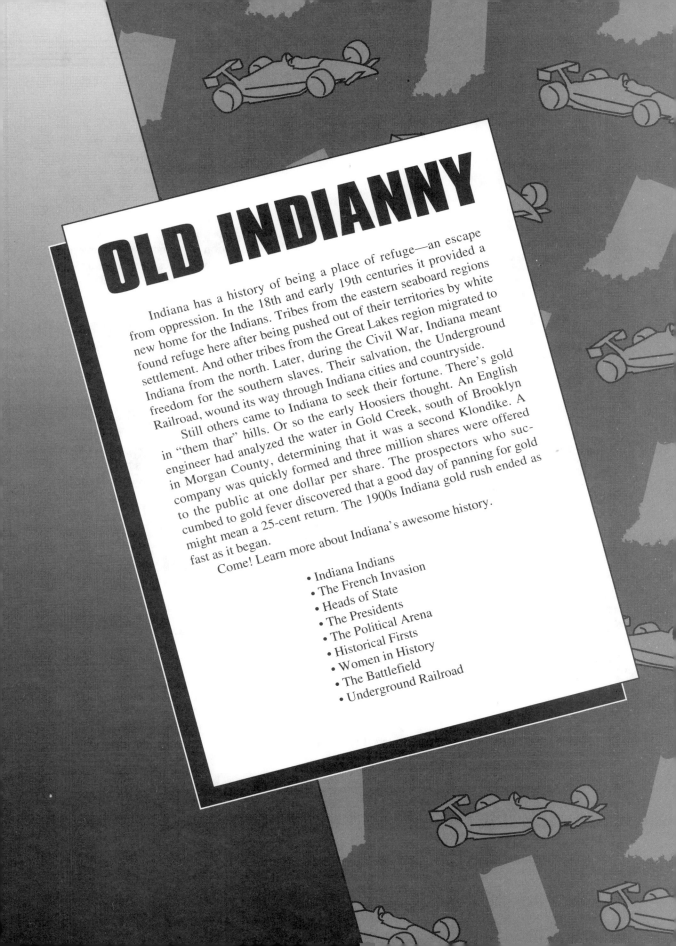

OLD INDIANNY

Indiana has a history of being a place of refuge—an escape from oppression. In the 18th and early 19th centuries it provided a new home for the Indians. Tribes from the eastern seaboard regions found refuge here after being pushed out of their territories by white settlement. And other tribes from the Great Lakes region migrated to Indiana from the north. Later, during the Civil War, Indiana meant freedom for the southern slaves. Their salvation, the Underground Railroad, wound its way through Indiana cities and countryside.

Still others came to Indiana to seek their fortune. There's gold in "them thar" hills. Or so the early Hoosiers thought. An English engineer had analyzed the water in Gold Creek, south of Brooklyn in Morgan County, determining that it was a second Klondike. A company was quickly formed and three million shares were offered to the public at one dollar per share. The prospectors who succumbed to gold fever discovered that a good day of panning for gold might mean a 25-cent return. The 1900s Indiana gold rush ended as fast as it began.

Come! Learn more about Indiana's awesome history.

- Indiana Indians
- The French Invasion
- Heads of State
- The Presidents
- The Political Arena
- Historical Firsts
- Women in History
- The Battlefield
- Underground Railroad

INDIANA INDIANS

Indians story told in historical mounds

⭐ Indiana's Indian heritage is found in mounds located in more than one-third of the state's counties. To the average observer they are simple cones rising from the ground. Some are only 4 feet high, while others stand 70 feet tall. But to the archeologist, they tell the story of the early Indians in Indiana.

Mounds State Park in Anderson contains the largest single earthen fortification. The wall is 9 feet high, 1,200 feet in circumference and 50 to 60 feet wide at its base. The fortification surrounds a central mound, 4 feet high and 30 feet in diameter. Eleven well-preserved mounds were discovered near Evansville on the Ohio River. The central mound is 44 feet high and covers over 4 acres. The site is located in Angel Mounds State Memorial Park. Extensive archeological work has been completed and the 430-acre site is open to the public. Other significant mounds include the Sonotabac Indian Mound in Vincennes and Fudge Mound in Winchester. A museum that displays artifacts from 8000 B.C. is located at the Sonotabac Indian Mound.

Founder of first agriculture school

A farmer at heart, Little Turtle, a Miami Chief, could very well be dubbed the founder of the first agriculture school in America. Sometime between 1795 and 1800, Little Turtle had the brilliant idea of bringing a Quaker family from Philadelphia to teach his braves how to be farmers. They already had experience working with the land, but Little Turtle wanted a more scientific approach. However, school lasted only one season. And why did it last only one season? Because that is all Little Turtle could endure. He ended up doing most of the manual work while his young braves fished and hunted.

The Miami influence

⭐ The Miami were the most influential tribe in Indiana. Of all the Native Americans in Indiana, the Miamis were the most permanent, staying nearly 150 years. The Miami Indians settled along the St. Joseph River, making Fort Wayne their main headquarters. To the Indians it was known as Kekionga, Kiskakon, Omee Town, Twightwee Village, French Town, or Miami Town.

When it came to war and making war, their sense of humor was unusual to say the least. A common practice was sending a messenger ahead to a village to announce falsely that its war party had suffered defeat and certain warriors had been killed. Actually the opposite was true so when the war party entered the downcast mourning village, the mood changed to rejoicing and happiness. (Someone must have wised up after the first few battles.)

The Maneaters

⭐ Some Miamis practiced cannibalism. They cooked and ate their prisoners of war. The practice stopped around 1789 when a young Miami woman, fasting for supernatural power, dreamed of a large fire heaped upon the bones of her man-eating ancestors. The concensus among her tribe was that the dream was a sign of punishment.

1680 Miami settle on St. Joseph River
1715 Delaware & Munsee settle on land between Ohio and White Rivers
1721 Mahican settle on banks of the Kankakee River
1748 Mahicans leave Indiana for Illinois
1751 Smallpox hits Indian tribes friendly to the French
1770 Kickapoo settle on the Vermillion and Wabash Rivers
1784 Nanticoke settle on the White River west of the Delaware Indians
1788 Shawnee settle on the White River and in southern Indiana
1795 Potawatomi settle at the headwaters of the Tippecanoe River
1809 Kickapoo move to Kansas
1811 Shawnee move west
1818 Treaty of St. Mary's gives the U.S the central third of Indiana in 1818. The Indians giving up their lands are the Miami, Wea, Wyandot, Senaca, Shawnee, Delaware, and Potawatomi. The Delaware & Munsee tribes move west to Kansas
1826 The Miami Indians sign the Treaty of Paradise Springs near the Wabash County courthouse. The 1826 treaty opens up new territory to the white men in the surrounding area
1836 Potawatomi sell their land and move west of the Mississippi
1838 Potawatomi (Tippecanoe) is forced out of Indiana and moves to Kansas
1846 Miami moves to a special reservation in Miami County, Kansas, and in 1867, move to Miami, Oklahoma

Tecumseh

⭐ Shawnee Chief Tecumseh hated American settlers. After being forced to leave Ohio, his people settled in Indiana, just to be pushed out again. He challenged all Indian treaties, declaring that the Indians owned the land collectively, and that no single Indian could release it to the Americans.

Although Tecumseh was well known for his war against the white settlers, he fell in love with Rebecca Galloway. The pioneer woman taught Tecumseh about the Bible and Shakespeare. The romance ended with an ultimatum—Rebecca or his people. Tecumseh's love of his people was greater.

A 368-pound chief

Chief LaFontaine was a huge man weighing 368 pounds. His chair, still located in Huntington, Indiana, was specially constructed with reinforced metal and bolts at the joints and measured three and a half feet wide between the arms. While LaFontaine was chief in 1846, the tribe of 300 was ordered to move to Kansas. LaFontaine missed Indiana so much he headed back home in 1847. His tribe, disappointed and broken-spirited, thought the chief was deserting them and so they secretly administered to him a slow-acting poison. (So much for loyalty.) He died in Lafayette, never reaching his beloved land in Huntington.

The saga of young Frances Slocum

⭐ Four-year-old Frances Slocum was stolen by the Delaware from her Quaker farm in Pennsylvania in 1773. Frances's mother never gave up searching for her young daughter. Only death ended the mother's search. Frances's brothers and sisters took up the gauntlet and continued the search. When their final efforts proved futile, they gave up in 1826.

And now here is the rest of the story. In 1833 a trader from Logansport, George Ewing, came to Deaf Man's Village on the Mississinewa River. Ewing had dinner in the cabin of an old Indian widow, Mac-con-a-qua, who coaxed him to stay long after dinner so she might unburden a long-held secret. She told him she had been kidnapped by three Delaware Indians as a small child. She had married twice, once to a Delaware and later to a Miami chief. Ewing immediately set out to find her siblings. He wrote of the tale to the postmaster of Lancaster, Pennsylvania, who ignored the letter. The postmaster's successor did not, and successfully located Frances's brother and sister and in 1837 they met. All of them were now over 60 years old. Mac-con-a-qua, called the "White Rose of the Miamis," spoke no English and the family spoke no Indian, so they all communicated through an interpreter.

THE FRENCH INVASION

Indiana's first white man

⭐ Robert Cavelier, Sieur de La Salle, famed French explorer, was considered the first white man to visit Indiana. La Salle wanted to build a series of forts from Lake Ontario, across Illinois country and down the Mississippi River to strengthen France's hold on the area. On a trip through the area, it is believed he and his 28 companions camped on the "south bend" of the St. Joseph River, December 3, 1679.

Early Vincennes

⭐ Most historians agree that Vincennes is the oldest permanent settlement in Indiana. The governor of Louisiana, Pierre le Moyne, Sieur d'Iberville, directed Charles Juchereau, a trader, to found a trading post at the "mouth of the Ouabache" in 1702. Many assume that it was Au Post, or present-day Vincennes. The Indians called the trading post Chippe Coke. Vincennes was more permanently settled in 1727.

⭐ The son of an early explorer, Jean-Baptiste Bissot, Sieur de Vincennes, was appointed by Perier, governor of Louisiana, to journey to the lower Wabash River area to establish a fort at the old site of Au Post. The stockade was built in 1732. François Marie Bissot, Sieur de Vincennes, was aware of the British trying to increase their influence with several Piankashaw villages by giving them money and presents, and that the Miami and Illinois tribes were "more insolent" than ever. He asked for increased supplies and men to control the situation but never received them. Vincennes had only eight families living with him and these were mostly traders whose wives were Indians. Vincennes was tortured and killed by Chickesaw Indians in 1736.

Vincennes's namesake

⭐ Alice Roussillon was the adopted daughter of Gaspard Roussillon, the leading citizen of Vincennes when the post was surrendered to the British in 1778. Rather than see the American flag brought down by Britain's General Hamilton, Alice hid it. When George Rogers Clark arrived, and the British were defeated, he heard of her exploit and gave her the honor of raising the flag. Alice of Old Vincennes is the heroine in the book by the same name by Maurice Thompson.

The real Alice of Vincennes

Mighty oak shelters peacemakers

In a 1681 attempt to bring about a truce, La Salle met with the Council Chiefs of the Illinois and Miami Confederacies in what is now South Bend.

This historical meeting was held under the branches of a tree known as the Council Oak. The meeting was not as successful as La Salle hoped. Raids still continued among the Indians, and the French were not successful in making the Indians their trusted and strong allies. Only the Council Oak remained strong, bending but never breaking for 400 years. It later became the focal point of Highland Cemetery. Damaged by numerous storms since 1934, residents of South Bend had regularly maintained it until a 1991 storm left the majestic old tree broken beyond repair. A saddened South Bend community had to cut down the mighty Council Oak. Its branches, however, have been preserved by the Northern Indiana Historical Society.

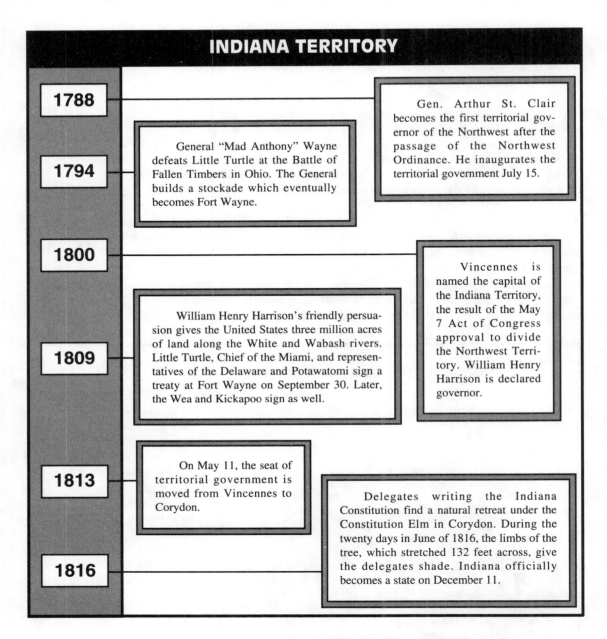

INDIANA TERRITORY

1788

Gen. Arthur St. Clair becomes the first territorial governor of the Northwest after the passage of the Northwest Ordinance. He inaugurates the territorial government July 15.

1794

General "Mad Anthony" Wayne defeats Little Turtle at the Battle of Fallen Timbers in Ohio. The General builds a stockade which eventually becomes Fort Wayne.

1800

Vincennes is named the capital of the Indiana Territory, the result of the May 7 Act of Congress approval to divide the Northwest Territory. William Henry Harrison is declared governor.

1809

William Henry Harrison's friendly persuasion gives the United States three million acres of land along the White and Wabash rivers. Little Turtle, Chief of the Miami, and representatives of the Delaware and Potawatomi sign a treaty at Fort Wayne on September 30. Later, the Wea and Kickapoo sign as well.

1813

On May 11, the seat of territorial government is moved from Vincennes to Corydon.

Delegates writing the Indiana Constitution find a natural retreat under the Constitution Elm in Corydon. During the twenty days in June of 1816, the limbs of the tree, which stretched 132 feet across, give the delegates shade. Indiana officially becomes a state on December 11.

1816

HEADS OF STATE

An Indiana dictator

⭐ Paul V. McNutt made a number of drastic changes in the state government while serving as governor from 1933 to 1937. He took his job and made it almost a dictatorship, turning 168 boards and commissions into nine departments. The powerful governor could hire and fire all state employees. If he saw fit that salaries should be raised or lowered, Gov. McNutt did so, on only his own whim. Legislative appropriations and the authority of the courts to review and void his decisions were the only way his powers could be limited.

⭐ Indiana's oldest governor, James D. Williams, was 68 years, 11 months old when elected to serve in 1877. He may have been the oldest, but under today's standards he was a "hip" politician. Governor Williams was nicknamed "Blue Jeans," because of his mode of dress. He was a prominent supporter of Indiana agriculture, serving as a member of the State Board of Agriculture for 16 years. Four of those years he held the office of president.

A "hip" politician

⭐ Oliver Perry Morton began practicing law in Centerville. He excelled as a railroad attorney, but his strongest interest was in politics. His opposition to the Kansas-Nebraska Bill in 1854 turned him toward the new Republican Party. He lost his 1856 bid for the governorship, but four years later he was the nominee for lieutenant governor with Henry Smith Lane. Shortly after Lane won the governorship, he left to be in the United States Senate. His departure put Morton in the governor's seat.

Governor snubs his legislature

A strong Lincoln supporter, Morton encouraged 150,000 Indiana men to enlist in the Union army. By 1862, he was facing an Indiana legislature filled with peace-loving Democrats. Rather than do battle with them, he bypassed them and ran the state his own way. He raised money by using his own credit and the state's credit. He was often called the "Assistant President" for his active support of the Civil War and Lincoln. His unconventional ways didn't prevent him from being re-elected in 1864, only this time the Republicans took over the legislature. Morton became a United States Senator in 1867, a position he held until his death on November 1, 1877. While in the Senate he was a strong advocate for the passage of the Fifteenth Amendment, making it illegal to deny voting rights because of race.

⭐ Indiana governor and later president William Henry Harrison left a beautiful legacy to Indiana. Grouseland, his home for eight years, was built to resemble an old Virginia plantation. It took more than a year to build at a cost of $20,000, an expensive venture in 1802. Located in Vincennes, the house became the political and social center of the Northwest Territory. He invited Chief Tecumseh to his home on August 12, 1810, to spend four days discussing the differences between Indians and white men. Tecumseh wouldn't enter the house so the two sat on the ground in a walnut grove on the front lawn of Grouseland.

Governor's home site of historical meeting

THE PRESIDENTS

Defending his case

⭐ At age 16, Abe Lincoln operated a ferry across Anderson Creek (now called Anderson River) where it emptied into the Ohio River. In order to make more money, he built himself a boat that took passengers to the steamboats in midstream. He was taken to court in Kentucky for operating without a license. Young "Honest Abe" won the case because he said he traveled on only half the river and didn't think the law applied to him. This part of his life is memorialized at Lincoln Ferry Landing State Wayside Park in Troy.

Lincoln's Indiana Home

Indiana had just become a state when Abraham Lincoln's family left Kentucky and settled in the Gentryville area. It was 1816 and young Abe was seven years old. Two years later he was without a mother. Nancy Hanks Lincoln had died of "milk fever." One year later, Thomas, Abe's father, went back to Kentucky and returned with a new bride, Sarah Bush Johnson. It was Sarah who encouraged Abe's thirst for learning by supplying him with books. It is said the young boy had great physical strength but didn't love work. What he did love was reading and talking.

Lincoln's gift of speech was encouraged by an Indiana schoolteacher, Azel Dorsey of Rockport, who taught school near Lincoln's boyhood home. The future president's family left Indiana for Illinois in 1830.

Young Abe remembered

⭐ Nancy Hanks Lincoln's grave lay weed-choked and unmarked near Pigeon Creek until 1878. At that time P. E. Studebaker of South Bend decided to place a headstone there. It was the beginning of memorializing Lincoln as a boy. A county park soon surrounded the pioneer cemetery. In the 1930s the Lincoln State Park and the adjoining Nancy Hanks Lincoln State Memorial were built at Pigeon Creek.

In 1962, the National Park Service acquired the property, making it the Lincoln Boyhood National Memorial. Five huge sculpted limestone panels tell about important events in Lincoln's life. Although Lincoln City, where Lincoln grew up on the family farm, was destroyed in a disastrous fire in 1911, a small U.S. Post Office remains to preserve the Lincoln City postmark. The Lincoln cabin site memorial consists of a bronzed sill and hearth believed to belong to the log cabin home built by Lincoln and his father.

⭐ William Henry Harrison, first governor of the Indiana Territory and ninth president, has the distinction of delivering the longest inaugural address ever. The speech was 8,578 words long and lasted one hour and forty-five minutes. His speech was long, but his term was short. The newly elected president was in office a total of 31 days, dying April 4, 1841, of pneumonia caught at the inauguration. The Virginia-born man was the first president to die in office of natural causes and the first to lie in state in the White House.

A long-winded inaugural address

⭐ Although Benjamin Harrison, President William Henry Harrison's grandson, twice failed to become governor of Indiana, he found success in being elected as the twenty-third president of the United States. It wasn't an easy election. Harrison, a Republican, received fewer popular votes than Grover Cleveland. It was the electoral college that put him in the White House. He is the only president in United States history to be preceded and followed in office by the same man, Grover Cleveland. Harrison's national budget was $1 billion. Born in North Bend, Ohio, 1833, Harrison moved to Indianapolis as a young lawyer. He died March 13, 1901, in Indianapolis and is buried in Crown Hill Cemetery.

An Indiana loser becomes U.S. President

⭐ The only native Hoosier ever nominated for president was Wendell Willkie. The Elwood man was a late starter in the race for president. He didn't campaign until May, much too late to enter most primaries and few of his friends knew he had turned Republican. However, in the general election of 1940 he carried Indiana by 25,000 votes and received more popular votes than any Republican before Eisenhower. He lost by a landslide to Franklin D. Roosevelt.

Hoosier falls to FDR

Secretary of State
    John W. Foster under Benjamin Harrison in 1892
Secretaries of the Treasury
    Hugh McCulloch under Abraham Lincoln and Andrew Johnson in 1865
    Walter Gresham under Chester Arthur in 1884
    Hugh McCulloch under Chester Arthur in 1884
    Joseph W. Barr under Lyndon B. Johnson in 1968
Secretary of the Navy
    Richard W. Thompson under Rutherford Hayes in 1877
Attorney General
    William H. H. Miller under Benjamin Harrison in 1889
Secretaries of the Interior
    Caleb B. Smith under Abraham Lincoln in 1861
    John P. Usher under Abraham Lincoln in 1863
Secretaries of Agriculture
    Claude R. Wickard under Franklin D. Roosevelt in 1940
    Clifford M. Hardin under Richard Nixon in 1969
    Earl L. Butz under Richard Nixon and Gerald Ford in 1971 and 1974
Secretary of Health and Human Services
    Otis R. Bowen under Ronald Reagan in 1985

The Presidents' Men from Indiana

Mr. President, you're in a mudhole

Along the National Road, now Interstate 70, a wooden marker has been placed on a large elm in Plainfield. Named the Van Buren Elm, the tree commemorates the fall of Martin Van Buren, literally. While Van Buren was president he vetoed a bill for improvements on the National Road. After being defeated in the 1840 presidential race, he was making a swing through Indiana in 1842 to size things up for a run in 1844. Knowing he was coming, the citizens of Plainfield decided to teach the former president a lesson. They wanted him to know the effect of his veto of the National Road bill. While passing around the town circle, Van Buren's coach ran into some poorly maintained road. The coach overturned near an elm tree and he was dumped into a mudhole. The driver of the coach received a new silk hat for his part in the plot.

"Mother of Vice Presidents"

Indiana has earned the nickname "Mother of Vice Presidents." The state has sent five men to Washington as vice presidents of the United States.

• **Schuyler Colfax,** known as a Radical Republican, served 1869-73 under Ulysses S. Grant. Born March 23, 1823, in New York, Colfax moved to South Bend in 1836. Later he founded the St. Joseph Valley *Register.* While vice president, he was implicated in a congressional investigation into corrupt transactions with Crédit Mobilier of America.

• **Thomas A. Hendricks,** a Democrat born in Ohio and lived in Indianapolis, served nine months in 1885, under Grover Cleveland, before dying in office.

• **Charles W. Fairbanks,** a Republican born in Ohio and lived in Indianapolis, called the "last of America's log-cabin statesmen," served 1905-09 under Theodore Roosevelt.

• **Thomas R. Marshall,** a Democrat from North Manchester, served a full eight years from 1913 to 1921 under Woodrow Wilson. He considered the position of vice president "a disease, not an office."

• During much of his term (1989-93) as vice president under George Bush, **J. Danforth Quayle** learned how mighty the pen can be. His spelling prowess was a constant thorn in his side. Now just how do you spell "potato?" His golfing abilities are another story. Quayle lived from age eight to sixteen in a home on the eleventh tee of the Paradise Valley Country Club in Phoenix, Arizona. He learned to play golf there and by 18 he had a handicap of four. While in the Senate, he co-sponsored a bill which would give a tax break to visiting golf pros.

THE POLITICAL ARENA

Brookville politicians

⭐ A name synonymous with Indiana politics for 25 years was the town of Brookville. John Test of Brookville was U.S. representative for  three terms. The state's first two U.S. senators, James Nobel (1816-1831) and his successor, Robert Hannah, both hailed from Brookville. From 1825 to 1840 every governor was a Brookville resident. They were James Brown Ray (1825-1831), Noah Nobel (1831-1837), and David Wallace (1837-1840). At one time every member of the state supreme court, Isaac Blackford, Stephen Stephens, and James McKinney, had practiced law in Brookville. One city founder, Jesse Brooks Thomas, left several years later and became a U.S. senator from Illinois.

The Greenback Party

⭐ November 1874 marked the birth of an American political party called the Greenback Party. A conference, called by the Grange of Indiana, included delegates from the Labor Reform Party and other minor parties in the nation. Small business, farming, and labor representatives experiencing financial strain were present. They called for the free issue and complete legal status of greenbacks (money). On May 17, 1876, in Indianapolis, Peter Cooper was nominated as their candidate for president. Although he wasn't elected, the party was able to send a large number of congressmen to the House of Representatives.

A Whig baptism

⭐ Howe was the site of the Whig baptism by whiskey. During the presidential campaign of 1840, the Whigs held a large demonstration in Howe supporting William Henry Harrison. Many of the 800 men assembled to hear the speeches were Democrats. One man became ill and his friends bathed his head with the pioneer remedy for all ills, whiskey. The Whigs then came up with the idea of "baptizing" all the Democrats present into the true Whig faith. The Whigs singled out the Democrats and washed away their "political" sins by pouring mugs of whiskey of their heads.

The eternal optimist

⭐ If you look at the Democratic Party emblem, you will notice a rooster. The Democrats' choice in feathered representation is due to Joseph Chapman from Greenfield. An eternal optimist, Chapman claimed every county for the Democrats at the beginning of each political campaign. The Whigs called his style of speaking "crowing." During the 1840 presidential campaign between Democrat Martin Van Buren and Whig William Henry Harrison, the Democrats were falling behind. Chapman was told by an Indianapolis newspaper editor to "Crow, Chapman, Crow!" The Whigs learned about the crowing phrase and used it to ridicule the Democrats. The Democrats, however, adopted the rooster as their party emblem and used the crowing phrase as their battle cry. It has remained an emblem for the Democratic Party.

It ought be a law

The Indiana General Assembly once tried to get involved in arithmetical values. They were close to passing a law changing the value of pi to 3 instead of 3.14159. Why would they want to make such a drastic change in the mathematical world? They thought 3 was a simpler number to work with.

Indiana has had its share of unusual laws. For instance, the moustache was once illegal if the bearer had a tendency to habitually kiss other humans. Or how about the one requiring hotel bed sheets to be at least 99 inches long and 81 inches wide. Lawmakers have even gone so far as to forbid baths during the winter.

KKK in Indiana

Under the leadership of D.C. Stephenson, the Ku Klux Klan was influential in choosing at least one governor, United States senators, and numerous lesser officials during a dark chapter of Indiana history. Stephenson's staff recruited 250,000 people and established a strong network of KKK members in Indiana. He was in control of twenty-three KKK state organizations. He announced from his Indianapolis office that he was the law in the state. In 1923, Stephenson became the Grand Dragon of the state. He created a private police force called the Horse Thief Detective Association to enforce his law. Many of Indiana's citizens were terrorized by the Klan at that time.

Stephenson's downfall happened because of a woman, Madge Oberholtzer. After meeting the employee of the Indiana State Department of Public Instruction, Stephenson invited her to dinner in 1924. The evening turned out to be a nightmare for the woman. He brutally assaulted Oberholtzer and attempted to rape her. On April 14, 1925, Oberholtzer committed suicide. Stephenson was held responsible for putting her into a mental state that would cause her death. He was convicted of her murder in 1925. After those in high places failed to do anything about his arrest and conviction, he revealed letters and records from top politicians who gave or received money from him. He was finally released from jail in 1956, disappearing into anonymity.

The union man

Eugene V. Debs, a strong supporter of the American worker, often preached from his Terre Haute home of the need for strong unions. Debs founded the Social Democratic Party in 1898. He had previously organized the American Railway Union which supported the Pullman strike in 1894. On March 6, 1900, his Social Democrats and the Socialist Labor Party joined forces to become the Socialist Party of the United States. Debs ran for president in 1900 on the Socialist ticket and received 88,000 votes. He ran again in 1904, 1908, 1912, and 1920. A violation of the 1917 Espionage Act for criticizing the government's prosecution of persons charged with sedition sent Debs to an Atlanta federal penitentiary. Directing

his 1920 campaign from behind bars, he had his most successful run for the presidency, gaining 915,000 votes. In 1921, a presidential order gave him his freedom from prison, but not his citizenship.

⭐ Voted one of the "ten dumbest Congressmen," Rep. Earl Landgrebe became the first elected official to be arrested in Moscow for selling Bibles. While making an official visit to Russia during Christmas of 1972, Landgrebe smuggled in Bibles for Christians. After returning from Moscow, he became the only opponent of a cancer research-funding bill. He said he had a good reason for voting no, "but I can't remember exactly what it was." Apparently he lived by his own axiom, "Don't confuse me with facts; I've got a closed mind." He was on the environmental "Dirty Dozen" list for three years, and in Nixon's last days, when his impeachment was certain, Landgrebe announced that Congress was shifting in favor of the beleaguered President. Nixon's escapades didn't bother him, he said—Nixon had just "lied to a few Congressmen, so what?"

One of 10 dumbest congressmen

⭐ In 1962, Democrat Birch Bayh scored one of the nation's biggest election upsets. At 34, he unseated Indiana's Republican Homer Capehart, who had held the seat for 18 years. The following song helped his victory: "Hey, look him over, He's your kind of guy . . . His first name is Birch, His last name is Bayh." Bayh, who served three terms, was a strong supporter of the Equal Rights Amendment and later ran a campaign to be the 1976 Democratic presidential nominee. His son, Evan, is now Indiana's governor.

A national upset

HISTORICAL FIRSTS

⭐ The first newspaper in Indiana was the *Indiana Gazette* published in Vincennes. It was established by Elihu Stout, a Kentuckian. The first newspaper plant in Indiana was located in Vincennes where the *Gazette* was first printed on July 4, 1804. It was destroyed by fire two years later, rebuilt and renamed the *Western Sun*. Another first occurred at the *Western Sun*. It was here that Abraham Lincoln first saw the process of printing.

The first newspaper

⭐ Samuel F. B. Morse, inventor of the telegraph, promised Ann Ellsworth of Lafayette, Indiana, that she could choose the first words to be sent by telegraph when his invention was perfected. When the telegraph line was completed between Baltimore and Washington in 1844, Morse told Ellsworth he was ready and she sent him the words, "What hath God wrought?"

First words by telegraph

Airmail by balloon

⭐ The first airmail flown in the United States originated in Lafayette. On August 17, 1859, a large balloon ascended carrying 23 circulars and 123 letters bound for New York City. But the balloon didn't reach New York—it landed 27 miles south in Crawfordsville and the mail was carried the rest of the way by train.

First black mayor in Indiana

⭐ On November 7, 1967, Gary residents elected Richard G. Hatcher as mayor. He was one of two Democratic African-Americans to become mayors of major cities that year. The other was Carl B. Stokes in Cleveland, Ohio.

Election campaign over air waves

⭐ 1922 marked the first time a campaign was waged over the radio. Senator Harry Stewart New, an incumbent Republican, tried to reach his constituents during the last five days of the campaign via radio. A good idea, but he was defeated by Democrat Samuel Moffett Ralston.

Legislating birth control

⭐ The 1907 Indiana legislature enacted a law to "prevent the procreation of criminals, idiots, imbeciles, and rapists." Before the law was challenged, 120 sterilizations were performed. The Indiana Supreme Court found it unconstitutional in the case of *Williams v. Smith*.

WOMEN IN HISTORY

Women's suffrage

⭐ Amanda Way had the first women's suffrage group meeting in Indiana at her home in Dublin in 1851. The next year the Women's Rights Society was formed and soon afterward a petition was filed in the Indiana General Assembly. But the Civil War came, slaves were freed, and the issue of women's suffrage was put on the back burner.

First women's club

⭐ Constance Fauntleroy, granddaughter of Robert Owen (see p. 128), founded the Minerva Club in 1859 in New Harmony. It was the first organized women's club in the United States with a constitution and by-laws. The inspiration for this club came from Frances Wright's earlier literary organization. Fauntleroy's club work didn't end in New Harmony. She went on to Madison, Wisconsin, where she organized the Bronté Club and later formed the Runcie Club in St. Joseph, Missouri.

⭐ Arabella Babb Mansfield was the first woman admitted to the bar in the United States. At the time she applied to the Iowa bar in 1869, little recognition was given her except by Susan B. Anthony. Having accomplished her goal, Mansfield never practiced law, instead she went back to teaching at Iowa Wesleyan University. She left Iowa to teach at DePauw University in Greencastle, Indiana.

First woman admitted to the bar

⭐ Alice B. Sanger of Indianapolis was the first woman ever to be employed in the office of the president. She began work on January 2, 1890, as a White House stenographer under President Benjamin Harrison.

First woman to work in president's office

⭐ Virginia Ellis Jenckes, representative in Congress, was the first woman in Indiana to be elected to Congress, as well as the first—unusually enough—to be elected without her husband having held the position before her. Born in Terre Haute, Jenckes was already widowed and managing her husband's farm in 1932 when she ran for Congress to help deal with the economic problems caused by the Depression. She promised to support the repeal of Prohibition with hopes of reviving the economy. After three terms she lost her seat to a Republican. Jenckes then went to work for the American Red Cross. She was recognized for her assistance in helping five priests escape the 1956 Hungarian uprising.

Jenckes wins on own merit

⭐ Rose McConnell Long, born in Greensburg, moved to Louisiana at age 9. At 21, she married the young Huey Long, put him through law school, and started to found a political dynasty. After her husband's assassination in 1935, her name was not mentioned in the Long political machine's plans to replace him. But the lieutenant governor, who had been left out of the plans, suddenly became governor on the death of Governor O. K. Allen. He named Rose Long to succeed Huey. She served for less than 12 months as Louisiana's first female U.S. senator.

Hoosier becomes Louisiana senator

Roll out the barrels

An exciting event happened in Mansfield during the Civil War but had nothing to do with the war. A large group of women, angry at the amount of time their husbands spent at the village saloon, raided the establishment and rolled the whiskey barrels out to the street where they emptied them. When another saloon was opened on the creek bank, the women hired a farmer to hitch his ox team to the building and drag it into the creek.

Supreme Court rules for brewery worker

⭐ Ann Bartmess, a brewery worker from Indiana, was the first person to make a U.S. Supreme Court challenge on the legality of a requirement that women retire earlier than men. She had been forced to retire at 62, to keep in line with the company-union pension contract. Men routinely retired at 65. In 1971, the Supreme Court ruled that such a pension requirement for women was a violation of women's civil rights.

Critic of nation's defense department

⭐ Indiana's Cecil Murray Harden was a harsh critic of the U.S. Defense Department. The Republican from Covington opposed the department's plans to shut down the Atomic Energy Commission's heavy water plant in Dana, Indiana, which would put 900 people out of work. As a representative in Congress, she worked hard for her constituents and didn't want her district to face even greater unemployment problems. After five terms (1949-59) in Congress, Harden was appointed special assistant for women's affairs to the Postmaster General in 1961. And in 1970, she was named to the White House Conference on Aging.

The most recent Indiana woman in the House of Representatives is Jill Lynnette Long of Warsaw, Indiana. She produced a surprise victory in 1989 during a special election to fill the vacancy created by Dan Coats who left the House to take Dan Quayle's Senate seat. Indiana has never had a woman in the Senate.

Congresswoman Katie Beatrice Hall

⭐ Gary's Katie Beatrice Hall, who served only one full term in the U.S. Congress from 1982 to 1985 (first black woman elected from Indiana), introduced the bill into Congress that made the birthday of Martin Luther King, Jr., a federal holiday.

THE BATTLEFIELD

The Battle of Tippecanoe

⭐ Although the Battle of Tippecanoe did nothing to settle the underlying Indian problems, it did boost General William Henry Harrison's political career. And 30 years later it provided him with a perfect campaign slogan, "Tippecanoe and Tyler Too." John Tyler was his running mate.

The events that led to the battle began when the Indians became agitated under the organization of Tecumseh and his brother, The Prophet. The loss of the last good hunting grounds in Indiana to the white settlers was the final straw. Indian tribes began to join Tecumseh's Indian confederacy quickly. Harrison was sent to the area with 900 men to keep peace.

Indians met Harrison on November 6, 1811, outside Prophet's Town, a village founded

The Prophet

by The Prophet on the junction of the Wabash and Tippecanoe rivers. The Indians talked truce and Harrison agreed. The truce was to begin the next day. Harrison camped a mile away from Prophet's Town, remaining on guard the entire night.

Tecumseh was away recruiting tribes for his confederacy. In his absence, the radical Prophet ordered an attack on Harrison the next morning. He promised the braves that they would be protected from the bullets by his magic charms which he brewed in a pot over the fire.

The Indians were defeated. The Prophet blamed his squaw, whom he said had touched the pot and ruined the magic of the charms.

Let the people declare war?

Congressman Louis Ludlow from Indiana believed the people should decide a declaration of war. He proposed an amendment to the Constitution calling for a popular referendum before war could be declared. The proposal was shelved by a 209-188 vote on January 10, 1938.

⭐ Confederate Civil War prisoners at Camp Morton in Indianapolis were treated so well that they donated a bust of the prison commander, Colonel Richard Owen, to the state. It is now located in the Indiana capitol building.

POWs honor their keeper

⭐ Indiana troops saw their first action in the Civil War in 1861. Their assignment to stop the Confederates from taking over the Baltimore and Ohio Railroad at Philippi, Virginia, was a success. The state sent 61,341 of its sons to fight. All volunteers, they surpassed the state quota of 38,832. The only Indiana general killed in the Civil War, General Pleasant A. Hackleman, was born in Brookville.

Civil War action

⭐ Liberty was the birthplace of Ambrose Burnside who later moved to Rhode Island. Burnside gained recognition as a Union general after he led the initial brigade in the first Battle of Bull Run on July 21, 1862. He succeeded Gen. George McClellan as Commander of the Army of the Potomac. Later, after the war, he became governor of Rhode Island and a U.S. Senator. He is also known for introducing sideburns.

Ambrose Burnside

⭐ Corydon was the scene of the only Civil War battle fought on Indiana ground. On July 9, 1863, a small band of Confederate raiders led by Gen. John Hung Morgan attacked the city. Corydon's Home Guard of 400 killed 8 and wounded 33 of the enemy while only three of their men were lost and two wounded. Although it may seem that the Home Guard had the advantage, records show that the Home Guard surrendered to General Morgan. Their decision to surrender was due primarily to the 2,000 troops the general brought with him

Only Civil War battle in Indiana

⭐ James F. D. Lanier was a wealthy pioneer banker in Madison and great-grandson of George Washington's maternal aunt. When Indiana needed money to equip its soldiers for the Civil War, Lanier advanced a $1,000,000 loan to the state of Indiana, unsecured.

A million for the Civil war cause

First to shed blood

⭐ Nicholas Biddle of Pottsville was the first Indiana man to be wounded in the Civil War. The African-American was one of a group of volunteers on his way to sign up as a soldier to protect the nation's capital. On his way to Washington the volunteers marched through Baltimore. Biddle was hit in the face with a brick. He is remembered in his hometown by a plaque erected in 1951.

"The Silent Victors"

The Soldiers and Sailors Monument, dedicated in 1902, stands 284 feet high in the center of Indiana's capital, Indianapolis, on Monument Circle. Created by Bruno Schmitz, the monument is a tribute to the state's valiant soldiers and sailors in wars prior to World War I.

The Grand Army of the Republic

The Grand Army of the Republic was a patriotic organization of Civil War veterans who served in the Union army. Created in Springfield, Illinois, in 1866, it dissolved in 1956. On August 31, 1949, the Grand Army of the Republic held its final meeting in Indianapolis. The meeting was attended by six delegates, each over 100 years old.

Inventor of the "ironclads"

During the Civil War, engineer and inventor James Buchannan Eads, born in Lawrenceburg, devised a "radical" defense plan for the Mississippi River calling for the use of steamboats covered with iron—ironclads. These boats helped Grant win victories at forts Henry and Donelson and were the first ironclads to fight in North America and the first to fight enemy war ships. He is best remembered today, however, for the innovative steel bridge he was chosen to build after the Civil War that spanned the Mississippi at St. Louis. He also devised a system of jetties to protect the New Orleans navigation channel. His idea for building a ship railway across Panama instead of the more expensive canal was rejected. Eads was the first American engineer to receive the Albert Medal of the Royal Society of Arts in London.

Another shot heard round the world

⭐ Sergeant Alex Arch of South Bend commanded the Battery C, 6th Field Artillery, United States Army, when that battery fired the first shot from American forces in France at 6:05 in the morning on October 23, 1917, during World War I. One of the first three men to die in World War I, James B. Gresham, was from Evansville.

Father of the draft

⭐ When Americans were drafted for World War II, their names were drawn in a fair and simple system devised by General Lewis B. Hershey. A Steuben County native, he was a teacher and National Guardsman before becoming an officer in World War I. He was instrumental in bringing the Selective Service Program under civilian control.

⭐ David M. Shoup helped plan the assault on Tarawa but little did he know that the assault commander would get sick, leaving the responsibility on his shoulders. The big-chested, cigar-chomping, strong-minded colonel from Battleground, Indiana, waded ashore on November 20, 1943, map case and gun over his head, to set up his first command post, amidst enemy fire. While Shoup set up another command post, his legs were torn with mortar fire. He fought off the pain to continue leading the assault. Shoup stayed on his feet, wounded, for over 60 hours without sleep. When his relief, Colonel Merritt Edson, arrived, the battle was well in hand, but, according to Edson, Shoup looked as if he had been hit by a tank.

Shoup had an outstanding post-war career. Appointed by President Eisenhower as Marine Corps commandant, he began serving in 1960. The hero was opposed to the build-up in Vietnam.

The Heroic deed of David M. Shoup

WORLD WAR II

Lt. Richard N. Antrim

Rear Adm. Norman Scott*

Pfc. Melvin Biddle

Sgt. Gerry H. Kisters

S.Sgt. Thomas McCall

Pvt. William D. McGee*

2nd Lt. Harry J. Michael*

Col. David Shoup

Killed in action

The Medal of Honor

The Medal of Honor is the United States's highest award for bravery in combat. It originated in the Civil War. Truman said, "I'd rather have this medal than be president." The criteria for receiving the Medal of Honor: clear risk of life, voluntary act beyond duty, and two eyewitnesses.

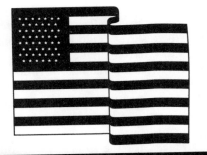

WORLD WAR I

1st Lt. Samuel Woodfill

KOREAN WAR

Cpl. Charles G. Abrell*

Lt. Col. Don C. Faith, Jr.*

VIETNAM WAR

Lance Cpl. Emilio De La Garza, Jr.*

Pfc. Daniel D. Bruce*

⭐ In July 1945, history was being made in the bowels of the USS *Indianapolis*. The ship was given the task of carrying, from San Francisco to Tinian, an island in the Marianas, an important component of "Little Boy," the atomic bomb destined for Hiroshima. The component, a large chunk of uranium, arrived safely on July 26. The USS *Indianapolis* was not so lucky. After completing its task, the ship left for the Philippines. A Japanese submarine torpedoed the unescorted ship four days later. The ship sank so quickly that its crew members didn't even get off an SOS, but 800 of the 1,200 crew members were able to escape. Victory over death, however, was short-lived. For 84 hours the sailors fought to stay alive in a shark-infested sea. When rescue came, only 316 had survived.

Lost at sea: The USS Indianapolis

USS Vincennes destroys Iran plane

⭐ Capt. Will C. Rogers III of the USS *Vincennes* ordered two missiles launched at Iran Air Flight 655 on July 3, 1988. He believed his ship was heading into a combat situation because the plane was heading directly toward them according to their radar and it did not respond to radio demands to identify itself. There was no combat situation. The plane, an Iranian airbus, carried 290 civilians: all were killed. The readings of the radar were attributed to human error. The plane was not descending upon the ship as thought. Although many errors were committed, the crew of *Vincennes* was absolved.

UNDERGROUND RAILROAD

The Coffins at Fountain City

⭐ Levi and Catherine "Aunt Katie" Coffin were Quakers who were opposed to slavery. Their home in Fountain City was later called "The Grand Central Station of the Underground Railroad." Three main lines of the Underground Railroad from Cincinnati, Ohio, and in Indiana, Madison and Jeffersonville, converged at Fountain City and the Coffins' home. They received more than 2,000 runaway slaves into their home during the Civil War. A frustrated Kentucky slave owner was the originator of the name "Underground Railroad," when he said "they must have an underground railroad running hereabouts, and Levi Coffin must be the president of it." Simeon and Rachel Halliday, characters in *Uncle Tom's Cabin* are based on the Coffins. Its heroine, Eliza Harris, also stayed with the Coffins as a fugitive for several days.

Crossing the river to freedom

⭐ Near West Franklin in Posey County, runaway slaves were helped across the Ohio River. Lake, Porter, and LaPorte counties all had places where slaves could be hidden until they could be smuggled on boats and carried farther north on the Underground Railroad network (see map). Evansville was another place where the slaves crossed the Ohio River. The city was the home of many freed slaves, who provided places for the runaways to hide. Another crossing of the Ohio River was between Owensboro in Kentucky, and Rockport in Indiana. Rockport had a regular crossing at the mouth of Indiana Creek.

Westfield: A slave hunter's last hope

⭐ The town of Westfield, founded by Quakers in 1834, was known as the north-central station of the Under-ground Railroad before the Civil War. This town was the last hope for a slave hunter to recapture a slave. Once a fugitive slave got this far north, he or she was considered safe.

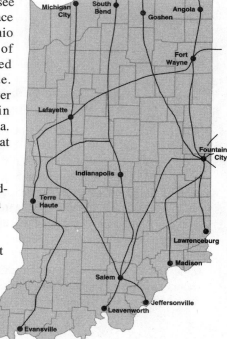

HOOSIER HAMLETS

On stage, in films, and in real life, Indiana cities and towns have the reputation of being typical middle-America.

Madison was chosen as the "typical American town" during World War II. Movies were made in 32 languages about Madison and sent to the troops to show the world what these American GIs were fighting to preserve. *Life* Magazine honored Madison as the ideal small town to live in.

In 1924, two sociologists, Robert and Helen Merrell Lynd used Muncie for their research into typical American behavior in a book called *Middletown*. Journalists and odds makers hang out in Muncie every election year just to get a middle-American opinion on the candidates.

Hold on one minute! If Indiana is so typical, what about Gnaw Bone, Pumpkin Center (of which there are two in Indiana), or Santa Claus. You can't call these towns typical, can you? Their names alone put them in the class of most unusual.

• Under Construction
• Indianapolis: The City
• Claims to Fame
• R & R Hoosier Style
• What's in a Name?
• Disastrous Events

UNDER CONSTRUCTION

Diamond in the rough

In the heart of rural Indiana sits a diamond in the rough. The contemporary architecture of more than forty public and private buildings has given Columbus the nickname of "Athens of the Prairie." Famous architects, artists, and designers, including I.M. Pei, Eliel Saarinen, and Kevin Roche, have left their mark on the city.

The change from a rather nondescript rural town to the "Athens of the Prairie" began in 1942 when the Finnish architect Eliel Saarinen was commissioned to design the First Christian Church. Its metamorphosis continued into the 1950s when J. Irwin Miller, an executive of the Cummins Engine Company, decided that the city needed a different look and offered to pay famous architects to come and design more contemporary buildings. Many were built almost 50 years ago but look brand new.

Outstanding in the Columbus architecture is the Commons, designed by Cesar Pelli, a completely enclosed ultra-modern shopping mall. A playground located within the mall has a constantly moving 7-ton sculpture built out of scrap metal by Jean Tinguely. Another noticeable design is Eero Saarinen's North Christian Church with a spire reaching 192 feet toward the sky.

North Christian Church

King Tut would approve

The College Life Insurance building, designed by Roche and Dinkeloo, opened its doors in 1972. What makes the Indianapolis building so unique is its three towers that look like quarter-pyramids. On the horizon of the Sahara Desert one wouldn't take a second glance at these towering pyramids, but in the heart of Indiana, they make a most unusual sight. Today, the Pyramids, as they are called, no longer house the College Life Insurance Company. It is now an office complex.

Canal dies, cities thrive

It took 20 years of constructing the Wabash & Erie Canal to connect Lake Erie and the Ohio River, a 460-mile stretch. In 1835, the first nine miles of the canal had been completed. A $10,000,000 federal bond gave the state the go-ahead to create a canal system run by a commission, but in 1837 the nation was in panic and the financial support was pulled. Bad investments by the clerk of canal commissioners, Isaac Coe, completed the collapse. However, the canal was completed from Fort Wayne through Logansport, Lafayette, Williamsport, Terre Haute, Bloomfield, and down to Evansville. And a portion was completed from Lawrenceburg to Hagerstown in the southeastern part of the state. The appearance of the railroads further stimied the success of the canal. The canal was a financial bust. However, for most of the cities along the canal it was a boon.

City of wrought iron

Madison is noted for its beautiful homes, many designed by Francis Costigan, a noted architect trained in Philadelphia and Baltimore. During the early 1800s, a great deal of beautiful iron-work was produced in Madison at the Neal Foundries—one of the largest in the United States. Much of it was shipped to Louisiana, contributing to that city's charm. Many houses in Madison still have beautiful wrought- and cast-iron work on exterior balconies and railings. The city's Shrewsbury Home features another unique design in its free-standing staircase at right.

**Free-standing spiral staircase
at Shrewsbury Home in Madison**

INDIANAPOLIS: THE CITY

🏠 On January 1, 1970, the Indianapolis and Marion County governments were redefined by the state legislature in the Unified Government Bill. Under the direction of Indianapolis mayor Richard Lugar, they consolidated into one unified government called Unigov. Unigov has a mayor, who can serve an unlimited number of terms, and a council of 29 members, all elected every four years. The City-County Council is elected from districts. The consolidation elevated Indianapolis's national population ranking from 26th to 11th in 1970. In 1991 it ranked 12th nationally. Unigov includes Indianapolis and Marion County excluding several cities and towns surrounded by the capital.

County and city form Unigov

🏠 A $1-million phase of the Indianapolis Canal Walk was opened in 1989 by Indianapolis Mayor William Hudnut III. Today's Canal Walk was originally part of the 1836 Indiana Improvement Act which included the Wabash & Erie Canal, the Whitewater Canal, and the Indiana Central Canal. Due to the state's financial difficulties, Indianapolis was the only part of the Indiana Central Canal that was completed. The canal was completed from Broad Ripple to Ohio Street. For every six linear feet, during construction, one life was lost to malaria, cholera, powder blasts, or kicks from mules.

The Canal Walk

The new Vermont Street Plaza, a part of the Canal Walk, features two fountains. One sprays 2,624 gallons of water per minute and the other 1,968 gallons per minute. Hot water discharged from the American United Life and State Office buildings is piped into the fountains, creating their magnificent spray.

Let the bells ring out!

Within the boundaries of Indianapolis is a most unusual cathedral. Completed in 1929, the Tudor Gothic-style Scottish Rite Cathedral has a 212-square-foot tower which contains a 54-bell carillon. The smallest bell is 6 inches in diameter and the largest is 7 feet. The cathedral also houses a 7,500-pipe organ. Following its construction, the International Association of Architects designated the cathedral "one of the seven most beautiful buildings in the world."

Legends leave names in concrete

They may not be Hollywood stars, but the signatures etched into Indiana's Walk of Legends are just as important to this state's residents. Orville Redenbacher and former Secretary of Agriculture Earl Butz are among those with their names written in the sidewalk at the state fairgrounds in Indianapolis.

The famous and infamous laid to rest

Crown Hill Cemetery is the burial place for many important figures in Indiana history. Benjamin Harrison, president; Charles W. Fairbanks and Thomas R. Marshall, vice presidents; Thomas T. Taggart and Albert J. Beveridge, U.S. senators; Oliver P. Morton, famous Civil War governor of Indiana; Kin Hubbard, author and humorist; and James Whitcomb Riley, poet. Among the not so desirables buried in Crown Hill is John Dillinger. The cemetery is located at the top of Strawberry Hill, the highest point in Indianapolis.

Children's Museum

Wonderful things are found at every turn in the Indianapolis Children's Museum, the largest of its kind in the world. The 203,000-square-foot building has five levels full of "hands-on" experiences. Explore a cave, visit a log cabin or tepee, and inspect a 55-ton locomotive. Scientific experiments are ready to be tested. Bakers busy themselves making croissants and other foods. You can check the accuracy of your watch with a 30-foot-tall water clock. On the top floor a carved carousel twirls around and around.

Museum's magnificent 55-foot atrium

First belt railroad

In 1877, the first belt railroad in the country (a 14-mile double track belt surrounding most of the city) was completed in Indianapolis. This greatly enhanced freight transportation and was copied by many other large cities. By 1902, Indianapolis gained the reputation of being one of the nation's largest interurban centers with the construction of electric rail lines connecting the city to all the major towns in Indiana.

CLAIMS TO FAME

🏠 Indiana cities have claimed to be first in a variety of areas. It had one of the first **electric interurban lines** in the United States. The 44-mile-long track ran between Brazil and Harmony and was completed in 1893.

The first **skyscraper** built in Indiana was located in Lawrenceburg. The 3-story brick, building erected in 1819 was an awesome sight to early Hoosiers.

Wabash was one of the first cities in the United States to use **electricity for public lighting**. On March 31, 1880, four large carbon lamps were installed on the courthouse dome. Each light produced over 4,000 candlepower.

Last but not least, did Sylvanus F. Bowser of Fort Wayne realize what he started when he invented the first **gasoline pump** in 1885? Without it, commuters might never get to work. Vacationers would never see the Grand Canyon. And a gas-price war would have been unheard of.

Indiana firsts

🏠 Elkhart is the musical instrument capital of the nation. There are 15 instrument factories busy producing half of all percussion and wind instruments made in the U.S. It has been first in the creation of many different instruments. An all-metal clarinet was manufactured by Charles Gerard Conn on August 27, 1889, and was named a "clarionet." The year prior to the clarionet, he produced the saxophone. 1908 was the year of the sousaphone. With design suggestions from "March King" John Phillip Sousa, Conn created a bell up sousaphone for parades. Later he designed the first bell-front instrument. The sarrusophone, an oboe-type instrument, was designed in 1921.

Who put the "sousa" in the sousaphone?

🏠 The Foellinger-Freimann Botanical Conservatory in Fort Wayne consists of three buildings connected by tunnels. Its 1,300 panels of glass make it one of the largest passive solar structures in the U.S.

Let the sun shine in

🏠 Petersburg is a small town with 5,000 inhabitants, 17 churches, and the only atheist museum in the Western world. Items displayed are related to the cultural anthropology of the United States. Murals show the history of the earth, man, and a DNA strand. The development of transportation and communication is depicted. Many books are available that discuss the world's major religions from an atheist's point of view. The owners describe their museum as the most "ungodly place north of the Mason-Dixon Line."

An ungodly place

A most unusual down-town district

🏠 Huntington's Jefferson Street Bridge spans the Little Wabash River. What makes this bridge unique is that one city block of stores and businesses is located on the bridge, suspended over the river and facing the bridge's traffic.

Tree's legacy lives on in its seedlings

Greensburg has the unique distinction of having a tree growing on the courthouse tower. It first appeared in 1870. The tree was removed, but five years later another tree started to grow. The citizens of Greensburg decided to let it stay. In 1929, it died of natural causes and was removed. During the removal, citizens discovered that another tree was already growing on the other side of the tower. Later, yet another tree started growing. Both trees were flourishing in the tower without any apparent nourishment. A visit from Smithsonian Institution scientists identified the trees as large-tooth aspens. Each September the town holds a Tree City Fall Festival in celebration of the phenomenon that grows on top of the courthouse.

A "bird's eye view"

🏠 DeVon Rose was planning to build a small replica of Wakarusa's Feed Mill, north of Nappanee, for his son's train set, but he got carried away. Instead, he built 60 miniature buildings on a one-inch-equals-five-foot scale out of toothpicks, popsicle sticks, and various other miniature building materials. His creations, one of the largest collections of miniatures in the world, are on display in the Bird's Eye View Museum at Nappanee.

Bees are their "bees-ness"

🏠 Since 1979, Boyd Musgrave and his wife, Madonna, of Banta have been catering to beekeepers. Even their daughter, Glenda Watson, reigned as Indiana's Honey Queen in 1980. Their general store provides beekeepers with a place to chat or purchase supplies. If they are having problems with their bees or need help in picking up a swarm, they just call Boyd. The Musgraves have a complete collection of smokers, used to repel bees and to cause the bees to engorge themselves, reducing their ability to sting. Musgrave's smokers date back to the 1800s.

World peace in Indiana

🏠 Michigan City is known for its sand dunes, coho and chinook salmon fishing, and world peace. To keep the peace, a spouse brings flowers home. It usually works, so why not try it at an international level? In 1934, the International Friendship Gardens project began. Thirty-five acres of plants given by countries and famous people from all over the world are arranged to look like each country. Among its more notable contributors are King Boris III of Bulgaria, Neville Chamberlain, King Gustav V of Sweden, Adolf Hitler, and Benito Mussolini.

Spiritualists gather in Chesterfield

🏠 Chesterfield is one of two major "spiritualist" meccas in the United States; the other is Lily Dale, New York. At Camp Chesterfield, many different methods are used by spiritualists to contact the dead, such as seances and trances. Clients come to visit the carefully hired mediums in cottages on the camp's 48 acres. Other areas of study include reincarnation, astrology, and faith healing. Courses in ESP, numerology, and spiritual healing are available to the campers. The camp has two hotels, an auditorium that seats 3,000 people, a cafeteria, and summer cottages.

🏠 In Nashville's courthouse yard sits the famous Liar's Bench. The bench is known to reward those who can tell the biggest lies. It seats six people and doesn't have an arm at one end. The person at the armless end is pushed off when a new liar takes his seat on the bench.

Six liars on a bench

🏠 The year 1836 is forever at Conner Prairie Pioneer Settlement. The 55-acre settlement south of Noblesville is run by Earlham College in Richmond. Costumed interpreters portray the real pioneers of old Indiana by demonstrating daily chores, crafts, and authentic customs on the William Conner Estate, built in 1823. Authenticity is crucial. When it was learned that the orchards of the time were not planted in rows as they are today, they were replanted in a random fashion. Beards were shaved off to keep in conformity with the 1836 gentleman. The ladies have to do without lace which was also missing from that era.

Conner Prairie Pioneer Settlement

🏠 Beverly Shores is a fashionable village on Lake Michigan. Many of its buildings are from the Century of Progress Exposition in Chicago including a Florida tropical house overlooking Lake Michigan (below).

Beverly Shores

The Exposition's Colonial Village, made up of reproductions of famous, historical habitats, was also moved to Beverly Shores:

Virginia Tavern—the tavern Washington visited in Georgetown.

Wakefield House—Washington's Virginia birthplace.

The House of the Seven Gables—the house in Nathanial Hawthorne's novel.

Wayside Inn—the tavern that inspired Longfellow's *Tales of the Wayside Inn.* Another Longfellow re-creation is the Village Smithy, a building constructed to resemble the blacksmith shop in his poem, the "Village Blacksmith."

Paul Revere House— Revere's Boston home.

The Old North Church— the famous Boston church.

Mount Vernon—George Washington's home.

R & R HOOSIER STYLE

Get healthy at French Lick

Even the early Indians found French Lick a great place for rest, relaxation, and recreation. Before the coming of the white settlers, the French Lick area had been a neutral Indian area where all could hunt and use the medicinal waters. It was a region where minerals were deposited on the rocks from the springs and the animals came to lick. The French operated a trading post in the area, hence the name French Lick.

The white settlers recognized the qualities of French Lick. Some had the foresight to reap the benefits from its natural resource. Dr. William Bowles built the first French Lick Springs Hotel in 1840. He even marketed the spring water as "Pluto Water." Dr. John Lane followed in 1851 with a hotel in West Baden and named his water "Sprudel Water." The West Baden was destroyed by fire in 1901.

The French Lick Springs Hotel was purchased in 1891 by a company headed by Thomas Taggart. Taggart was an influential national Democratic Party head, mayor of Indianapolis, and U.S. senator. When gambling came to the resort, it became a hot spot for celebrities and gangsters. Today, gambling has ceased to exist at French Lick, but it continues to be an elegant recreation spot.

West Baden Hotel: Carlsbad of America

The dome above the atrium of the West Baden Hotel (above) was called "the eighth wonder of the world." It was bigger than the dome at St. Peter's Basilica in Rome—200 feet in diameter, 130 feet from floor to top. The atrium floor was covered with 12 million Italian marble tiles and had sunken gardens planted with rare species from Asia and Europe. There were over 700 rooms on six floors which surrounded the atrium and gardens. Construction of the West Baden Hotel began in 1902, after the first hotel was destroyed by fire, at a cost of $414,000, in

200 working days. The builder agreed to complete the hotel, with a late penalty of $100 per day. He succeeded in meeting the agreed time.

The hotel was prosperous for nearly 30 years. Famous visitors included General John J. Pershing, Diamond Jim Brady, Al Capone, and J. M. Studebaker. The hotel's golden era was snuffed out by the Great Depression.

It became a headquarters for the Hagenbach-Wallace Circus, a Catholic school, and home for the Northwood Institute, a school that trains restaurant-hotel students. Many architectural changes have been made to accommodate the new tenants. Roman-style baths were taken away, gardens not tended, furniture sold, Moorish-type towers removed, arabesque brickwork changed and straightened to make it more of an institution rather than a resort. The huge dome and atrium remain intact, making the building a National Historic Site.

Gobbler glut celebrated at the Turkey Trot Festival

Daviess County wanted to be famous for something. Parke County had its many covered bridges. All Daviess County had was a gobbler glut. The county had 40 turkeys for each person. The perfect claim to fame was right under their noses in the barnyard. The residents decided to celebrate their bounty with the Daviess County "Turkey Trot Festival." The festival is a four-day event of turkey races with numerous preliminary heats featuring turkey racing stars—Dirty Bird, White Lightning, and Turkey Lurkey. The raceway is a 213-foot straight track which can be traversed by the winner in just 20 seconds. Another event is the best-dressed turkey contest. This turkey festival is famous world-wide. The races are sanctioned by the National Turkey Federation. People from all over the U.S. flock to the festival. Coverage of the event has been translated into five different languages.

🏠 Roselawn's Sun Spot is now a family-oriented nudist camp, but it used to be Naked City where thousands of spectators would flock to see its annual contests which included Miss Nude America and Miss Nude Teenybopper. The Sun Spot has dropped the contests and placed the emphasis on picnics, parties, and dances.

A nude retreat

WHAT'S IN A NAME?

🏠 Which came first—Buena Vista, Buena Vista, or Buena Vista? There are actually four Buena Vistas in Indiana. Being original doesn't come easy. The state has three Fairviews, four Millersburgs, three Needmores, three Mechanicsburgs, two Klondykes (and one Klondike), three Jamestowns, three Georgetowns, five Mt. Pleasants, four Salems, and two Pumpkin Centers.

The copycats

🏠 The only way you can get into Logansport is over a bridge. All its entrances cross water. Let's hope the Wabash and Eel Rivers stay in their banks. Or that all its residents have access to a boat. If you have a phobia about crossing bridges, stay away.

Logansport: City of Bridges

Gateway to the Northern Indiana Lake Region

The first large Indiana city on the Wabash & Erie Canal is Fort Wayne. Three rivers converge on the city—the Maumee, St. Mary's, and St. Joseph. The rivers are crossed within the city by some 20 bridges. Surrounding Fort Wayne are over 300 lakes, hence its nickname, Gateway to the Northern Indiana Lake Region.

Hymera rather than Pittsburg

Hymera was once a prosperous coal-mining town originally named Pittsburg. But when the postmaster discovered another town in Indiana already named Pittsburg, he renamed the town High Mary, after his very tall adopted daughter. The name was later shortened to Hymera.

Believe it. . . Santa Claus is in Indiana

How can a town with a population of 300 receive about one million pieces of mail yearly? Easy, just name it Santa Claus.

But the mail doesn't stay in the town for long. In fact, envelopes come packaged in bulk for the sole purpose of receiving the "Santa Claus" cancellation. Since 1856, its post office has been processing mail with a unique Santa Claus postmark. The post office and Santa Claus even made it into *Ripley's Believe It or Not* in 1929. The late Jim Martin, postmaster at Santa Claus, was known nationally as the real Santa Claus for 35 years.

The name Santa Claus actually began as a joke. At first the name Santa Fe was suggested, but another Indiana town beat them to the punch. Someone suggested, with tongue in cheek, the name Santa Claus. It stuck.

The town became the home of a Santa Claus College in the 1930s when Charles W. Howard opened up a school to train department store Santas. Its graduates received Bachelor of Santa Clausing degrees. Today, Santa Claus is known more for its Holiday World, a 180-acre amusement park. The park opened in 1946. At that time it was named Santa's Country; it was later changed to its present name. Holiday World has the distinction of being the first amusement park in the nation.

The town's streets and landmarks are reminiscent of Christmas. A drive through Santa Claus reveals such names as Lake Rudolph, Snowflake Drive-in, Christmas Lake Village housing development, and Sled Run. The town's newspaper is named *Santa's Country*.

Indians name Elkhart

History has it that an Indian noticed the island where the Elkhart and St. Joseph Rivers meet was shaped like an elk's heart. The island was named Elkhart. Isaac McCoy, a Baptist minister to the area, recorded the name, which white settlers adopted.

Gnaw Bone sticks to its guns

Although the State Highway Commission tried to change Gnaw Bone to West Point, the citizens refused. They say the town was named when one of the early settlers, who was looking for someone, was told: "I seed him a-settin' on a log above the sawmill a-gnawing on a bone."

A Loogootee sounds like some character out of Dr. Suess, but it's not. It is a town in the southern portion of Indiana. The name Loogootee is a combination of Lowe—name of the engineer of the first train through town—and Gootee—owner of the land upon which the town was built.

What's a Loogootee?

The Eiteljorg Museum of American Indian and Western Art in Indianapolis houses a $40 million collection. These prancing deer are found outside the museum, which is considered the finest of its kind in the nation. It is named after Indianapolis businessman Harrison Eiteljorg.

DISASTROUS EVENTS

Lockheed discovered too late for the passengers of Flight 710 on March 17, 1960, that their Electras had wings which broke in certain types of flight vibrations. The wing tore away over Tell City driving the aircraft into the ground. It hit at a speed of 600 mph, killing all 63 aboard.

Flight vibrations tore off wing

The squirrel invaders

In 1833, the same year that Salem was hit with a cholera epidemic, a huge squirrel invasion occurred in Washington County. Thousands of squirrels came from the north, filling the trees, fences, and ruining the corn crop. The settlers tried killing and capturing them but more came. As quickly as they came, they disappeared with no one knowing what had brought them in the first place.

David and Goliath 🏠 An Allegheny Airlines DC-9 flight crashed on August 9, 1969, because the student pilot of a Piper Cherokee plane sheared off the jet's tail. Attempting to land in Indianapolis, the jet spiraled out of control and crashed outside of Shelbyville killing all 83 people aboard. The disaster could have been prevented if the jet had been equipped with a transponder, a piece of radar equipment now found on all flights.

Explosion causes panic 🏠 Panic from the explosion of a steam boiler used with a portable sawmill on exhibit at the Indianapolis State Fair, October 1, 1869, caused the death of 27 people. The majority were women and children trampled by the crowd. Fifty-six more people were injured.

INDIANA GETS STAMPED

Indiana has been honored by the United States Post Office many times. The following stamps were issued in Indiana towns:

World War II	Souvenir sheet	August 17, 1992	Indianapolis
Cole Porter	29 cent stamp	June 8, 1991	Peru
Knute Rockne	22 cent stamp	March 9, 1988	Notre Dame
Racing Car	17.5 cent stamp	September 25, 1987	Indianapolis
Milk Wagon	5 cent stamp	September 25, 1987	Indianapolis
Pan American Games	22 cent stamp	January 29, 1987	Indianapolis
Horace A. Moses	20 cent stamp	August 6, 1984	Bloomington
Christmas (Santa)	20 cent stamp	October 28, 1983	Santa Claus
Summer Olympics	13 cent stamp	July 28, 1983	South Bend
Casimir Pulaski	2 cent stamp	January 16, 1931	Gary
			(issued in 9 other cities)
Ohio River	2 cent stamp	October 19, 1929	Evansville
			(issued in 6 other cities)
George Rogers Clark	2 cent stamp	February 25, 1929	Vincennes
			(also in Charlottesville, VA)

Air Mail Stamps issued in Indiana:

Balloon Jupiter	7 cent stamp	August 17, 1959	Lafayette
Blanche Stuart Scott	28 cent stamp	December 30, 1980	Hamondsport, NY
Benjamin Harrison	13 cent stamp	January 11, 1926	Indianapolis
			(also in North Bend, OH)

IN THE SPOTLIGHT

Dancing, music, and play-acting—what kind of foolishness is this? Even the *Indianapolis Journal* refuses to advertise theatricals.

It was the early 1800s and most Indiana settlers knew little about having a good time. That is, until showboats began stopping in Ohio River towns. Evansville, Madison, and New Albany residents couldn't resist the temptation of the magnificent floating theaters.

By 1898, Hoosiers were hungry for entertainment. Their appetites were appeased by the likes of the Boston Lyric Opera Company and John Philip Sousa's Band. In the years to follow, Indiana produced great entertainers—Carole Lombard, James Dean, Michael Jackson, and David Letterman. Its towns and cities were the backdrops for two hit movies, *Breaking Away* and *Hoosiers*. The next few pages will give you a look at all that "foolishness."

- Actors and Actresses
- Awards and Honors
- Indiana in the Movies
- Behind the Camera
- Comics, Clowns & Circuses
- Singers, Musicians & Their Songs
- Indiana on TV

ACTORS AND ACTRESSES

A tough guy

⭐ An ex-reform school boy, drifter, and marine describes Steve McQueen in his early days. He came into the world March 24, 1930, in the Indiana town of Beech Grove, an Indianapolis suburb. His father, who walked out six months after McQueen's birth, named him Terrence Steve after a one-armed bookie friend. Young Steve's acting career began in New York where he attended acting school and debuted as a walk-on in a Second Avenue theater. The calm, cool, and collected McQueen hit Broadway as a replacement for Ben Gazzara in *Hatful of Rain*. However, Broadway would not be his greatest success. The TV series "Wanted—Dead or Alive" brought him national recognition as bounty hunter Josh Randall, from 1958 to 1961. His portrayal and his motorcycle-riding escapades as a POW stood out in the 1963 movie *The Great Escape*. Other movies included *The Magnificent Seven, Bullitt,* and *The Sand Pebbles.* McQueen, who died in 1980, was married to actresses Neile Adams, Ali McGraw, and Barbara Minty.

The Brady's mom

⭐ Being the mom of six "Brady Bunch" kids kept Florence Henderson pretty busy. "The Brady Bunch" TV series ran from 1969 to 1974. Henderson, a native of Dale, Indiana, performed in many Broadway musicals, including *Oklahoma* and *The Sound of Music.*

J.R.'s arch-rival

⭐ Ken Kercheval portrayed J. R. Ewing's nemesis, Cliff Barnes, in the TV series "Dallas." The Wolcottville native's most popular Broadway appearances were in *Who's Afraid of Virginia Woolf?, Fiddler on the Roof,* and *Cabaret.*

Calling Dr. Joe Gannon

⭐ The dashing Dr. Joe Gannon of "Medical Center," Chad Everett starred in the TV series from 1969 to 1976. He was known as Ray Canton in his hometown of South Bend. His TV appearances include "Hawaiian Eye," "77 Sunset Strip," "Lawman," "Route 66," and "Ironside." On film he performed in *The Singing Nun, The Impossible Years,* and *Airplane II—The Sequel.*

TV's most lovable grandpa

⭐ Goodnight, mama. Goodnight, pa. Goodnight, grandpa. "The Waltons" TV series ended every episode with goodnights echoing through the old Walton homestead. Among the most loved was Grandpa Zeb Walton played by Will Geer, born March 9, 1902, in Frankfort. He won an Emmy in 1975 for his portrayal of the head of the Walton clan. Geer died in 1978 and was not replaced in the series. Instead, the seventh season's opening show dealt with the family's loss of Grandpa.

He was a rebel

James Dean, the idol of the 1950s, was born February 8, 1931, in Marion, where only a small boulder, in what is now a parking lot, identifies his place of birth. Dean stayed in the home until 1936. He spent most of his growing up years after his mother died with his uncle in Fairmount.

Dean was educated at the University of California, Los Angeles. He appeared in TV commercials, but his big break was in New York where he acted in two plays. His role as a homosexual procurer in *The Immoralist* won Dean a Tony in 1954.

His first movie in Hollywood was *East of Eden*. After it opened, Dean became an instant teenage idol and then a legend. *Rebel Without a Cause* opened four days after he crashed in his sports car on his way to a race meet on September 30, 1955. Later *Giant* was released. After his death, Dean's fans worshiped him. Many gathered around the spot where the accident occurred. His fans quickly made his memory into a cult, a cult that exists even today.

His family brought his body back to Indiana to bury him in Park Cemetery at Fairmount. Approximately 3,000 people attended the funeral. For 10 years after Dean died, Warner Bros. continued to receive 7,000 letters per day addressed to the movie star. His grave in Park Cemetery has been defaced, handfuls of soil taken, and people from as far away as Germany have tried to buy burial plots next to Dean.

The town of Fairmount holds a "Remembering James Dean" festival in connection with the September Fairmount Museum Days.

⭐ Actress Carole Lombard (Jane Alice Peters of Fort Wayne) began her career as a Mack Sennett bathing beauty and played in 13 of his comedies where she experienced custard pies in the face and drenchings from buckets of water. She joined Paramount in 1930. Both funny and glamorous, she was first married to William Powell. But her most notorious and greatest love was with Clark Gable. They were married and lived happily together for five years until she was killed in a plane crash in 1941. The plane crashed into Table Rock Mountain outside of Las Vegas after flying from a patriotic pageant in Salt Lake City where she sold U.S. defense bonds. President Roosevelt awarded her a posthumous medal as the "first woman to be killed in action in the defense of her country in its war against the Axis powers." Among her most popular films was *My Man Godfrey* (1936) and *To Be or Not To Be* (1942).

Beauty, comedy, and tragedy

A ditzy barmaid

The "Cheers" bar is a long way from Fort Wayne where Shelley Long was born. But after all, wasn't the job supposed to be temporary? And Long's character, Diane Chambers, was much too intelligent to stay. Somehow time got away, and the ditzy barmaid finally left the TV series after five years. Long didn't leave empty-handed. She received an Emmy for her performance as Diane in 1983 and had the pleasure of jilting Sam. A less pleasing honor bestowed on Long in 1987 was making Mr. Blackwell's Worst-Dressed Women list. Long has also starred in the movies *Irreconcilable Differences, Outrageous Fortune,* and *Troop Beverly Hills.*

Will the real Malden Sukilovich please stand up?

Karl Malden's real name, Malden Sukilovich, would not be so easily recognized on the American Express card he promotes. Born in Gary, March 22, 1914, he was successful on the stage in *A Streetcar Named Desire, Desperate Hours,* and *Desire Under the Elms.* He won an Oscar for the movie version of *A Streetcar Named Desire* in 1951. He starred with Michael Douglas on TV in the series "The Streets of San Francisco" from 1972 to 1977.

A "terribly, terribly British" Hoosier

A "terribly, terribly British" Hoosier, Clifton Webb was born November 19, 1891, in Indianapolis. Born Webb Parmallee Hollenbeck, he was performing on stage at age eight. His mother took a great interest in developing his theatrical career. His father disagreed and split. At age 19 Webb began a career in dancing. He danced in many Broadway and London musicals. Webb was over 50 before he entered the film industry. He was best known for his characterization of Mr. Belvedere in *Sitting Pretty.*

AWARDS AND HONORS

Oscar winner among first worst-dressed

In 1946, *The Razor's Edge* earned Anne Baxter the Best Supporting Actress Oscar. She didn't always remain the best. Baxter, born in Michigan City on May 7, 1923, was named in 1960 to Mr. Blackwell's first list of the Worst-Dressed Women. She appeared in *All About Eve* and the television series "Hotel." Granddaughter of architect Frank Lloyd Wright, Baxter died December 12, 1985, in New York.

Musicals bring honors to Hoosier

Director Robert Wise brought the silver screen alive with music and earned two Oscars for *West Side Story* in 1961 and *The Sound of Music* in 1965. Born September 10, 1914, in Winchester, Wise was editor of Orson Welles's *Citizen Kane* (1941) and *The Magnificent Ambersons* (1941) at RKO prior to directing films.

At least once, possibly more, Americans gather around the TV and watch *Miracle on 34th Street,* especially at Christmas time. Screenwriter George Seaton, born April 17, 1911, in South Bend, earned an Oscar in 1947 for this heart-warming tale of Santa Claus. *The Country Girl* in 1954 earned him a second Oscar.

An Oscar-winning Christmas tradition

Making his contribution to the theater, dramatist and screenwriter Paul Osborn, a native of Evansville, received a Tony for his play *Morning's at Seven* in 1980. He also wrote the screenplays for two outstanding films: *The Yearling* (1947) and *South Pacific* (1958).

Dramatist wins Tony

The dual role of Adam and Stuart Chandler on ABC's "All My Children" has been good to David Canary. He earned Emmys for his performance in 1986, 1988, 1989, and 1992. He also played Candy on the TV classic "Bonanza."

Emmys for soap star

INDIANA IN THE MOVIES

Beating the odds and winning is what the 1987 film *Hoosiers* is all about. It is a story of three "comebacks." A small southern Indiana town takes the ball and runs with it. Against all odds, their high school basketball team becomes state champions. Norman Dale, played by Gene Hackman, is starting over as a coach, but he makes it happen. And the town drunk, Shooter, played by Dennis Hopper, tries to rebuild his life. (Learn more about the real Hoosiers team on page 88)

Beating the odds

Gary in the 1940s is the setting for the 1983 movie *A Christmas Story*. Based on a comic novel, *In God We Trust, All Others Pay Cash*, by Jean Shepherd, it tells of a simpler time when people weren't trying to keep up with the Joneses. The main character, Ralphie, played by Peter Billingsley, wants a Daisy Brand Red Ryder repeating BB gun and pays a visit to a workaholic Santa Claus.

A Red Ryder BB gun, a workaholic Santa, and a Christmas story

Coming of age in Bloomington, Indiana, is the basis of the 1979 movie *Breaking Away*. Filmed on location, four local youths facing adulthood decide to have one last summer fling. Actor Dennis Christopher plays Dave, who has ambitions of being a champion bicycle racer. His three buddies are played by Dennis Quaid, Jackie Earle Haley, and Daniel Stern. The screenplay was written by Indianan Steve Tesich, who won an Oscar for the movie. The movie was the basis of the ABC series with the same name. Featured as the cyclist was Shawn Cassidy. The show on the fall line-up in 1980, but was canceled in January, 1981.

Bloomington is setting for Steve Tesich film

Four friends growing up in Hoosierland

Another Steve Tesich screenplay, *Four Friends,* was filmed on location in East Chicago. Having lived in the neighborhoods of East Chicago, Tesich tells the story of four friends growing up in the turbulent 1960s. This 1981 film was directed by Arthur Penn.

BEHIND THE CAMERA

A genius behind the camera

Sydney Pollack left behind his home in Lafayette to become one of the all-time great directors. A 1954 graduate of Neighborhood Playhouse Theatre School in New York, Pollack began as an actor on Broadway and live TV. His area of expertise changed from performing in front of the camera to working on the other side. He has an uncanny ability for turning great actors and actresses into even greater ones. Paul Newman and Dustin Hoffman are only two of his many successes. As a motion picture director, his credits include *They Shoot Horses, Don't They?, The Way We Were,* and *Absence of Malice.* He was producer and director for *Tootsie* and *Out of Africa.* He won a Best Director Oscar for *Out of Africa* in 1986, which also took Best Picture. In 1966 he won an Emmy for "The Game." In TV he is most widely known for his episodes of the "Ben Casey" series.

Gentlemen Prefer Blondes director

The first film Howard Winchester Hawks directed, *The Road to Glory,* was the beginning of a long and prosperous career. Born in 1896, in Goshen, Hawks is best remembered for *Dawn Patrol, Scarface, Bringing Up Baby, Sergeant York,* and *Gentlemen Prefer Blondes.*

Lafayette native earns Emmys

John Korty, a native of Lafayette, won an Emmy for best director in 1974. *The Autobiography of Miss Jane Pittman* also gave Korty a Directors Guild of America Award. In 1977 he received an Emmy for outstanding individual achievement for *Who Are the DeBolts . . . and Where Did They Get 19 Kids?*

What do Indiana, Reagan, and Valentino have in common?

Now, where would Ronald Reagan, Joe DiMaggio, Red Grange, Tom Mix, and Rudolph Valentino go for an instant marriage? All of these famous men chose Lake County's famous courthouse, "The Grand Old Lady of Lake County," for their nuptials. Was it the no-blood-tests or the lack of a three-day waiting period that made Indiana a wedding chapel in the first half of the century?

Morality in films

Are today's films adhering to the Hays Code? Actually called the Production Code, it was tagged the Hays Code after one of its authors, Will H. Hays. He joined others in putting a strict code of morality on American films in 1933. The code lasted until 1966. Hays, a former

Sullivan, Indiana, attorney and U.S. postmaster general, became the first president of the Motion Picture Producers and Distributors of America (later called the Motion Picture Association of America) in 1922. In his new position he developed a moral blacklist in Hollywood and put morals clauses in actors' contracts. In American films today morality is rated rather than enforced.

COMICS, CLOWNS, & CIRCUSES

In the late 1800s, the circus became a major focal point in the life of Peru, Indiana. Ben Wallace, a livery stable owner, inherited the animals of an animal show in 1883 when the owner couldn't pay for his services. Taking on a partner, James Anderson, Wallace decided to start his own circus. It became one of the world's best, the Hagenbeck-Wallace circus.

Circus life in Peru

Wallace's reputation for having good facilities turned Peru into the off-season home for many major circuses. Many famous circus entertainers spent part of the year in Peru. Among them were Emmett Kelly, the clown; Tom Mix, who later became a Hollywood star in westerns; Clyde Beatty, the animal trainer from Peru who moved on to become world-famous and form his own circus; and Willi Wilno, a human cannonball.

The circus no longer flourishes in Peru except the third week of July each year when the circus comes to town once again. Its performers, ranging in age from six to ninety-six, must be Miami County residents. Many are descendants of the early circus performers. The old-time circus is recreated, complete with human pyramids, clowns, tightrope walkers, and aerialists. A giant parade with calliopes, old circus wagons, and the Circus City Band kick off the event. NBC once filmed a documentary on the Peru circus.

June 22, 1918, marked a dark day in the otherwise upbeat life of the Hagenbeck-Wallace Circus. The circus train, while sitting in the Ivanhoe train yard, was hit in the rear by a Michigan Central Railroad troop train and 53 circus performers were killed. The engineer, A.K. Sargent, was accused of falling asleep at the wheel.

Hagenbeck-Wallace Circus tragedy

One of the elephants performing in the ring of the Tarzan Zerbini International Circus at Lafayette, Indiana, on July 15, 1992, decided to make an unscheduled stop. A chain reaction occurred when the next elephant failed to put on the brakes, sending the first into a barricade. Several spectators in the crowd of circus lovers were injured slightly by the flying barricade, but the only hospitalization was one woman experiencing a panic attack.

Elephant collision sends spectators scrambling

Red Skelton: A clown through and through

Richard (Red) Bernard Skelton has clowning in his blood, literally. His father, a circus clown, died two months before Skelton was born in Vincennes in 1913. By ten, Skelton, already known as "Red" for his flaming hair, was on the road with a medicine show. His first circus stint was with the Hagenbeck-Wallace Circus in Peru. Best known for his television series, "The Red Skelton Show," from 1951 to 1971, he recreated the characters he had brought to vaudeville, such as Clem Kaddiddlehopper, Sheriff Deadeye, Junior the Mean Widdle Kid, and Cauliflower McPugg.

Late night host David Letterman

Comedian and talk-show host David Letterman was born April 12, 1947, in Indianapolis. The graduate of Ball State University, Muncie, began his career as a radio and TV announcer in Indianapolis. He performed in 1975 at The Comedy Store in Los Angeles. Appearances on "Rock Concert" and "The Gong Show" are among his credits. Several guests host stints on "The Tonight Show" led to hosting his "The David Letterman Show" and "Late Night with David Letterman." Letterman won six Emmys from 1981 to 1988.

"Laugh-In" star, Jo Anne Worley

One of the original "Laugh-In" cast members, comedienne Jo Anne Worley was born in Lowell in 1937. "Laugh-In" was a popular television series in the late 60s. Even President Nixon had a cameo spot on the show, uttering the immortal words, "Sock it to me?"

SINGERS, MUSICIANS & THEIR SONGS

Hoosiers who hit the top of the charts

The name stayed the same, but the town changed. Joe Dowell was born in Bloomington, Indiana, but grew up in Bloomington, Illinois. Dowell wrote his first song at the age of 13 and titled it "Tell Me." He had a #1 hit in 1961, "Wooden Heart," right after another Indiana-born singer, Bobby Lewis, hit the top of the charts.

Indianapolis-born Bobby Lewis spent twelve years in an orphanage before being adopted and moving to Michigan. He had a #1 hit song in 1961 called "Tossin' and Turnin'."

John Cougar Mellencamp eloped at age 18 but his in-laws threw him out. The singer and songwriter born in Seymour often tells the story of small-town life in his songs. A man of many names, his first record called him Johnny Cougar. He later became John Cougar Mellencamp and in the 1990s, he dropped the Cougar. "Jack and Diane" hit the top of the charts in 1982.

Deniece Williams joined Johnny Mathis in the 1978 hits, "Too Much, Too Little, Too Late" and "Let's Hear It for the Boy" from the movie *Footloose* in 1984. She was born in Gary on June 3, 1951.

⭐ July 1991, a concert outside St. Louis, Missouri, 20,000 angry Guns N' Roses fans rioted. Why? . . . Axl Rose jumped into the crowd to stop a person from filming the band while they were performing. The crowd exploded when the band walked off the stage after security failed to throw out the camera-wielding fan. The stadium was left in a shambles and $200,000 worth of property was damaged. Rose finally paid his due in 1992. He was arrested on a damage-to-property charge and four counts of misdemeanor assault in connection with the St. Louis Guns N' Roses riot. Rose had planned to turn himself in, but was caught at JFK airport in New York before he could do so.

A rose isn't always a rose

Two Lafayette, Indiana, friends, Bill Bailey (who changed his name to Axl Rose) and Jeff Isabelle (Izzy Stradlin), formed this volatile and controversial band in Los Angeles in 1985. The name Guns N' Roses was a combination of two bands some of its members belonged to, L.A. Guns and Hollywood Rose. Members of the band include lead guitarist Slash, bassist Duff McKagan, drummer Matt Sorum (who replaced Steven Adler), and keyboardist Dizzy Reed. Guns N' Roses's first album, *Appetite for Destruction*, and those to follow include violence, racism, sexism, homophobia, and drug abuse. It turned them into the kings of heavy metal rock. *Appetite for Destruction* sold 14 millions copies. In 1991 they released two albums, *Use Your Illusion I* and *Use Your Illusion II*, making rock history by selling about 500,000 copies within three days. The marriage of Erin Everly (Don of the Everly Brothers' daughter) and Axl Rose lasted a whole 27 days.

⭐ Home was a 40-acre farm in South Whitley for Janie Fricke, country/western star. As an Indiana University student, she began making extra money by singing commercial jingles which led her to Nashville, Tennessee, after graduation in 1975. Her recording career began anonymously while singing back-up for a number of vocalists including Tanya Tucker. Fricke moved on to sing duets with Johnny Duncan. Finally, Fricke went solo. Among her country hits are "I'll Need Someone to Hold Me," "Please Help Me I'm Falling," and "Pass Me By." She continues to sing duets. Charlie Rich, George Jones, and Merle Haggard have been some of her famed partners.

From back-up singer to country star

⭐ Lyricist Noble Sissle, born in Indianapolis in 1889, became the partner of ragtime composer Eubie Blake in 1915. They worked together on and off for many years, including a stint as "The Dixie Duo" in vaudeville. Their show, *Shuffle Along*, broke the color barriers in every theater it played in the 1920s. One of their most popular songs was "I'm Just Wild About Harry," which was used by Harry Truman as a campaign song.

Wild about Harry

MCA founder

Though trained as a physician, South Bend-born Jules Stein (known to his parents as Julien Caesar Stein) went into business in Chicago with a partner, Billy Goodheart, Jr., to book musical acts, under the name of Music Corporation of America. It was a grandiose name for two young men starting out, but MCA eventually lived up to its name. What became the biggest theatrical and musical agency in the world began with total capital of $1,000.

Paul Dresser gives state its song

The idea of priesthood didn't set right with Paul Dresser, brother of the famous American novelist, Theodore Dreiser. Born in Terre Haute in 1858, he was sent to St. Meinrad Academy in the town of that name in Indiana. At 15 he ran away from the academy, changed his name to Dresser, and joined a medicine show in Indianapolis. In 1892 he joined a music publishing company and for 10 years he enjoyed nationwide recognition as a songwriter. "My Gal Sal," "Just Tell Them that You Saw Me," and "The Blue and the Gray" were favorites at the time. Although he died in 1906 broke and in ill health, his song "On the Banks of the Wabash, Far Away" has lived on as Indiana's state song.

Cole Porter

Cole Porter, born in 1892 into a wealthy family in Peru, was promised a fortune from his grandfather if he would become a lawyer. He tried but in 1916 he left the law and turned to composing and writing music. With a friend he wrote his first show, *See America First*. Hundreds of songs and many musicals followed. Among his best known songs are "Night and Day" and "Don't Fence Me In." After a fall from a horse in 1937, Porter was left with both legs smashed.

Time spent in a wheel chair and a life of pain didn't stop him from composing. When his friends thought he was at the end of his rope dealing with his pain, Porter composed one of America's best musical scores, *Kiss Me Kate*. His last two musicals were *Can-Can* and *Silk Stockings*. In 1956, Porter faced two more operations making a total of 33 since his accident. Two years later, his right leg was amputated following a bone tumor diagnosis. Porter became a recluse. In 1964, Porter underwent routine surgery for kidney stones. It would be his last. He died two days later, on October 15, 1964.

A regular with Jack Benny

The man best known for his song "That's What I Like about the South" was born in Linton, Indiana, but Phil Harris's youth was spent in Nashville, Tennessee. Comedian and bandleader, Harris was a regular on "The Jack Benny Show." He and wife, Alice Faye, worked together on radio's "Bandwagon Show" and their own "Phil Harris-Alice Faye Show." He never has explained just what "The Thing" found in his perennially favorite song was.

The Jackson clan

Driven by their father, Joseph Jackson, five brothers from Gary formed a group in 1966 singing in and around their home. In the next two years, they recorded three singles on the Steeltown Records label. "Let Me Carry Your Schoolbooks" was sung by the Jackson brothers under the name Ripples and Waves. In 1968, "Big Boy", their first song under the name Jackson 5, and "You Don't Have to be Twenty-One to Fall in Love" were recorded.

The brothers, Michael, Tito, Marlon, Jackie, and Jermaine, exploded on the scene after being discovered by Motown in Detroit. Their debut single, "I Want You Back," was a smash in 1969. Diana Ross and Motown boss Berry Gordy, Jr., helped the Jackson 5 become hit-makers rivaling the Osmonds. In 1977, they became "The Jacksons" striking gold with their first album.

Jermaine married Gordy's daughter, Hazel Joy, in 1973. The wedding was extravagant to say the least. The wedding decor featured 175 doves in white cages and 7,000 camellias. Jermaine opted to stay with his father-in-law and go solo when the Jacksons split from Motown in 1976. He was replaced by brother Randy. Sister LaToya appeared with the group occasionally. She made her solo recording debut with "If You Feel the Funk." The youngest sister, Janet, also soloed. She hit the charts with "Control" in 1987. Her record, "Miss You Much," climbed to the top of the charts in 1989. She took up acting and was a star of the comedy series "Good Times" as a battered child.

Michael Jackson: The thriller

Every time he goes on tour, Michael Jackson is greeted by thousands of screaming fans. The thrill of his performances has never diminished. Michael's fans have copied his "moon walk," worn a single beaded glove, and danced to his music (young Michael Jackson is pictured above center wearing a tie).

Michael's mother and father, Katherine and Joe Jackson, were the inspiration for Michael. His father used an iron hand while his mother was more gentle. Michael began playing bongos when he was five years old. He was lead singer with The Jackson 5 at the age of 10 when Motown put them on the charts. His singing ability made him a stand-out in the group. Michael began to branch out in 1978 when he appeared in the Motown/Universal film *The Wiz*. With the film's music director, Quincy Jones, Michael produced his first solo album, *Off the Wall*. It sold 5 million copies in the U.S. alone. He brought Jones in again to work on another album, *Thriller*. The album, which appeared in 1983, is the best-selling album of all time. The first hit single of the album was "Billie Jean." Lionel Ritchie and Jackson created "We are the World" for the first Live Aid concert.

Michael is not without his eccentricities. He has a love for exotic animals. Many roam freely at his California home—snakes, giraffes, monkeys, the works.

Inspired before he saw the real thing

Songwriter Albert Von Tilzer wrote "Take Me out to the Ball Game" twenty years before he ever attended a game. Von Tilzer was born in Indianapolis in 1878, to a family named Gumm. Both he and a brother changed their names to their mother's maiden name. He worked primarily in vaudeville and early Broadway before going to Hollywood.

Mood music for your vegetables

Only in Indianapolis could an album be released for houseplant lovers. Funny Forum of Indianapolis released an album entitled *Vegetable Conversation: Music and Thoughts for Things in Pots*. The album was created for latchkey plants—those left home alone. Hits include: "Lament to a Plant," "Oh, the Coleus," and "No Matter How Fertile, There's No Place Like Loam."

INDIANA ON TV

One day at a time in Indianapolis

Single-parent families was the subject of the CBS sitcom, "One Day at a Time," starring Bonnie Franklin. It took place in an Indianapolis apartment where Franklin (Ann Romano) worked at raising her two daughters (Valerie Bertinelli and Mackenzie Phillips) alone. The show began in 1975 and ended in 1984.

Documentary on the all-American town

Six programs were filmed by producer Peter Davis of Muncie. A book, *Middletown,* written by two sociologists, Helen and Robert Lynd, in 1929, inspired Davis to choose Muncie in 1981 as the all-American town. The documentary aired in 1982. One segment was not aired because of complaints by students and parents. Davis had filmed high-schoolers smoking marijuana.

Reporting the news

Frank Reynolds was a familiar face on local Chicago TV. The East Chicago-born Reynolds joined ABC as a Chicago correspondent in 1963. He moved up the ladder securing a post as ABC correspondent in Washington and later became the anchor of "World News Tonight." He won a Peabody Award and an Emmy for his news broadcasting in 1969.

The second first lady of news

Jane Pauley, Chicago's first woman co-anchor on WMAQ-TV, replaced Barbara Walters as NBC's "Today" show host after four years of TV reporting. The Indianapolis-born Pauley went on to host her own show, "Real Life with Jane Pauley," and more recently has co-hosted NBC's "Dateline" with Stone Phillips (shown with Pauley).

MAKING IT IN INDIANA

Bakers will never tell at Tell City. A secret recipe brought over from Europe by a Swiss baker over 100 years ago has never gone beyond the walls of the Tell City Pretzel Company. The company produces 8,000 pretzels each day, all still hand-twisted.

Pretzels, roses—even goldfish—are among the multitude of products Indiana offers to the world. The northwest region ranks high in the nation's industrial output. Steel mills and oil refineries nestle along Indiana's Lake Michigan shoreline. And Elkhart is the band instrument capital of the world. Indiana ranks high among agricultural states as well.

- Birth of the Automobile
- Industrial Stronghold
- With Heads in the Clouds
- Indiana Farming
- Inventions, Firsts & Great Ideas
- Made in Indiana
- Hoosier Communicators
- Riding the Rails

BIRTH OF THE AUTOMOBILE

**The birthplace of the
horseless carriage**

$ Although Indiana leaves the title "automobile capital of the nation" to its neighbor to the north, it does claim the title of "American birthplace of the automobile." It began with inventor and all-round general practical person, Elwood Haynes of Kokomo. Haynes is recognized as the creator of the first successful car. In 1892, the inventor was fascinated with the idea of a self-propelling vehicle. After trying electricity and steam, he settled on a gasoline-powered single-cylinder upright marine engine. Other firsts in the Haynes vehicle were a clutch and an electric ignition.

On the Fourth of July, 1894, he tested his car on the Pumpkin Vine Pike, east of Kokomo. Down six miles of the Pike, Haynes roared into the history books at seven miles per hour. The vehicle is now in the Smithsonian Institute.

Wind snuffs out chance to be first

Charles H. Black built an automobile with an internal combustion gasoline engine in Indianapolis in 1891. Because his automobile engine used a kerosene torch for ignition, it was considered impractical since the torch would blow out on a windy day. This prevented him from being noted as inventor and builder of the first successful automobile.

**An early version of
Detroit**

$ Early in the days of automobiles, Indiana was tops. And the town of Auburn was its leader, producing 21 different types of cars. As early as 1900, Frank and Morris Eckhart started building the beautiful Auburn automobile. In 1903, they introduced their Auburn at the Chicago Auto Show. By 1919, the Eckhart brothers sold the Auburn Automobile Company to a group of Chicago bankers.

The company struggled until Errett Lobban Cord took it under his wing. He was considered by many a "shaker and mover" in the automobile field. His motto was "If you can't be big, you have to be different." His Cord L-29 became the first production car to have front-wheel drive. It was added to the Auburn line in 1929 along with the Duesenberg Model J. Cord had purchased the Duesenberg Motors

Duesenberg Model J. Cord had purchased the Duesenberg Motors Company of Indianapolis when it was in the bankruptcy courts in 1926. It became a subsidiary of Auburn.

The Duesenberg was a status symbol costing $15,000 to $20,000 even during the Great Depression. Named after Fred Duesenberg, a race driver and inventor of the supercharger and hydraulically controlled brake, the Duesenberg Model J was pure class. Custom-designed for each owner, all 480 Duesenbergs were handcrafted. It was a popular automobile among Hollywood stars and the wealthy.

The Great Depression, however, was too much for the Cords, Auburns, and Duesenbergs. These sleek road machines disappeared from the market in 1937. Duesenbergs now sell for hundreds of thousands of dollars—if a collector can find one available to buy.

Clark Gable and the 1935 Duesenberg

A great art deco building was built in Auburn to house the Auburn Automobile Company administration before its demise. Now it is a famed car museum containing over 130 classic, antique, and special interest cars dating from as early as 1898. Models displayed include the Cord, Duesenberg, Auburn, Locomobile, Rauch-Lang, McIntype, and a 1956 Bentley once owned by John Lennon. Each year an Auburn-Cord-Duesenberg Festival is held with an auction of collector cars that produces world-record prices.

What's a Crosley?

$ What's a Crosley? It has four wheels, two doors, and one rear light. It looks as if someone put it in a vise and squished it. The reason for being tall and skinny was to fit its inventor, Powell Crosley, Jr. The inventor of the Crosley radio wanted a car that was big enough for his 6-foot-4-inch stature. Crosley cars averaged 12 feet long from bumper to bumper, and weighed 1,100 to 1,200 pounds. They had a 2-cylinder, air-cooled engine. Oh, let us not forget the propeller on the front which was standard in all Crosleys.

The Crosley was first built in Richmond before World War II. After the war, from 1946 to 1952, it was built in Marion. In 1952, the Crosley couldn't hold public appeal, and production ended. Today, if this inexpensive and very fuel-efficient automobile were on the market, there might have been a different ending to the Crosley story.

Studebaker legacy

$ In 1852, Clement and Henry Studebaker came to South Bend to start a blacksmith and wagon shop with $68 and two forges. Studebaker wagons were used by the Union in the Civil War. Their prairie schooners transported thousands of emigrants westward . Henry left the business for farming. As the company grew, additional brothers, John, Peter, who opened the first branch in St. Louis, Missouri, and Jacob helped create one of the largest makers of wagons and carriages.

The Studebaker family's wealth was well displayed in 1888 when they built a mansion in South Bend with 20 fireplaces, 40 rooms, and 24,000 square feet of living space. Turrets, stone walls, and irregular roof lines gave it the look of a medieval castle.

In 1899, the Studebaker company started manufacturing bodies for electric automobiles. Electric trucks and vehicles called electric runabouts were made from 1902-1912. Electric power was abandoned after 1912. The company's experimentation with gasoline-powered automobiles was a success and production, which began in 1904, continued. In 1911, the original company was merged into the Studebaker Corporation.

The Studebaker Corporation was the basis for South Bend's prosperity. Studebaker's automobile production peaked in 1923 when 145,167 cars were produced. In 1954 the Packard Motor Car Company joined Studebaker. Production ceased in the United States in 1963, and their Canadian branches were shutdown in 1966.

The Studebaker National Museum houses the Studebaker carriage in which Lincoln rode to Ford's Theater the night he was shot, along with carriages made for Benjamin Harrison and Ulysses S. Grant.

The Avanti

$ Studebaker introduced the Avanti, America's only handmade luxury car, in the fall of 1962. It was produced for 15 months until the plant was shut down. Leo Newman bought the Avanti rights from Studebaker in 1964 and began producing the car by hand. It was produced in South Bend for 15 years until J.J. Cafaro of Youngstown, Ohio, bought Newman out. He moved the Avanti company to Youngstown.

INDUSTRIAL STRONGHOLD

$ In 1941, Standard Oil Company built a huge oil refinery in Whiting, occupying 750 acres. Parts of the plant were actually in East Chicago and Hammond.

Standard Oil

Whiting was chosen because Chicago residents did not want their air polluted with the smell of oil and sulfur. In 1941, it was said that the coal used in this one plant could produce enough power for a city of 500,000 people and the water used to cool gasoline every day would supply a city of 1,250,000 people.

$ Inland Steel began in 1893 when eight partners purchased 40 railroad cars full of used steel-producing machinery from a bankrupt company and set up operations in Chicago Heights. In 1901, 50 acres of land were offered by the Lake Michigan Land Company at Indiana Harbor to any firm that would develop it by building an open-hearth steel mill. Inland then built Indiana Harbor Works in East Chicago, where it still produces all its raw steel products. The company now focuses its attention on specialty steel products and in the late 1980s established several joint ventures with Nippon Steel of Japan.

Inland Steel

$ When the developers of Gary saw the Calumet region, they faced a totally uninviting and uninhabited land. It was nothing but dunes, sloughs, and small streams with a strong, cold wind blowing in off the lake. What they planned in this undesirable place was an industrial city.

U.S. Steel and its dream city

The United States Steel Corporation originally purchased land for a new steel plant in 1905 and later an additional 7,000 acres were bought on which the town would grow. U.S. Steel directed the Gary Land Company to develop a community for 100,000 people. The city was named after Judge Elbert H. Gary, chairman of the board of U.S. Steel.

Building the mills and the city were not easy tasks. Massive drain and fill operations were used. The mill site was elevated an average of 15 feet by material pumped in from Lake Michigan. Huge sand dunes were pulled down. A river was moved to a different location. Since grass wouldn't grow in the sandy soil, huge trainloads of black topsoil were hauled in. With the erection of U.S. Steel and the development of homes and city services, other large companies such as Republic Steel soon built factories.

Gary's job opportunities were a strong draw for the nation's immigrants. Its population, about 50 percent foreign in 1920, made it the sixth largest city in the state.

WITH HEADS IN THE CLOUDS

Oops! Blame it on the wind

$ The first American woman to fly an airplane was Blanche (Betty) Stuart Scott of Indiana in September 1910. During a lesson from Glenn Curtiss, she was taxiing along the ground when, as she related it, the wind caught the plane, giving the lift necessary to get the plane airborne. (There were rumors that she planned the "accidental" flight.)

Two weeks later, however, Bessica Raiche, wife of a Long Island aircraft designer, deliberately soloed her airplane, if only a few feet off the ground. The Aeronautical Society of America recognized her as America's first female pilot because her flight was not a matter of chance.

Betty Scott, however, did go on to make the first accepted flight by a woman in public, at Fort Wayne the following October. She lifted her craft twelve feet in the air. This intrepid flier never did get a pilot's license because she felt the requirements were too stiff. Scott died at the age of 84 in 1970.

Amelia Earhart's flying laboratory

$ Purdue University in West Lafayette found the perfect woman, Amelia Earhart, to counsel its women students and be a special advisor in aeronautics. They even bought a Lockheed Electra to be used by Earhart as a flying laboratory. They invited her to join the university staff in 1935. Their plans ended with the tragic 1937 disappearance of Earhart in her Electra.

Crop-dusting leads to Delta Air Lines

$ Bloomington native C.E. Woolman was the principal founder of the first commercial crop-dusting company, Huff Daland Dusters. Organized in 1924, the company later became Delta Air Lines.

Helicopter founder

$ Lawrence Bell, founder of Bell Aircraft Corporation, is responsible for 20 aviation firsts such as the world's first commercial helicopter and the U.S.'s first jet-propelled plane. Born in Mentone, Bell was also responsible for the plane that first broke the sound barrier, piloted by Chuck Yaeger.

INDIANA FARMING

A rose is not a rose

$ The peacemakers of hundreds, thousands, even millions of lovers' spats came from Indiana. E. Gurney Hill is noted for his introduction of new varieties of roses into America. He often worked years on new hybrids trying to develop just the right color or more shapely bud. It is said that during his long years of experimentation he rejected as many as 16,000 rose plants from all over the world. The Richmond Rose, named after his company, Hill Floral Products, Inc. in Richmond, was introduced in 1905 and helped Hill attain international prominence. Over 40 acres of greenhouses contain 60 varieties of roses. Hill ships over 20 million cut roses to Midwestern and Southern locations yearly. The American Beauty Rose was developed there.

⑤ When James Oliver arrived in the United States, he settled in South Bend where he bought a quarter interest in a foundry. In 1864, Oliver, owner of Oliver Chilled Plow Works, discovered a process for chilling and hardening steel so that it could be used for the curved iron plate of plows. The use of steel instead of softer iron made the plow keep its sharp edge longer and its moldboard free of clods of earth. The Oliver Plow was internationally famous and, along with other Oliver Farm implements, played a major role in revolutionizing agriculture worldwide.

Plow revolutionizes farming

⑤ Grassyfork Fisheries, Inc., turns into a likeness of a Monet painting during the hot months of the year. It is a major producer of water lilies. However, their main product is goldfish. Over 40 million fish are produced and shipped worldwide each year. The hatchery, located in Martinsville, has spring-fed ponds and tanks that cover 1,500 acres.

Millions of Goldfish

Which came first, the chicken or the Easter egg?

Gale Ferris calls his farm in Canaan the United Nations of the Poultry World. Forty rare breeds which include silver spangled hamburgs (Germany), bearded mottled houdans (France), blue-skinned Chinese silkies (China), black cochin bantams (Asia), and araucanas (South America). If these aren't an impressive display of fine feathered creatures, he has some that even lay colored "Easter" eggs.

INVENTIONS, FIRSTS & GREAT IDEAS

⑤ Charles C. Hill has the dubious honor of being the first man to realize the insulating qualities of rock wool, now known as asbestos. The rock wool was made from melted limestone blown by steam pressure into fine wool-like threads. Hill opened the Crystal Chemical Works, located in Alexandria, in June 1897. Alexandria's Mud Creek was underlaid with an almost inexhaustible supply of the type of limestone from which rock wool is made. The Johns-Manville Corporation acquired the works in 1929. Unfortunately, Johns-Manville and other asbestos manufacturers, as well as consumers, have suffered because of the material's cancer-causing effects.

Asbestos: A good idea at the time

⑤ Clessie Cummins, a chauffeur in Columbus, was certain he could improve the diesel engine for use in transportation, and was able to get his boss, Columbus banker W. G. Irwin, to lend him money to start Cummins Engine Company in 1919. He succeeded in refining the smelly engine but ran into strong resistance from truckers. It took Cummins many years and lots of Irwin's money to finally make a profit in the late 1930s. The company now produces more than half of the diesels made, most of which are on trucks.

Major leader in diesel market

Automatic phone tested in LaPorte

$ Invented by Kansas City undertaker Almon Strowger, the automatic telephone (one not requiring an operator) was first used in LaPorte. He had developed it because an operator was bypassing his undertaking establishment and diverting calls to her husband's rival business.

A profitable fat lip

$ Charles G. Conn returned to Elkhart after the Civil War and began a bakery business, but his favorite hobby was playing cornet in the town band. After a fight with a town bully left his upper lip badly bruised, he fashioned a soft rubber mouthpiece for his cornet in order to retain his position with the band. He started receiving numerous requests for this mouthpiece, which he produced from his home.

In 1875, Conn rented one room and began building instruments. In 1888 he undertook the production of the saxophone, originally used by military bands. From this humble beginning came the largest band-instrument factory in the world, the C. G. Conn Band Instrument Company. Other instrument makers settled in Elkhart, and by 1940, 70 percent of all wind and percussion instruments made in the United States were being produced in Elkhart.

A wife's request inspires inventor

$ Because his wife requested silverware that wouldn't tarnish, Elwood Haynes, prominent in the history of cars (see p. 74), invented stainless steel in 1912. He also invented stellite, a metal alloy now used in jet engines, dental instruments, and nuclear power plants. New ways to use Haynes's stellite are still being discovered.

Indiana men start Mayflower Transit

$ Mayflower Transit, one of the largest movers in the nation, was started in 1917 by two truck drivers from Indiana, Don Kenworthy and Conrad Gentry. Theirs was the first moving company to get approval to go national, as well as the first to establish a school to train their movers in the proper handling of household goods. Be careful. That's grandpa's priceless mustache cup!

"Indiana Fried Chicken?"

$ You're never too old to have a good idea. Colonel Harland Sanders was 66 when he came up with the idea of fried chicken franchises. By the time he was 73, six hundred Kentucky Fried Chicken franchises covered the United States and Canada. The title of Colonel was bestowed on him by the state of Kentucky because of his "services to the state's cuisine." The Colonel was born near Henryville, Indiana.

Indy grocer develops Van Camps

$ The tinplate industry came to Indiana before the Civil War. The material was used in creating a tin can with a soldered lid for canning foods. An Indianapolis grocer, Gilbert Van Camp, became interested in the process. By the 1890s, Van Camp Packing Company was among the most successful suppliers to wholesale grocers in the United States. Son Frank found that beans packed in tomato sauce were quickly accepted by the public. Today, Stokely-Van Camp pork and beans are found on most kitchen shelves.

National Guardmen tear-gas picketers

$ A general strike of coal workers was called in July of 1935 at Terre Haute to support 600 Columbian Enameling and Stamping company workers who wanted a 10 percent wage increase and the right to form a union. This was the first general strike east of the Rockies. On July 18, the company brought in 58 professional strikebreakers. The company ignored warnings by the AFL unions that a general sympathy strike would be called if the strikebreakers didn't leave. On July 22, nearly 26,000 workers and many merchants quit work. The *New York Times* described the strike as virtually "100 percent effective." National Guardsmen were ordered by the governor to end the picketing. The Guard tear-gased 1,800 pickets. The general strike ended two days after it began. Martial law was maintained for six months.

Popcorn king Orville Redenbacher

We've heard of basket weaving in college, but a course in popping corn? Native of Brazil, Orville Redenbacher took one at Purdue University, and it proved to be most profitable. His fascination with those tasty, puffed morsels that you can't get enough of continued on past graduation. In his field of agronomy and genetics, he became employed as an agricultural teacher, a Terre Haute County farm agent, and a manager of a corn farm. The creation of his hybrid yellow popping corn came after teaming up with a college friend, Charles Bowman. They discovered a way of making their corn pop wider than the plain varieties. Turned down by established companies because of their hybrid's high price, Redenbacher began packaging and marketing it himself. Hunt-Wesson Foods acquired the business in 1976 with Redenbacher staying on as their spokesperson.

World's Foot Doctor

$ With 12 brothers and sisters, the need for shoes was immense. So it seemed only natural that William "Billy" Scholl, who showed an aptitude for sewing leather, become the unofficial cobbler. Raising their children on a dairy farm in LaPorte County, Scholl's parents quickly recognized Billy's ability at making and repairing shoes. At 16 he was apprenticed to a local cobbler, which began a career that took him to Chicago. After working in a shoe store as a cobbler-salesman, he noticed the horrible condition of his customers' feet. It was then he decided to enter Illinois Medical College and become "foot doctor of the world." His first invention was the Foot-Eazer, an arch support. He established a podiatric correspondence course for shoe-store clerks. A persuasive spokesman, Dr. Scholl turned the nation foot-conscious.

World's largest builder

($) Bechtel Corporation is one of the world's largest construction and engineering firms. Its roots can be traced back to Aurora with the birth on September 24, 1900, of Stephen Davison Bechtel, the man behind the company. The list of Bechtel projects includes the Hoover Dam, the Alaskan oil pipeline, and the rapid transit systems of San Francisco and Washington, D. C. It has designed or built half the nuclear power plants in the United States.

The Wonder of it all

($) The Taggart Baking Company of Indianapolis took advantage of a new-fangled idea. In 1913, the automatic bread-wrapping machine was

invented. Taggart decided to market a one-pound loaf called Mary Maid. Its success led to their development of a one-and-a-half-pound loaf in 1920. The next challenge was what to name this loaf and how the wrapping should be decorated. Elmer Cline was given the task to come up with a marketing idea. A huge balloon race in Indianapolis gave Cline the inspiration he needed. As he viewed the many balloons floating in the sky, he thought of the word, *wonder*. The balloons became polka-dots on the wrapping and the jumbo loaf became Wonder Bread. "Wonder" is now a registered trademark of Continental Baking Company, which took over Taggart in 1925.

Walker agents sell cosmetics

($) A short-term industry in Indianapolis was focused on cosmetics for the black woman. Madame C.J. Walker, who had been a poor black orphan from Louisiana, built a factory in Indianapolis to be the home base of her cosmetic firm. Previously her offices were in Denver and Pittsburgh. Madame C.J. Walker Manufacturing Company employed approximately 3,000 people, mostly women. They were named "Walker Agents" who traveled around the country selling their products. Her most valued preparation was Madame C.J. Walker's Hair Grower. Walker Agents sold the hair grower and 16 other products door-to-door. However, she stayed in Indianapolis for only five years before moving to New York. The move proved to be a prosperous one. She became one of the first women millionaires and owned a townhouse in New York. She was a great philanthropist, giving to the NAACP, the aged, and the needy.

MADE IN INDIANA

Shipbuilders of the midwest

($) The *Eclipse*, the largest and most ornate ship of its time on western waters, was built in New Albany between 1851-52. It cost nearly $400,000, an astronomical price for its day. The ship was the fastest long-distance boat on the Mississippi. A famous race from New Orleans to Louisville between the *Eclipse* and another New Albany-built boat, the *A.L. Shotwell*, was won by the *Eclipse* in 4 days, 9 hours, and 20 minutes.

$ In 1832, Dr. William Foote convinced a Louisville stonecutter to come to Bedford because of the endless supply of limestone that lies just under the soil. Limestone is the material preferred by stonecutters. Soon after, Bedford became an active producer of limestone shipped out on the New Albany & Salem Railroad. In 1877, Davis Harrison developed the Dark Hollow Quarry Company and Bedford was on its way to becoming the "Limestone Capital of the World." Its limestone has become the foundation of a number of very famous structures, including the Empire State Building, Chicago's Tribune Tower, and St. John the Divine Cathedral in New York City. One can say that Indiana is scattered all over the United States.

Solid as a rock

$ Whiskey and the distilling of it has been associated with the Greendale and Lawrenceburg area of Indiana since 1809. This is mainly because there was a supply of cold, clear well water. The industry grew steadily with big growth coming after the repeal of the Eighteenth Amendment. Joseph E. Seagram started in Greendale with the alcohol plant of the Commercial Solvents Company. The Seagrams, Canadian distillers, purchased this plant in 1933. In 1940 the plant had 54 buildings and covered 25 acres. Today, Seagrams produces their popular wine coolers at the plant.

Canadians produce wine coolers in Hoosier land

$ The *Elkhart Truth* must take the credit for giving A.H. Beardsley, president of Dr. Miles Laboratories, the inspiration that has tamed the savage hangover and calmed the rocky stomach. A visit to the Elkhart newspaper during December 1928 surprised Beardsley. The town was in the midst of colds and influenza of epidemic proportion, but for some reason the newspaper staff had escaped the flu. Why? he asked. It turned out the editor was giving the staffers a dose of aspirin and bicarbonate of soda when signs of a cold appeared.

The Miles company had great respect for home remedies, so Beardsley asked his chief chemist to develop an effervescent tablet with those same ingredients. He tested them in the office and even on a Mediterranean cruise when seasickness hit. Alka Seltzer went on the market in 1931. From its beginning, advertising the wonder tablet was top priority. It sponsored "The Saturday Night Barn Dance" on WLS in Chicago and "The Quiz Kids." Sales, along with a number of hangovers, increased with the end of Prohibition. In the 1970s Alka Seltzer was attacked by Ralph Nader, saying that aspirin, one of its ingredients, irritates the stomach. Miles came back with Alka-2 Antacid containing no aspirin.

Who put the plop, plop, fizz, fizz in Alka Selter?

**Ball Brothers moves on
with the times**

💲 The Ball canning jar is popular among antique collectors, as well as today's home canning enthusiast. Immediate success was found by the five Ball brothers when they moved their company from Buffalo, New York, to Muncie, Indiana. The move was prompted by Indiana's gas boom of 1886. Muncie offered free natural gas for the first five years of operation, 70 acres of land, and $7,500 in cash to bring new business in, an offer the brothers couldn't refuse. When the supply fizzled out, Ball Brothers stayed in Muncie, but changed to coal for their fuel. By 1910, Ball Brothers was turning out 90 million fruit jars. As the nation turned away from home canning, the Balls changed their focus to producing bottles for the post-Prohibition alcoholic beverage makers. In the 1950s, the Ball company formed an aerospace division building satellites, antennas, and cameras. On the 1973 Skylab, a Ball camera took photographs of the sun's surface.

The Louisville Slugger

The famed Louisville Slugger used by major league players nationwide was the result of a broken bat. In 1884, John "Bud" Hillerich asked Pete "The Old Gladiator" Browning to come by his father's woodworking shop in Louisville, Kentucky, after the star player of the Louisville Eclipse team broke his favorite bat. The two picked out a piece of white ash and Hillerich began making a new bat under the direction of Browning. The next day, Browning went 3 for 3 ending a batting slump...and beginning the Hillerich bat business.

The Louisville Slugger was first called the "Falls City Slugger." Bats were created to fit each player's preference. Among the early players using the Louisville Slugger were Willie Keeler of the Brooklyn Dodgers, Hugh Duffy of the Chicago Nationals, and Honus Wagner. Wagner signed a contract with the company giving them permission to use his autograph, making it the first to be used on a baseball bat. Other greats using the bats included Ty Cobb, Babe Ruth, Mickey Mantle, Hank Aaron, and Johnny Bench. Bats from many of these greats are on display at the company's Bat Museum.

In 1916, the company's name was changed to the Hillerich & Bradsby Company to include Frank W. Bradsby, a buyer of athletic equipment.

The manufacturing operations are in a 56-acre facility, called "Slugger Park," in Jeffersonville. Its corporate offices are in Louisville. Today, 1.4 million wooden bats are made every year. The professional baseball players still have their bats crafted by hand. Major league players use an average of 72 bats per season. The company also makes aluminum bats, gloves and mitts, and golf clubs.

$ Union officer Eli Lilly became disgusted during the Civil War with the quality of the pharmaceuticals that the army was required to use. In 1876, he opened his own firm in Indianapolis to produce drugs of good and consistent quality. One way he did that was to invent gelatin capsules that melted in the stomach. In 1923, Eli Lilly & Company became the first company to produce and sell insulin, extracting it by an involved process from cattle and hogs. Sixty years later, the firm accomplished another first by selling a genetically engineered version of human insulin. For eighteen years until 1988, Eli Lilly owned Elizabeth Arden, the huge cosmetics firm.

Eli Lilly developed human insulin

HOOSIER COMMUNICATORS

$ Indiana pioneers had a tendency to name their weekly newspapers strange names. A few of the most unusual were the *Broad Axe of Freedom*, the *Grubbing Hoe of Truth*, the *Whig Rifle*, and the *Coon-Skinner*. It was hard to keep newspapers afloat in the early 1800s. Most pay was in produce. Pork, flour, and cornmeal at market price was the expected pay. Firewood wasn't a bad price especially when winter was in the offing, but it didn't pay for paper and ink.

Extra! Extra! Read all about it!

Not only was it hard to get paid, but it was hard for newspaper editors to get paper. It is said that the first newspaper in Rushville, the *Dog-Fennel Gazette*, was distributed on single sheets given out one at a time. When the readers were through, they returned them to the *Gazette's* office and the sheets were printed on the other side for the next issue.

A popular column of the time, the "Sheriff's Log," had an entry that read, "Girl at restaurant requests a conservation officer. An owl is sitting on the pizza oven."

$ The *Indianapolis Times* won a Pulitzer Prize in 1928 for its campaign against the Ku Klux Klan. The paper was influential in ending the Klan's power in Indiana. Two years later, the *Times* received another Pulitzer Prize for its campaign to promote tax reform. In 1932, the *Indianapolis News* won the Pulitzer Prize in Meritorious Public Service for its campaign to reduce waste in city government and taxes. More recent Pulitzers went to the *Indianapolis Star* for local reporting in 1975 and the Fort Wayne *New-Sentinel* for its flood report in 1983.

Pulitzers for Indiana

$ The human side of war was vividly recorded by Ernie Taylor Pyle. The Dana native looked at war through the eyes of the average GI. He was heralded by those at home during World War II as one of the most beloved American correspondents. His journalistic career began on the LaPorte *Herald* after leaving Indiana University just short of graduating. He moved on to New York and Washington, writing for the dailies. In 1935, he became a roving reporter, which eventually took him to the front lines. In 1944, Pyle watched the Normandy Invasion at first hand. Japanese machine-gun fire killed him on a small island of Okinawa April 18, 1945. He received a Pulitzer in 1943.

Ernie Pyle: War from the eyes of a GI

RIDING THE RAILS

The first Indiana railroad

$ The first railroad in Indiana was completed on July 4, 1834, in Shelbyville. The owner, Judge W.J. Peasley wasn't able to get a locomotive for the 1.5-mile line so he had the passenger coach pulled by horses.

The longest steam railroad

$ Whitewater Valley Railroad is the longest steam railroad in the Midwest. Thirty-four miles of track lie between Connersville and Metamora. Each Saturday, Sunday, and holiday from May to November the old steam engines fire up. Old-time sights and sounds are recreated when two rare Baldwin locomotives (1907 and 1919) pull passenger cars along the towpath of the Whitewater Canal.

The shortest railroad

$ The Louisville, New Albany & Corydon Railroad is one of the nation's shortest railroads. Built in 1881, "The Dinky," as it is called, has a track eight miles in length. It is a working railroad hauling freight continuously from Corydon to Corydon Junction

Indiana Union Station

America's first union railway depot was built in 1853 in Indianapolis. By 1888, the depot was replaced by a Romanesque-style Union Station. In more recent times, it has been renovated into a multi-million dollar festival marketplace. Covering a four-block area it has 60 specialty retail shops, nine restaurants, three nightclubs, and 22 eateries. Its architectural beauty has not been changed, including the original leaded stained glass windows.

Disaster on the rails

$ Two Baltimore & Ohio trains, one carrying freight, the other passengers, failed to obey the lights due to a blinding snowstorm November 6, 1906. They collided outside Woodville. One train burned entirely within minutes, killing 43 people.

Human error caused the New York Central's Interstate Express to collide with the Michigan Central's Canadian at Porter on February 27, 1921. The engineer and fireman of the Michigan train failed to see the stop lights at a crossing. Its passenger cars were already derailed at the intersection leaving a wooden coach directly on the tracks. The New York Central train plowed through at 50 mph, killing 35 Michigan Central passengers. The New York two-man crew was also killed.

THE SPORTING LIFE

The essence of Indiana sports lies in its feverish love of basketball. Tagged "Hoosier Hysteria," Indiana's love affair with the sport begins with high school basketball. Small towns have built field houses with seating capacity equal to and at times even greater than their population. Come basketball game night the seats are filled to capacity. "Hoosier Hysteria" doesn't stop at the high school level. Bobby Knight and his Indiana University teams have kept the fever up. And so have former high school greats who went professional, among them Larry Bird and Oscar Robertson.

Let us not forget Indiana football fame and Notre Dame—Knute Rockne and his "Four Horsemen." Hoosier football greats include Alex Karras and Paul Hornung.

"Gentlemen (and ladies), start your engines." The grandfather of all car races, the Indianapolis 500 draws hundreds of thousands to the Hoosier capital. Indianapolis is a sports mecca which has hosted the Pan Am Games, the Final Four NCAA tournament, and the U. S. Skating Championships. The Indiana Pacers and the Indianapolis Colts have made it their home. Sports and Indiana have made an awesome combination.

- Hoosier Hysteria
- Go! Zebras! Go!
- Knight Time in Indiana
- Great Indiana Cagers
- Indiana Pro Basketball
- Basketball Hall of Famers
- The Indianapolis 500
- Take Me Out to the Ball Game
- Baseball Hall of Famers
- Indiana's Football
- Hoosiers in Sports

HOOSIER HYSTERIA

Basketball comes to Indiana

◀ Rev. Nicholas McKay, an English Presbyterian minister, was sent in 1893 to start a YMCA in Crawfordsville. Preparing for his new venture, he visited Dr. James Naismith's YMCA camp in Massachusetts. Naismith had invented basketball two years earlier. When he arrived in Crawfordsville and opened up the YMCA, Rev. McKay decided the peach baskets and ladders for retrieving the ball could be improved. He eliminated the ladder and replaced the peach baskets with two metal hoops with coffee sacks around them. He did, however, need a tall player to knock the ball out of his basket hoop. His tallest player, the center, usually had to get the rebound in and get the rebound out.

Squirreling away to victory

Indiana high school basketball is never without its stunts. In the 1922-23 season Butlerville High left its opponents in a quandary with its "squirrel stunt." The team's 5-foot, 110-pound guard, Merlin Swarthout, would find a way to get his guard out of position. He then scrambled up the back of the team's center, 6-foot-4-inch Raymond Rees. The bent-over Rees allowed him to take a quick pass and Swarthout would lay it in the basket. Butlerville used it to get into the semifinals, but that was the end for the "squirrel stunt." A rule was made the next year prohibiting the stunt.

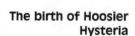

The birth of Hoosier Hysteria

◀ The term "Hoosier Hysteria" was given to Indiana's high school basketball state tournaments in the 1920s. Sixteen regional tournament winners traveled to Butler University in Indianapolis for a two-day elimination. The university built America's largest basketball fieldhouse in 1928. Seating capacity was 15,000. When "Hoosier Hysteria" hit during tournament time, the house was filled to capacity with fans. The pitched excitement and competitive spirit was at the point of hysteria. It continues today.

Indiana is one of only a few states that does not divide its tournament by enrollment. It is possible for the smallest schools to come face-to-face with the big city teams. In 1954, a large school, Muncie Central, was brought down by small Milan High School in the last three seconds of the game. Milan had 161 enrolled students, only 73 of them boys. Its champion, Bobby Plump, made the game-winning final basket.

Indiana loves its high school basketball. State champions in 1940, Hammond Technical High, were greeted by 50,000 residents when they returned from their victory. In 1938, Fort Wayne held a parade for their South Side High champions.

A top priority in most Indiana high schools is a big gymnasium. By 1986, Indiana had 18 of the 20 largest high school gymnasiums in the United States.

BASKETBALL TIME IN HOOSIERLAND

1911 First state tournament played. Crawfordsville beat Lebanon, 24-27.

1914 Wingate High School became state champions. Home court was a barn heated by pot-bellied stoves and out-of-bounds was non-existent.

1920 **Hoosier Hysteria Hits!**
First glass backboards in the state were installed at Owensville High School gym.

1928 Butler Fieldhouse in Indianapolis was completed. With a seating capacity of 15,000, it became the home of the Indiana High School Athletic Association's boys state basketball tournaments.

1930 Smallest schools to reach the "Sweet 16" in the 1930s were Dugger, Cicero, Hazelton, Sandusky, Mentone, Plainville, and Ossian. Winamac and Huntington advanced to the final four.

1933 Beaver Dam, 52 students strong, reached the "Sweet 16" and repeated it in 1934.

1940 Fans got in the act by flying an airplane around the gymnasium floor to pump up the Eden Flyers.

1954 Milan Indians beat Muncie Central. The small school was labeled "Miracle Milan" for beating the favorite by Bobby Plump's jump shot in the last seconds. Score 32-30.

1955 Crispus Attucks, the first Indianapolis school to win tourney and first all-black school to participate, defeated Gary Roosevelt, 97-74. Professional star Oscar Robertson was a member of the team.

1960 Hoosiers Oscar Robertson and Terry Dischinger helped win the gold medal at the Rome Olympics.

1966 Rick Mount of Lebanon High School became the first high school athlete to make the cover of *Sports Illustrated*. He averaged 35 points a game, two years in a row.

1971 Bobby Knight came to Indiana University.

1876 Indiana held the first sanctioned girls' tournament. Judy Warren led her Warsaw Tigers to victory over Bloomfield, 57-52.

1980 At the sound of the buzzer, a 57-foot shot by Stacey Toran gave Indianapolis Broad Ripple its first state championship.

1986 "Hoosier Hysteria" depicted in the film *Hoosiers*, based on the Milan victory in 1954.

1990 State Finals became Hoosier-dome Hysteria. 41,046 fans set a world record for the largest attendance watching a high school basketball game.

Recession touches Hoosier Hysteria

◄ The General Motors townspeople of Anderson live and breathe basketball. Even when the bottom nearly dropped out of the auto industry in the 1970s and 1980s and Anderson was close to collapse, basketball thrived. It was an escape from an otherwise difficult time in Anderson's history. The high school sold nearly twice as many season tickets as the Indiana Pacers.

GO! ZEBRAS! GO!

◄ Every high school has its nickname. The Knights. The Panthers. But what about the Zebras, the Alices, and the Jeeps? The following are a few of Indiana's most unusual high school nicknames. Go! Zebras!

Rochester "Zebras"

In the early 1900s, schools didn't have nicknames. But colors were very important. The Rochester basketball team chose Purdue's colors of black and gold. But when they appeared at the State Tourney in 1912, the team's uniform were not black and gold. They were half white and half black in vertical strips. Someone in the crowd said they looked like Zebras. The name stuck.

Frankfort "Hot Dogs"

◄ Where else but in Frankfort could you have the high school nickname "Hot Dogs." According to an old timer, the nickname has always been "Hot Dogs" and it is a play on the name, Frankfort. Don't put mustard and relish on this Hot Dog mascot. He might take a bite out of you.

Shoals "Jug Rox"

◄ Come on, Jug Rox! Fight! Fight! Fight! Shoals High School chose its nickname from one of the most mystifying rock stands in the nation. Within the city limits of Shoals an eroded sandstone oddity is located. Known as the Jug Rock, it stands 60 feet high and is capped with a massive flat stone. The rock stands 20 feet in diameter at its base and resembles a jug.

◀ The mighty Alices were named after Maurice Thompson's Revolutionary War novel, *Alice of Old Vincennes* (see p. 33).

Vincennes "Alices"

◀ Fifteen basketball players put their heads together in 1936 to come up with a nickname. Their decision didn't come easy. It was even heated at times. The comic strip "Popeye" gave them the winning nickname and mascot. The imaginary character, Jeep, had a long nose and curly tail, and boasted great intelligence. In fact, it could even predict the future. The Dubois Jeeps couldn't foresee their future, but the year the Jeep became their mascot, they achieved a 17-4 win-loss record. Dubois experienced reorganization and became Northeast Dubois High School in 1969. Although a change had occurred, Jeepism prevailed.

Dubois High School "Jeeps"

KNIGHT TIME IN INDIANA

Explosive to say the least, Bobby Knight, Indiana University coach, is college basketball's most colorful coach. During a game most cameramen are unable to draw away from Knight for fear they will miss his "in your face" style, chewing a player out or giving his reaction to a bad call by an official. It's Knight time at Indiana.

Coming from West Point where he coached for six years, he turned Indiana University basketball around through discipline, high principles, demands, and expectations. Knight won three national championships at Indiana in 1976, 1981, and 1987, which makes him one of only three head coaches to win the "Triple Crown." He became the winningest coach in Big Ten history in 1988-89. During his 20 years at Indiana, the Hoosiers have won 459 games and lost only 153. 1975 and 1976 were undefeated regular seasons with 37 consecutive wins. Knight coached the 1979 U.S. Pan American gold medal team and the U.S. Olympic team that took the gold medal in 1984.

He has been named Coach of the Year numerous times. He is most proud of the graduation rate of his players. It is close to 95 percent. All but four of his four-year players have completed their degrees.

Among his more colorful antics was an incident involving a flying chair during a Indiana-Purdue game. Made furious by a referee's call, Knight flung the chair onto the court. Chaos and national attention followed. Knight received a one-game suspension and had to apologize for his action.

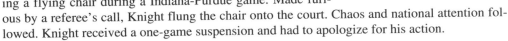

GREAT INDIANA CAGERS

Larry the Legend

◀ Larry Joe Bird is the "hick from French Lick," Larry the Legend, and forever a Hoosier. He grew up with four brothers in French Lick, a southern Indiana town known for its springs and limestone quarries. His basketball career started in the fourth grade. As a high school sophomore with the Springs Valley High Black Hawks, he was 6 feet, 1 inch tall and 135 pounds. By the time Bird was a senior, he had grown six more inches in height. He averaged 31 points, 21 rebounds, and 5 assists per game.

In 1974, Bird went to play at Indiana University. It wasn't to his liking and he stayed less than a month. Northwood College, a junior college near home, was his next stop. He stayed a little longer but landed back home as a garbage collector. The next year he went to Indiana State in Terre Haute. He waited a year getting academically settled before taking to the basketball court. Bird's talents began to shine. He averaged 32.8 points a game as a 6-foot-9-inch forward.

During his first NBA season with the Boston Celtics, they tied with the 76ers for the best record in the league. He went on to accumulate a career total of 21,791 points, 8,974 rebounds, and 5,695 assists. He was an NBA Most Valuable Player in 1984, 1985, and 1986. And he made the All-Star Team eleven times.

Back surgery in 1991 kept him out of the second half of the season and the playoffs. It didn't prevent him from being a member of the 1992 Olympic U.S.A. "Dream Team." He played all eight games, scored 67 points, captured 30 rebounds, and made 14 assists. However, his back continued to bother him and after the Olympics, on August 18, 1992, Bird announced his retirement after 13 years with the Celtics.

"The Big O"

◀ Oscar Robertson moved to Indianapolis when he was three. The great-grandson of Marshal Collier, a slave who died in 1954 at the age of 116, Robertson began handling the basketball at an Indianapolis YMCA at an early age. He was a stand-out star with his Crispus Attucks High School team. In a state where the absolute focus was on basketball, Robertson fulfilled the Hoosier dream by helping his team to become the first high school to have an unbeaten season in Indiana history. The team had two consecutive state championships. And for three years he was All-State and named a high school All-American.

By his sophomore year, Robertson was the University of Cincinnati's leading scorer. Named college All-American three years in a row, he graduated after having scored the most points by a single player in college basketball history. He co-captained the U. S. men's basketball team to a gold medal in the 1960 Olympic games in Rome.

At 6 feet, 5 inches tall, Oscar Robertson was considered short for professional basketball. Nevertheless, he was drafted by the last-placed Cincinnati Royals in 1961. He was selected Rookie of the Year. When Robertson was traded to the newly franchised Milwaukee Bucks for the 1970-71 season, he teamed up with Kareem Abdul-Jabar to win the NBA title.

One player said, "If you give him a twelve-foot shot, Oscar will work on you until he's got a ten-foot shot. Give him ten, he wants eight. Give him eight, he wants six . . . give him six, he wants four . . . give him four, he wants two . . . give him two, you know what he wants? . . . a lay-up."

He had over 26,710 career points and 9,887 career assists. Of those points he was the top free-thrower with 7,694 points in his career. Retiring in 1974, Roberston became a TV sports announcer.

INDIANA PRO BASKETBALL

◀ The American Basketball League, formed in 1926, included the Fort Wayne Knights of Columbus. The Great Depression ended funding and the league. Two Indiana teams won championships as members of the National Basketball League created in 1937. They were the Fort Wayne Zollners who won championships in 1943, 1944, and 1945, and the Anderson Duffey Packers in 1949. In 1946, the Basketball Association of America was formed and included the Fort Wayne Pistons and Indianapolis Jets.

Indiana goes pro

◀ From 1967 to 1976, the Indiana Pacers were members of the American Basketball Association. Bob Leonard began coaching the team in 1969, and made the change with the Pacers to the National Basketball Association in 1976.

Indiana Pacers

◀ Ann Meyers signed with the Indiana Pacers in 1979 for $50,000 becoming the first woman to sign in a men's professional league. Other clubs accused the Pacers of signing a woman to gain publicity. The owner of the New York Knicks called it "a travesty."

Prior to joining the Pacers, Meyers was an All-American player at UCLA, leading the Bruins to their first women's national championship, and was a star on the 1976 U. S. Olympic women's team. She never had her chance on the men's basketball court. Meyers was cut after one week of training camp with the Pacers. She married Baseball Hall of Fame pitcher Don Drysdale.

First woman to sign with men's pro-team

The Hoosier Dome

The Indianapolis Hoosier Dome, opened in 1984, has the distinction of housing the largest audience ever to attend an indoor basketball game. When the U.S. Olympic team played the NBA All-Stars in 1984, 67,596 people attended. The Dome hosted the Final Four NCAA 1991 tournament. They will return in 1997. The NCAA I Collegiate National Championship for track in 1991 was also held at the Dome.

Indiana Pacers: The glory years

In 15 seasons, the Indiana Pacers have found their way into the record book:

- Most points in overtime period—Indiana vs. Boston, March 20, 1984 (14 points).
- Highest three-point field goal percentage in one game—Indiana vs. Phoenix, February 11, 1987 (6-6).
- Most steals in a rookie season—Dudley Bradley 1979-80 (211).
- Fewest field goals in a game—Indiana vs. New York, December 10, 1985 (19).
- Most offensive rebounds for both teams—Detroit (29) vs. Indiana (28), January 30, 1977.
- Most three-point field goal attempts for both teams—Indiana (26) vs. Golden State (20), March 2, 1989.—Indiana (44) vs. Kansas City (40), October 22, 1977.
- ABA championship over LA Stars 4 games to 2, 1970.
- ABA title of 1972 defeating NY Nets 4 games to 2.
- ABA title of 1973 defeating Kentucky Colonels 4 games to 3.

Other teams of Indianapolis

Indianapolis has hosted two other National Basketball Association teams before the Indiana Pacers. They are the Indianapolis Jets who finished sixth in the 1948-1949 season. Then, the Indianapolis Olympians competed from 1949 to 1953.

BASKETBALL HALL OF FAMERS

◀ University of California, Los Angeles, head coach from 1948 to 1975, John R. Wooden, was named Coach of the Year by the U.S. Writers Association six times. He was the first player to be elected into the Basketball Hall of Fame in 1960 and was re-honored in 1972 as a coach. Many of the Martinsville native's early accomplishments took place while playing with a professional ball club, Kautsky Grocers of Indianapolis. He made 138 consecutive free throws in competition. While coaching UCLA, he dominated college basketball. From 1964 to 1975 his Bruins won 10 NCAA national championships; of those, seven were consecutive titles.

First player to be inducted

◀ In 1930, Branch McCracken was named an All-American forward. The Big Ten scoring champion, born in Monrovia, went on to become the head coach at Ball State Teacher's College. In seven seasons his record was 93 wins and 41 losses. His greatest achievement was leading the basketball teams at Indiana University. His running style of play gave his teams the nickname of "Hurrying Hoosiers." They hustled their way to NCAA titles in 1940 and 1953. He was named Coach of the Year during both those years. His record at Indiana was 364 wins and 174 losses. He is in the Basketball Hall of Fame and the Helms Hall of Fame.

The "Hurrying Hoosier"

◀ 1971 Hall of Fame inductee W. R. Clifford Wells began his coaching career at Bloomington High School. Twenty-nine years of high school coaching included Bloomington, Columbus, and Logansport. As a high school coach he won 617 games. In 1945, he went on to coach at Tulane University where his win-loss record over 47 years of coaching was 885-418. He was the co-founder of the Indiana High School Coaches Association. From 1935 to 1964, he conducted numerous basketball clinics in the United States and overseas.

29 years of "Hoosier Hysteria"

Other Hall of Famers

Charles "Stretch" C. Murphy (inducted 1960) – One of first "big men." Marion High School, 1926. Purdue University, 1930.

Paul Hinkle (1965) – Known as Dean of Indiana Coaches.

Everett Dean (1966) – Won NCAA crown in 1942 with Stanford University.

Robert Vandivier (1974) – Member of the All-Time All-Star Five of Indiana.

Arad A. McCutchan (1980) – One of two coaches in college basketball to win at least five NCAA championships.

Everett N. Case (1981) – Won four Indiana State High School championships at Frankfort, later coached North Carolina State University.

Clyde E. Lovellette (1987-88) – Was a member of the 1952 U.S.A. gold medal team in Helsinki.

King of the basketball sneaker

Chuck Taylor, the "Ambassador of Basketball," spent 11 years running up and down the court as a professional after several seasons on the Columbus High School team. But as history would have it, it wasn't Taylor on the court, it was his sneakers that became famous. He developed the Converse All-Star Basketball shoe. When working for the Converse Rubber Co., he offered the first basketball clinic in 1922. It was the beginning of a long series of clinics held all over the world. He was also the editor of the *Converse Basketball Yearbook*, a publication in which he chose All-American teams. Inducted into the Basketball Hall of Fame in 1968, Taylor was an outstanding Columbus High School, Indiana, player.

Helped develop athletic association

◀ In the early 1900s, the Indiana High School Athletic Association along with Indiana's high school basketball tournament became models for other states. Instrumental in developing the association was Arthur Trester. Born in Pecksburg, he became secretary in 1913 and later commissioner of the association. He was inducted into the Basketball Hall of Fame in 1961 for his contributions to the game.

THE INDIANAPOLIS 500

◀ A simple dirt track used by the Indianapolis automobile industry for testing cars in 1909 became the granddaddy of racetracks, the Indianapolis Motor Speedway. Later the track was paved with brick. Located in Speedway, just outside Indianapolis, the track is called the Brickyard after its original pavement. As a test course it has brought about such automotive innovations as four-wheel brakes, front-wheel and four-wheel drive systems, and hydraulic shock absorbers. During World War II, the track provided a testing ground for synthetic rubber tires while raw materials were rationed.

The first 500-mile race, held May 28, 1911, was won by the Marmon Wasp, an Indianapolis-made car. Its driver, Ray Harroun, sped past the checkered flag beating two other contenders by a narrow margin. The victor took home a $10,000 purse. The average speed of the race was 74.59 mph. Accidents, near collisions, and wheels flying off the race cars kept the event's 80,000 fans from losing interest. Hundreds of militiamen and policemen were kept busy with crowd control as many of the fans ran back and forth for a better view of an accident. (The crowd must have looked like an early version of "the wave.")

Since the inaugural race, the Indy 500 has become the most prestigious of all automobile races. It has been held every year, except during World War I and World War II. World War I flying ace and race car driver Eddie Rickenbacker bought the Speedway in 1927, expanded the facilities, and sold the track in 1945 to Terre Haute's Tony Hulman, Jr.,

The 2.3-mile oval track has sweeping curves of 1,320 feet each, two short straightaways, and two long ones. Today, race cars negotiate the curves and straightaways in qualifying times of over 200 mph.

 The use of a crash helmet came after Wilbur Shaw, race driver, suffered a skull fracture in a 1923 crash. Another crash halted the needling given to him by other drivers for wearing a helmet. Shaw was ejected from the car, landed on his head, and survived. Born in Shelbyville, he began his racing days at the young age of 18 with a car he built and drove at many Midwestern tracks. Shaw won the Indianapolis 500 in 1937. He went on to win twice more, 1939 and 1940, finishing in the top four seven other times. He was president and general manager of Indianapolis Speedway Corporation after World War II. He was inducted into the Auto Racing Hall of Fame and the Helms Hall of Fame. Shaw died October 30, 1954, in an airplane crash.

Survivor of crash wears helmet

Indy 500 at a snail's pace

Close to nine hours after Ralph Mulford started the 1912 Indy 500, he crept across the finish line. Although nine cars had already finished the race, Mulford was determined to get his share of the pot. Tenth place was $1,200 and nothing to sneeze at in 1912. All the other entrants had dropped out, leaving him in tenth position. He had started experiencing clutch trouble 100 miles from the finish line but wasn't about to give up. Circling the track at 60 mph with 17 laps to go, Mulford made a pit stop for dinner and then proceeded to chug across the finish line. The race went into the record books as the slowest race in Indy history.

When the Indianapolis Motor Speedway opened in 1909, Theodore "Pop" Myers was in charge of ticket sales. By 1914 he was general manager and a year later he took the position of treasurer. He became vice-president of the Speedway Corporation in 1927, serving until his death on March 14, 1954. "Pop" is in the Auto Racing Hall of Fame and Helms Hall of Fame.

Ticket seller turns CEO

Indy 500's first woman driver

Janet Guthrie of New York became the first woman to qualify in the Indy 500. In the 1977 race she went to the pits to stay after 27 laps and 8 pit stops. She promised she would be back.

INDY CHAMPS

YEAR	DRIVER	AVERAGE SPEED (mph)	YEAR	DRIVER	AVERAGE SPEED (mph)
1911	Ray Harroun	74.59	1954	Bill Vukovich	130.840
1912	Joe Dawson	78.72	1955	Bob Sweikert	128.209
1913	Jules Goux	75.93	1956	Pat Flaherty	128.490
1914	Rene Thomas	82.47	1957	Sam Hanks	135.601
1915	Ralph Depalma	89.84	1958	Jimmy Bryan	133.791
1916	Dario Resta	84.00	1959	Rodger Ward	135.857
1917-18	(not held)		1960	Jim Rathmann	138.767
1919	Howard Wilcox	88.05	1961	A.J. Foyt	139.130
1920	Gaston Chevrolet	88.62	1962	Rodger Ward	140.293
1921	Tommy Milton	89.62	1963	Parnelli Jones	143.137
1922	Jimmy Murphy	94.48	1964	A.J. Foyt	147.350
1923	Tommy Milton	90.95	1965	Jim Clark	150.686
1924	L.L. Corum/ Joe Boyer	98.23	1966	Graham Hill	144.317
1925	Peter DePaolo	101.13	1967	A.J. Foyt	151.207
1926	Frank Lockhart	95.904	1968	Bobby Unser	152.882
1927	George Souders	97.545	1969	Mario Andretti	156.867
1928	Louis Meyer	99.482	1970	Al Unser	155.749
1929	Ray Keech	97.585	1971	Al Unser	157.735
1930	Billy Arnold	100.448	1972	Mark Donohue	162.962
1931	Louis Schneider	96.629	1973	Gordon Johncock	159.036
1932	Fred Frame	104.144	1974	Johnny Rutherford	158.589
1933	Louis Meyer	104.162	1975	Bobby Unser	149.213
1934	Bill Cummings	104.863	1976	Johnny Rutherford	148.725
1935	Kelly Petillo	106.240	1977	A.J. Foyt	161.331
1936	Louis Meyer	109.069	1978	Al Unser	161.363
1937	Wilbur Shaw	113.580	1979	Rick Mears	158.889
1938	Floyd Roberts	117.200	1980	Johnny Rutherford	142.862
1939	Wilbur Shaw	115.035	1981	Bobby Unser	139.029
1940	Wilbur Shaw	114.277	1982	Gordon Johncock	162.029
1941	Floyd Davis/ Mauri Rose	115.117	1983	Tom Sneva	162.117
1942-45	(not held)		1984	Rick Mears	162.962
1946	George Robson	114.820	1985	Danny Sullivan	152.982
1947	Mauri Rose	116.338	1986	Bobby Rahal	170.722
1948	Mauri Rose	119.814	1987	Al Unser	162.175
1949	Bill Holland	121.327	1988	Rick Mears	144.809
1950	Johnnie Parsons	124.002	1989	Emerson Fittipaldi	167.581
1951	Lee Wallard	126.244	1990	Arie Luyendyk	185.981
1952	Troy Ruttman	128.922	1991	Rick Mears	176.457
1953	Bill Vukovich	128.740	1992	Al Unser, Jr.	134.477

The Roachdale 500

On July 4th each year a major event is held in Roachdale, Indiana. Although it doesn't get quite the coverage the Indianapolis 500 gets, the city's residents are just as serious about their annual 500 race. Their participants don't need high performance fuel, nor do they lose any wheels. Life-threatening accidents are a rarity. However, you may need binoculars even if you are 10 feet away to watch Roachdale's best cockroaches speed along a plywood course as fast as their tiny, little legs can carry them.

TAKE ME OUT TO THE BALL GAME

On the evening of June 2, 1883, League Park at Fort Wayne was filled with 2,000 baseball fans cheering on the Methodist Episcopal College and the Quincy professionals. Remember, it is 1883 and how could these people possibly see the ball? Easy, 17 arc lights, equivalent to 4,857 gas burners, lit up the park. It was a momentous occasion. This was the first night baseball game in history. It lasted seven innings and Quincy won 19 to 11.

First night baseball

The Negro National Baseball League was established on February 12, 1920. The Indiana franchise was the Indianapolis ABCs. Oscar Charleston, born in Indianapolis, October 14, 1896, was an outstanding center fielder and first baseman. He played for the ABCs, Harrisburg Giants, Hilldale, Homestead Grays, and the Pittsburgh Crawfords.

Playing baseball in the NNL wasn't easy. They would play three games in a day. While some games were all in the same town, others were in three different towns, but on the same day. Unlike today's million-dollar players, they would make, maybe, $5 a day. And what about expense money? How does 60 cents a day sound? The league ultimately improved players' income and the parks they play in.

Negro National League

Evansville-born Don Mattingly, first baseman for the New York Yankees and an All-Star, was benched in 1991 for wearing his hair too long. Mattingly went quickly back into the lineup after promising to cut his long locks.

The long and short of it

New York Yankee Don Larsen pitched the only perfect game in World Series history on October 8, 1956. He faced 27 batters. None were able to reach first base on hits. Larson was born in Michigan City.

A perfect game

Gil Hodges broke the grand-slam home-run record in 1957. Known as the "Artless Dodger," he joined the Dodgers in 1943, but he had only played only one game before entering the Marines. In 1947, the Princeton native was back playing with the Dodgers as first baseman. He averaged more than 100 RBIs a season and over 32 home runs between 1949 and 1955. Among his darkest moments was the 1952 World Series against the Yankees. He was unable to hit safely in 21 times at bat.

The "Artless Dodger"

Women in the pros

◄ The All American Girls Professional Baseball League's first game was won by the South Bend Blue Sox in 1943 against the Racine Belles. Annabelle Lee of the Fort Wayne Daisies pitched the first perfect game in 1946. South Bend won pennants from 1949 to 1951 and the championship in 1951. Fort Wayne won pennants in 1952, 1953, and 1954 and a 1952 championship.

Rockford Peaches
Kenosha Comets
Racine Belles
Milwaukee Chicks
Minneapolis Millerettes
Grand Rapids Chicks
Muskegon Lassies
Peoria Redwings
Chicago Colleens
Springfield Sallies
Battle Creek Belles
Kalamazoo Lassies

The women of this league created by Philip K. Wrigley used an official ball larger than a baseball but smaller than a softball. Pitchers were 55 feet from home plate and a runner had to run 85 feet to the bases. The league lasted until 1954.

BASEBALL HALL OF FAMERS

"Three Finger" Brown

◄ Mordecai "Three Finger" Brown, born 1876 in Nyesville, began his career with the National Baseball League in 1903, playing for the St. Louis Cardinals. He was dubbed "Three Finger" because of an accident in his youth which took the use of half of an index finger. The loss proved to be the pitcher's asset, giving him a variety of unorthodox pitches. The Cardinals failed to recognize his potential and traded him to the Chicago Cubs. The move was a positive one for Brown. His Cubs won four pennants in nine seasons. He averaged more than 20 victories a season from 1906 to 1911. His best season was in 1908 when he won 29 games. His greatest rival was the dreaded Giants. Brown moved to the Cincinnati Reds in 1913 for only one season. In 1914 he went to the Federal League as the St. Louis manager. Brown was named to the Baseball Hall of Fame in 1949.

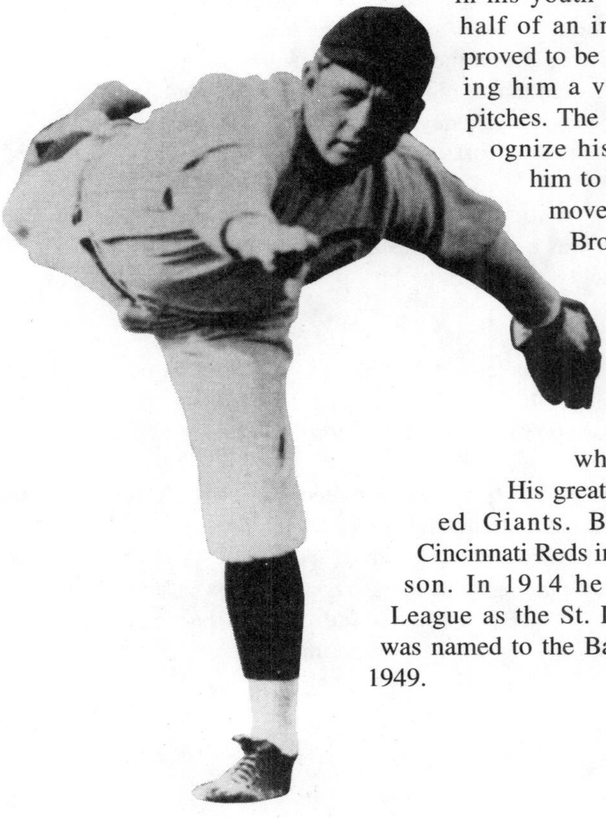

◀ A hard-hitting Hoosier, Edd J. Roush surprised most fielders by his ability to place the ball. The Cincinnati player had a knack for making pitchers very nervous. Always knocking off invisible clods of dirt and fidgeting in the box, Roush kept them on edge. The batter from Oakland City had a .323 lifetime batting average. In the early 1920s, he averaged .350 in a four-year stretch. The center fielder had a reputation as a major hold-out. In 1930 he missed an entire season over a salary dispute with the Giants. As a Hall of Fame inductee, Roush was recognized for his talents in 1962.

Edd Roush kept the mound shaking

The commish

Ford C. Frick, commissioner of baseball from 1951 to 1965, was born in Wawaka in 1894. Prior to becoming commissioner, he was president of the National League. He followed baseball as a *New York Journal* sportswriter and radio commentator from 1921 to 1934. The National Baseball Hall of Fame was his passion. He nurtured its growth as chairman of the board. While commissioner, Frick was called an idealist when it came to baseball. Sportsmanship was all-important. He was in favor of the 12-team league. Frick was admitted into the Hall of Fame in 1970, eight years before his death.

◀ New Albany's Billy Herman, Chicago Cubs second baseman in the 1930s, began his career in the Cotton State League playing for a Vicksburg, Mississippi, team. He played for the Chicago Cubs from 1931 to 1941. In his first appearance with the team, he stood at the plate and fouled off an inside pitch. The ball bounced back, hit him in the jaw, and knocked him out momentarily. Herman recovered and went on to appear seven times in the All-Star Game representing the Cubs. He still holds the National League All-Star Game batting average record (.433). After his stint with the Cubs, including three unsuccessful World Series bids, he was traded to the Brooklyn Dodgers in a contract dispute. He became a player-manager with the Pirates in 1946. A year later, he left baseball but returned to coaching minor league teams. He also played for the Milwaukee Braves and later managed the Boston Red Soxs. Herman was inducted into the Hall of Fame in 1975.

KO'd at the plate

◀ After 31 seasons, Ken Schreiber, La Porte high school baseball coach, ranked fourth in the list of winningest coaches (797-171). He was voted the National High School Coach of the Year in 1977 and 1987. He was selected State High School Coach of the Year six times. He is a member of the Indiana Baseball Hall of Fame and the American Baseball Coaches Association Hall of Fame. The La Porte Slicers won five state titles under his tutelage.

Winningest coach

Stealing came easy

◀ The 1961 Hall of Fame baseball player, Max Carey, was known for his uncanny ability to steal bases. While playing for the Pittsburgh Pirates, he stole 738 bases, and in 1922, he was thrown out only twice in 53 attempts. His outfielding wasn't too shabby either. In six seasons, Carey caught 400 or more flies per year. In his career, the boy from Terre Haute made 6,363 put-outs. One feather in his cap was Carey's 1925 World Series batting average of .458 while playing for the Pittsburgh Pirates. Carey, who had finished his playing years with the Brooklyn Dodgers, went on to manage the club in 1932 and 1933

Other Hall of Famers

◀ Other Hoosiers who have made their mark in the nation's favorite pastime are as follows, with their year of induction into the Baseball Hall of Fame:
- Edgar "Sam" Rice, right fielder from Morocco, 1963
- Sam Thompson, right fielder from Danville, 1974
- Oscar Charleston, Negro League from Indianapolis, 1976
- Amos Rusie's, pitcher from Mooresville, 1977
- Chuck Klein, right fielder from Indianapolis, 1980

INDIANA'S FOOTBALL

The force behind the Fighting Irish

◀ To get his Notre Dame team inspired to beat Army, Knute Rockne told his team to "Win just one for the Gipper," using a comment made by star player George Gipp, who had died of an infection eight years earlier. Rockne's 1928 team was experiencing a poor season, but his half-time speech worked. Notre Dame won. Rockne turned the South Bend college into a football force to be reckoned with. During his thirteen years as head coach, the Fighting Irish lost only twelve games.

Five times he had undefeated seasons. He was responsible for the 1922-24 backfield known as the "Four Horsemen," Harry Stuhldreher, Don Miller, Jim Crowley, and Elmer Layden.

Rockne's stats went beyond the win-loss column. At the time of his death, the result of a small plane crash on March 31, 1931, 23 of his boys were head coaches at colleges, more were assistant coaches, and 150 were high school coaches.

Rockne himself had been a Notre Dame athlete. He played end on the football team and was a track star. He began his coaching career at Notre Dame in 1918. Even the Studebaker company recognized his coaching ability and hired him to give inspirational talks to their salesmen and management.

◄ The luster of Notre Dame football was fading fast when coach Lou Holtz left the University of Minnesota to take the helm in 1986. A perfectionist, he is known for his tough practice sessions and attention to detail. Like Ohio State's Woody Hayes, Holtz often joins his team in the huddle. Once he sacked his quarterback Tony Rice for not taking a passing drill seriously.

Coach Lou Holtz takes the helm

In 1990, Holtz faced the heat of controversy. Charges were made by former Notre Dame lineman Steve Huffman concerning the use of anabolic steroids by Irish players. He claimed Holtz turned his head to their use. Holtz denied the accusations. The university backed Holtz.

◄ Just out of high school in 1953, Paul Hornung was the target in a recruiting fight between the University of Kentucky and Notre Dame. His mother was the reason he chose Notre Dame. The freshman threw three touchdown passes during the traditional Notre Dame varsity-alumni game, earning him the name "Golden Boy." In 1956, Hornung lived up to his nickname. He ran, passed, punted, kicked off, kicked placements, caught passes, returned punts and kickoffs, and played defense. The Fighting Irish were a bit tarnished that year, having had the worst season in Notre Dame history, but the Golden Boy still won the Heisman Memorial Trophy. At the time, he earned the honor of becoming the only player from a losing team to receive the Heisman.

Notre Dame's "Golden Boy"

The media debated whether he would choose Hollywood or pro football. He signed with the Green Bay Packers (1957-1966). Coach Vince Lombardi considered him the best football player he had ever coached. However, off the field he had some problems. In 1963 commissioner Pete Roselle suspended him for gambling. After retirement, he got into showbiz co-hosting "Weekend Heroes" (1981) with Jayne Kennedy—half-hour TV episodes on famous gridiron stars.

◄ Notre Dame's big man, Leon Hart, at 6 foot 5 and over 250 pounds, won the 1949 Heisman Trophy. He said, "I never brought the Heisman Trophy home from New York. I gave it to Notre Dame." During his tenure with Notre Dame, they never lost a game in four years, going 46-0-2, an amazing feat. He was named AP's Male Athlete of the Year.

Leon Hart: 1949 Heisman Trophy

Under the glow of the Heisman Trophy, Hart tried his hand in Hollywood. But the call of the football turf was greater. He was drafted by the Detroit Lions in 1949 and played eight years with that team, winning three NFL championships. He left pro sports embittered because he felt that athletes were becoming greedy. Today's pro football players don't impress him. He fought to get the two platoon system out of football, which he believes has been its ruination. He would rather see players play both defense and offense as in the old days of football.

John Huarte: The Heisman upset

◀ Notre Dame's quarterback, John Huarte, won the 1964 Heisman Trophy. It wasn't your typical Heisman win. In fact, it was one of the greatest upsets in the history of the honored trophy. Huarte won the Heisman as a returning non-letterman, the only player to do so. He knocked out the likes of Roger Staubach, Gale Sayers, and Joe Namath.

Notre Dame had just finished another losing season when it headed into the 1964 season. Quarterback Huarte, who had an unorthodox sidearm throwing motion, was not expected to do great things on the field. Ara Parseghian, the new coach, gave Huarte a chance even though he received little encouragement from the previous coaching staff. The results were astounding. The Fighting Irish were undefeated until the last game of the regular season.

After college, Haurte played for six different pro teams in eight years and threw 48 passes. He later went on to become a "tile king" as the owner of Arizona Tile Company.

A success on the field and on TV

◀ Emerson High School in Gary was the foundation for the successful football career of Alex Karras. Moving from the industrial city to corn country, Karras became an All-American tackle at the University of Iowa in 1956. One year later he won the Outland Trophy for best interior lineman in the nation. He also placed second in the voting for the Heisman Trophy that same year, earning him the distinction of placing the highest for any tackle.

For 12 years Karras played with the Detroit Lions, and was named to the Lions all-time team. After retirement he became an analyst for ABC's "Monday Night Football" and began his acting career. He had roles in the films *Paper Lion, Against All Odds, Babe, Blazing Saddles*, and *Victor/Victoria*. He is most widely known for his gentle but stern father image in the TV series "Webster." His career doesn't end there. Karras has his own production company and is an author. He has written three books: *Even Big Guys Cry, Alex Karras by Alex Karras*, and *Tuesday Night Football*. The latter is being made into a movie. He was inducted into the College Hall of Fame in 1991.

Football Hall of Fame

Notre Dame has more player members (31) in the National Football Foundation's College Hall of Fame than any other university in the nation. Other members from Indiana are as follows:

• DePauw University—Robert Steuber, 1943
• Indiana University—Zora Clevenger, 1903; John Tavener, 1944; Peter Pihos, 1946; George Taliaferro, 1948
• Purdue University—Cecil Isbell, 1937; Robert Griese, 1966; Leroy Keyes, 1968

Indiana coaches named to the Hall of Fame:
Ken Mollenkopf, Purdue, 1988
Dan Devine, Notre Dame, 1985
Ara Parseghian, Notre Dame, 1980
Jesse C. Harper, Notre Dame and Wabash, 1971
Knute Rockne, Notre Dame, 1951
Andrew Smith, Purdue, 1951

◀ The Colts galloped their way from city to city over the years of their existence. They began in Boston as the Boston Yanks in 1944. In the next nine years they stopped to graze in New York and Dallas until 1953 when the Colts settled in Baltimore. On March 29, 1984, in the early morning hours, the Baltimore Colts packed up and moved to their new home to become the Indianapolis Colts, leaving Baltimore angry, but Indianapolis fans loved them. Two weeks after they arrived in town, season tickets were requested by 143,000 fans.

The Indianapolis Colts

HOOSIERS IN SPORTS

◀ Indianapolis became an international mecca for the world's greatest athletes in August of 1987 as the tenth host of the Pan Am Games. Since the mid-1970s the city had been preparing for the event. $136 million was dropped into the constuction of pools, track and field stadium, and other facilities. The games were a pre-Olympic test for the athletes and on the political front. Ten athletes from the Dominican Republic landed in Indianapolis and quickly hopped a bus for New York to look for work. A small airplane flew over the opening ceremonies with a banner urging Cuban athletes to defect. It even gave a phone number to call for help in defection.

Pan Am Games

◀ The Olympic gold is only a shiny memory for Wilma Rudolph, the first American woman to win three medals in a year. Gold in 1992 means a bright future for most athletes, but the 1960 gold-medal winner has battled her way through bankruptcy and is trying to keep one of her few assets, a house in Indianapolis. Since the early 1980s, Rudolph has been battling over "$419,451, plus 11 percent annual compounded interest" the Internal Revenue Service claims she owes. In August 1992, an Indiana appeals court stopped a lower court's decision to allow foreclosure. Rudolph is now a vice president of Baptist Hospital in Nashville, Tennessee.

Only a golden memory

◀ James "Doc" Counsilman Day was held in Bloomington, February 3, 1990, after his last home meet ended a 33-year career as swimming coach at Indiana University. His Indiana team won 20 consecutive Big Ten championships from 1961 to 1980. He won 23 Big Ten championships in all. He brought his team to six consecutive NCAA championships starting in 1969. Each year, Counsilman would hold a "Jelly Bean Day" during practice. He would set a goal for each swimmer. Their reward would be jelly beans. Just to receive a handful of jelly beans, his swimmers would break world records for him. Counsilman produced 59 Olympians, one of whom is Mark Spitz, who received seven gold medals in Munich. Spitz earned eight NCAA titles for the Hoosiers. Among Counsilman's personal accomplishments are being named Coach of the Year in 1969 and 1970, induction into the International Swimming and Diving Hall of Fame in 1976, and becoming the oldest person to swim the English Channel, in 1979 at age 58.

Swimming coach honored

Up to 5,000 spectators can watch exciting cycling competition at the Major Taylor Velodrome in Indianapolis. The 28-degree banked velodrome was named after Marshall "Major" W. Taylor, born in Indianapolis, who was the most respected black athlete at the turn of the century. He won his first bicycle race at age 13. Two years later he raced a five-lap mile in 2 minutes, 11 seconds from a standing start. Taylor went on to break records. In 1901, he went to Paris where he demanded that his national anthem be played during his appearances and he waved his own American flag during cooling-off laps.

Polio victim wins Olympic gold

◀ Purdue University student Ray Ewry won eight gold Olympic medals in three Olympiads for track and field. He won three in 1900, sweeping the standing high jump, standing long jump, and the standing triple. He repeated the feat in 1904. In 1908, he settled for two golds. The triple jump was eliminated from the 1908 Games. Born in 1873, Ewry contracted polio as a young boy in Lafayette and was confined to a wheelchair. Courage and exercise gave him his legs back and a chance at the gold.

Mike Tyson KO'd by beauty queen

◀ July 19, 1991, was a dark day in the life of heavyweight champion boxer Mike Tyson. Indianapolis's Canterbury Hotel was the location of Tyson's raping of an 18-year-old beauty-pageant contestant on that day. He was arrested for the crime. After deliberating 10 hours, an Indianapolis jury found him guilty of two counts of deviant sexual behavior. Tyson received a sentence of six years in an Indianapolis prison. Within the first six weeks of his sentence, he threatened to beat up a guard, earning him four days in solitary. His earliest possible release date was pushed back fifteen days. The ex-champ will get out April 9, 1995.

Tragedy hits Evansville basketball

◀ University of Evansville lost its basketball team in a tragic accident. The chartered DC-3 they were riding in crashed just after take-off from Evansville on December 13, 1977. The coach and 14 members were killed, along with a number of fans and other people associated with the university.

CREATIVE INDIANA

Imagine James Whitcomb Riley, Meredith Nicholson, Booth Tarkington, and Lew Wallace all on the same stage. What a coup! And it happened in Indianapolis! In the 1900s Indiana was a literary gold mine. Writers' clubs popped up everywhere. Just about everyone—from merchants to lawyers to housewives—wanted to write. From this fascination with literature, the state produced many quality writers.

The arts in Indiana didn't stop with literature. Great opera singers, composers, and dancers trace their humble beginnings to the Hoosier State. And its landscape gives artists the inspiration for their work. Come, learn about Indiana's cultural side.

- A Verse and a Rhyme
- Pen and Ink
- Hoosier Winners
- On the Lighter Side
- On Stage
- Top Designers
- With Brush and Canvas

A VERSE AND A RHYME

A frontier poem

🌟 "The Hoosier's Nest," often called the first genuine frontier poem, was written by John Finley, a transplanted Virginian who lived in Wayne County for 40 years. It was a simple account of a stranger's visit to an Indiana settler's cabin. The *Indianapolis Journal* published it for the first time in 1833. Within a year, it was published all over the United States and England.

The unofficial poet laureate of Indiana

🌟 Even as a young girl living on Six-Mile Creek north of Vernon, Sarah Tittle Barret Bolton was composing verses. At nine, she moved with her father to Madison where she attended school. Within two months, young Sarah was able to put her verses down in writing. At 13 her verse was first published in the city's newspaper, the *Madison Banner*. In 1851, while husband Nathaniel Bolton was state librarian and custodian of the State House and grounds, Sarah Tittle Barrett Bolton was inspired to write her famous poem, "Paddle Your Own Canoe." The poem came to her as she was sewing strips of carpeting for the State House and Senate Chambers. She was considered the unofficial poet laureate of the Hoosier State and one of the first literary women in the Mississippi Valley.

Adventurous poet

🌟 Hulings Miller, a Quaker schoolmaster living in Liberty, chose the name Cincinnatus Hiner for his son on September 8, 1837. Little did he know that Cincinnatus would grow up to become a renowned poet and an adventurer. Unlike many Indiana-born poets, Miller did not use the state as a basis of his poems. In fact, his family answered the call to "go west" when he was young. He led an adventurous life after leaving home at 17, working in a California mining camp, living with Indians, and even establishing a pony express route. Miller began writing verse in 1868 using the pen name Joaquin Miller. His peers called him the "Poet of the Sierras." His best known poem was "Columbus."

Poet catches Lincoln's eye

🌟 Byron Forceythe Willson moved from Genesee Falls, New York, to New Albany, Indiana, in 1852. Living in a white cottage, he wrote his best verses, "In State" and "The Old Sergeant." The latter was distributed as a Christmas souvenir by the *Louisville Journal* where Willson was an editorial writer. Among the most noteworthy people who read "The Old Sergeant" was President Lincoln. Lincoln asked Oliver Wendell Holmes if he knew who the author was. Once the President inquired, the poem's and Willson's popularity skyrocketed.

"Ain't God Good to Indianny?"

William Herschell's poem, "Ain't God Good to Indiana?" was inspired by the beautiful scenery along the Blue River outside Knightstown. He got the phrase from an old man who was enjoying the sun while fishing on the Blue River. With a wide sweep of his arms, the old gentleman looked over the countryside and declared, "Ain't God good to Indianny?" Herschell, born in Spencer in 1873, is also the author of the poem "Long Boy" which became a popular World War I song.

Keeping a job was not an easy task for James Whitcomb Riley. He had no formal training in any occupation and had a tendency to drift in and out of jobs. But when it came to taking up a pen and jotting down his observations of the world around him, Riley was an expert. The "Hoosier Poet" as he was known, let the heartbeat of Indiana flow from his creative mind. He was loved by the common, uneducated man, because it was his story Riley was telling in such works as "The Old Swimmin' Hole," written in 1883.

Indiana's favorite poetic son

Riley was born in Greenfield on October 7, 1849. It was there that he earnestly began his career, submitting poems to the Greenfield *Times*. He later became editor of the newspaper in 1874. He moved on to the Anderson *Democrat* three years later where his tenure was short-lived due to a literary hoax (see below).

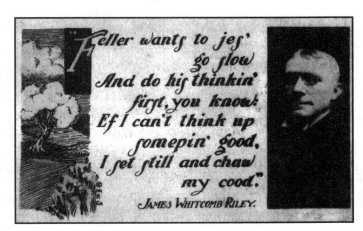

"Feller wants to jes'
go slow
And do his thinkin'
first, you know!
Ef I can't think up
somepin' good,
I set still and chaw
my cood."

JAMES WHITCOMB RILEY.

Riley, a lifelong bachelor, was loved by children. His statue, located on the Hancock County Courthouse grounds, was purchased entirely from funds raised by Indiana schoolchildren. He has earned a reputation as a poet for children and extremely simple adults.

Riley's best known poems are "Little Orphant Annie" and "The Raggedy Man." Both were the inspiration for John Gruelle's *Raggedy Ann* books. An employee of Riley's family, Annie Gray, was the real-life "Little Orphant Annie."

He lived his last 20 years on Lockerbie Square in Indianapolis, a six-block area of one of the best preserved collections of 19th-century Victorian homes in the United States. Lockerbie Square is literally a slice of that era.

Hoax loses job for the Hoosier Poet

The editor of the Kokomo *Dispatch* jumped at the opportunity to put Edgar Allan Poe in print. In 1877, James Whitcomb Riley of the Anderson *Democrat* told him "Leonainie" was an unpublished work of Poe. It made the front page of the *Dispatch* and copies were sent to other publications. Excitement, as well as skepticism, grew over the discovery. Riley was asked to take the original manuscript to Kokomo to prove its authenticity. Great pains were taken by friends to make Riley's "Leonainie" pass the inspection. It never had a chance. The true story was leaked to a competitive newspaper, the Kokomo *Tribune*. The hoax was widely denounced, Riley resigned from his post at the *Democrat,* and everyone knew where Kokomo was located. The practical joke gone awry left Riley heartsick. He had only wanted to prove that editors buy poetry not on its merits, but on the author's reputation.

AWESOME

PEN AND INK

Alice of Old Vincennes

In 1900, James Maurice Thompson wrote an historical romance about the early days of Vincennes. *Alice of Old Vincennes* is a fictionalized account of the true story of Alice Roussillon, who hid the French flag from the British during the Revolutionary War. Before the success of his novel, Thompson gained prominence as a poet and editor of the *New York Independent*. Like Indiana authors Meredith Nicholson and Lew Wallace, Thompson made his home in Crawfordsville, where he stayed until his death on February 15, 1901. His birthplace home in Fairfield was relocated to Vincennes where it is a museum on the Vincennes University campus.

Royalties in 1901

George Barr McCutcheon received $5,000 for his romantic novel, *Graustark*, in 1901. His publishers were so pleased they agreed to pay him royalties on sales of the book. In 1902 he also wrote *Brewster's Millions* which has been filmed twice. Prior to his success as a novelist, McCutcheon was editor of the Lafayette *Daily Courier*.

Author's life like unfinished novel

Writer Ambrose Bierce spent his boyhood and young manhood in Elkhart. He hated the city and so many other things in his life that he was known as "Bitter Bierce." When he returned to Elkhart after being wounded in the Civil War, a friend told him he should have been more careful. He replied, "The damn Rebels can't shoot." He later wrote *What I Saw of Shiloh*, which was recognized as an excellent portrayal of the Civil War.

Bierce disappeared in Mexico in 1913 and was never found. He had written farewell letters constantly implying the possibility of never coming back. He called his final adventure traveling through Mexico during Pancho Villa's revolt against the dictator, Victoriano Huerta, a *Jornada de Muerte*, a journey of death. Villa provided him with credentials to accompany the bandit's army. His last letter was written December 26, 1913.

No one knows what happened to Bierce. Some say he was executed by Villa after an argument. Others say he shot himself in the head at the highest ledge of the Grand Canyon. There will always be speculation concerning Ambrose Bierce's death.

Eggleston among first realistic fiction writers

Edward Eggleston was born in Vevay on the Ohio in 1837 into an educated and cultured family. Because his health was poor and there was an extensive library in his home, his love of literature blossomed early. His first book, *The Hoosier Schoolmaster*, a realistic portrayal of illiterate southern Indiana people in the 1850s, was published in 1871. It was an important step in the development of American realistic fiction. He was one of the first to skillfully and vividly present the frontier experience. It was first published in France under the title *La Revue des Deux Mondes*. The book was printed in eight languages. The basis of *The Hoosier Schoolmaster* was the experiences of his brother, George, who, at age 16, taught school at Ryker's Ridge District School in Jefferson County. Other novels followed. Sixteen years later, he wrote one of the most important works about American social history, *The Beginnings of a Nation*.

❧ Theodore Dreiser's grim realism may have been the product of growing up poor in a fanatically religious family. He is considered the founder of the naturalism movement or pessimistic realism. *Sister Carrie*, published in 1900, was his first novel. Although the wife of the president of Doubleday did not want the book published because of its immorality, Dreiser insisted that the provisions of his contract be honored. The book was published but was suppressed for several years in the United States without any advertising or effort to distribute it—the book was, however, applauded abroad as a masterpiece in realism. This conflict with Doubleday is said to have upset Dreiser so deeply that he suffered a nervous breakdown and quit writing for a time. *Sister Carrie* wasn't as much immoral as it was a realistic look at everyday life— something readers didn't want in their novels.

His later novel, *An American Tragedy* (1925), was considered his best work and made him the most important author of realism in the country. *An American Tragedy*, which has been called the great American novel, was adapted for Broadway and sold to Hollywood. Dreiser paved the way for other American realists such as John Steinbeck, Sherwood Anderson, and John Dos Passos.

Theodore Dreiser attacked for immorality

❧ Limberlost Cabin was Gene Stratton Porter's home from 1895 to 1913 in Geneva. She had a fascination for Limberlost Swamp and wrote many nature books. The books contained excellent watercolor wildlife illustrations and her own photography. Where novels were concerned, she was the hottest selling author of her day. *Freckles* (1904) and *The Girl of the Limberlost* (1909) depict life in the Limberlost lake and marsh region of northern Indiana. These books were sentimental, romantic, and beautiful fluff. When Limberlost Swamp was drained and her idealized wilderness gone, Porter moved to Sylvan Lake, near Rome City, where the natural environment was still intact.

Nature's beauty lost and found

The Gene Stratton Porter State Memorial is at Sylvan Lake where her second home was located. She named the home "the cabin in Wildflower Woods." From 1914 to 1921, she enjoyed nature, taking great care in nurturing flora and fauna on the grounds, and completed three more novels. Seven silent films were based on her books. Intent on making her own movies from her books, she moved to California. There on December 6, 1924, Porter died in an automobile accident.

Riley biography brings writer success

❧ Together with Eggleston, Riley, and Wallace, Meredith Nicholson helped advance Indiana's reputation as a literary center. At the age of 19, Nicholson left his home in Crawfordsville to join the ranks of newspaper writers in Indianapolis. There he wrote *The House of a Thousand Candles* in 1905. *The Poet,* a fictionalized biography of James Whitcomb Riley, brought him his greatest success in 1914.

First film critic

❧ Writer Janet Flanner, searching for her place as a young writer, spent a brief stint in 1914 working for the *Indianapolis Star* as what she later called "probably the first cinema critic ever invented." The work didn't last long and she soon left for New York. Eventually she spent most of her career living in Paris, where she wrote long fascinating letters to *The New Yorker* as correspondent "Genet." The first political profile she wrote as Genet was of Hitler, several years before most people took him seriously. She was the author of *An American in Paris* and *The Cubical City.*

Hoosier writes for children

❧ Along with Margaret Weymouth Jackson and Gene Stratton Porter, Annie Fellows Johnston made Indiana one of the nation's leading producers of fiction. Johnston was the author of the popular *Little Colonel* series begining in 1896. It portrayed a romantic view of life on a Southern plantation. She was born in Evansville.

Mystery is his game

❧ After years of working in a variety of occupations from bellhop to clerk in a cigar store, Rex Todhunter Stout took a chance at writing mysteries. In 1927 he wrote his first mystery novel, *Fer de Lance.* His main character, Nero Wolfe, became an instant success. Wolfe is a very large gourmand with a love for growing orchids and a hatred of leaving his New York townhouse. Rex Stout was named the Grand Master of the Mystery Writers of America in 1958.

Slaughterhouse Five

❧ Kurt Vonnegut, Jr., began his writing career as the editor of the Shortridge High School newspaper, the *Echo,* in Indianapolis. Vonnegut is noted for the satirical and pessimistic approach he has made in his 20th-century novels. He uses fantasy and science fiction to show the horrors and ironies of civilization. In his own life, he was a survivor of the fire bombings of Dresden, Germany, during World War II, an experience he tried to re-create in his novel, *Slaughterhouse Five* (1969). Other novels earning national aclaim include *Cat's Cradle* (1963) and *Breakfast of Champions* (1973).

The Quaker life in Indiana

❧ Jessamyn West brought to her readers very human and perceptive stories of Quaker life. Her first and most popular novel was *The Friendly Persuasion,* an account of Quaker life during the Civil War. She also wrote the screenplay for the film adaptation starring Gary Cooper in 1956. West followed up in 1969 with a "prequel" called *Except for Me and Thee.* Other accounts of life in Indiana by West include *The Massacre at Fall Creek,* which tells about men being tried for the murders of Indians, and *The Witch Diggers,* dealing with farm life in southern Indiana.

✤ Crawfordsville is often called the "Athens of the Hoosier State" because of the unusual number of authors who chose to live there at one time or another. Among those was historical novelist Lew Wallace. He was also a lawyer, statesman, and Civil War general. His greatest accomplishment was the epic novel *Ben Hur: A Tale of the Christ,* published in 1880. It twice became the basis of a movie, in 1927 and 1959. The 1959 version was the all-time classic, *Ben Hur,* starring Charleton Heston. Lew Wallace is also noted for *The Fair God* and *The Prince of India.*

Regal Crawfordsville home worthy of Ben Hur author

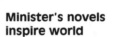

In 1896 the General Lew Wallace Study was built under his own supervision on the grounds of his home in Crawfordsville. It was a two-story red brick building which used Byzantine, Greek Revival, and Romanesque styles. He spent his last years of writing in the Study.

Today, the Study is the Ben-Hur Museum—General Lew Wallace Study. It houses mementos of Wallace's career as a writer, traveler, and soldier. He is buried in Oak Hill Cemetery.

✤ After accepting the call, Columbia City's Lloyd C. Douglas began his first ministry in 1903 at the Zion Evangelical Lutheran Church in North Manchester. Here he produced his first book and experienced his first failure with *More Than a Prophet.* Douglas continued his ministry serving churches in Ohio, Washington, D.C., Michigan, California, and Montreal, Quebec. Starting in 1933, Douglas focused all his time on writing and lecturing.

Minister's novels inspire world

Among Douglas's novels are the ever-popular inspirational books, *The Magnificent Obsession* in 1926 and *The Robe* in 1942. Both novels were made into films. *The Magnificent Obsession* starred Rock Hudson, and Richard Burton played a memorable part in *The Robe.*

✤ Ross Lockridge wrote a Civil War epic, *Raintree County,* in 1948. His fictional Indiana county focused on cities modeled after New Castle and Straugh. The novel was later made into a film starring Elizabeth Taylor and Montgomery Clift.

Raintree County

✤ Indianapolis-born Margaret Anderson dreamed of founding a magazine because she "could spend my time filling it up with the best conversation the world has to offer." In 1914 in Chicago she succeeded as founder of the *Little Review.* It became one of the most influential literary magazines of all time. The editor was willing to experiment with all forms of literature. Anderson even dared to use her magazine to publish James Joyce's *Ulysses* in several installments, knowing that the copies would be confiscated. Anderson lived much of her later life in Paris, except for 13 years in which she lived with the widow of the great tenor Enrico Caruso.

Literary daredevil

PULITZERS OF INDIANA

❧ Novelist **A.B. Guthrie, Jr.**, born in Bedford, grew up in the state of Montana, where his father was first a school principal and then a reporter. Guthrie returned to the Midwest, to Lexington, Kentucky, as a newspaper editor, but his heart and his novel writing were rooted in the West. He won a Pulitzer in 1950 for *The Way West*. In 1952 he gained fame for his novel *The Big Sky,* which became a movie starring Kirk Douglas and produced by fellow Indianan, Howard Hawks. Guthrie credits his writing to a year at Harvard as a Nieman Fellow.

❧ Composer **Ned Rorem** won a Pulitzer for his Bicentennial commission *Air Music* in 1976.

❧ **Newton Booth Tarkington** wrote about the life of the American middle class as he saw it during his time—a comfortable life with neat houses, front porches, plush furniture, calico dresses, and kerosene lamps. *The Magnificent Ambersons* best portrayed Tarkington's view of life in the Midwest centering on his hometown, Indianapolis. It earned him a Pulitzer Prize in 1919. He received a second Pulitzer for *Alice Adams* in 1922. By 1939 Tarkington was called the dean of American writers. At that time he had produced 36 novels and collections of short stories and written 19 plays. He was awarded the gold medal of the National Institute of Arts and Letters. Tarkington also delved into politics, albeit briefly. He was a State Representative for Indiana from 1902 to 1903.

James Whitcomb Riley was not one of Booth Tarkington's biggest fans. However, he still paid a weekly visit to Tarkington's home during the early 1900s. Tarkington's work was never discussed. Riley didn't like his fellow writer's "pretty" portrayal of Indiana. His opinion was somewhat altered when Tarkington published *The Flirt* in 1913. *The Flirt* made fun of the struggles of middle class women for prestige and was more like Riley's style of exposing the foibles of city people.

❧ Cartoonist **John McCutcheon** spent most of his career affiliated with the *Chicago Tribune*. His Indiana ties are in the town of South Raub. He spent much of his life traveling the world from the Gobi Desert to South Africa in an attempt to cover events personally. In 1932, he won a Pulitzer for his cartoons. McCutcheon's famous "Indian Summer" cartoon strip is still reprinted each year in the *Tribune*.

HOOSIER WINNERS

Indiana biographer earns awards

❧ Indianapolis native Shirley Graham completed her first biography for young people in 1944. *Dr. George Washington Carver*, Scientist was a collaboration with George Lipscomb. She received the Julian Messner Award for *There Was Once A Slave* in 1947 and the Anisfield-Wolf prize for *Your Most Humble Servant* in 1950. The latter was a biography of Benjamin Banneker. She married W. E. B. DuBois. In 1960 she went with him to Ghana where she lived until her death in 1977.

❦ Making his contribution to the theater, dramatist and screenwriter Paul Osborn, a native of Evansville, received a Tony award for his play *Morning's at Seven* in 1980. He also gave the motion picture industry two outstanding films: *The Yearling* (1947) and *South Pacific* (1958).

Dramatist wins Tony for Morning's at Seven

ON THE LIGHTER SIDE

❦ George Ade was most widely known for his colorful characters and use of satirical humor. In his 1899 serial comic, *Fables in Slang,* he depicted the simple folks from the Indiana countryside. They skillfully mocked the airs of the "city fellers." Ade was a master at the use of the Hoosier slang. Born in Kentland, he began his career at a newspaper in Lafayette after graduation from Purdue University. He also wrote plays with some success and once had three plays running in New York at the same time. *The County Chairman* (1903) and *The College Widow* (1904) were popular satirical comedies.

George Ade's country folk

❦ The floppy, bright-eyed doll with the mop of red hair has Indiana connections. John Gruelle, creator of *Raggedy Ann,* grew up in Indianapolis. He became a cartoonist with the *Indianapolis Star* and *Indianapolis Sentinel*. His father, R. B. Gruelle, was an impressionist painter who became associated with the "Hoosier Group." Among the family friends was James Whitcomb Riley, whose poems, "The Raggedy Man" and "Little Orphant Annie," became the inspiration for the nationally loved doll. Raggedy Ann was originally a tattered doll belonging to John Gruelle's daughter, Marcella. After her death at a young age, he began writing *Raggedy Ann* stories.

Raggedy Ann creator raised in Indianapolis

❦ Garfield the cat has brought laughter to young and old alike since June 19, 1978. The lovable feline's comic strip is featured in 500 newspapers. He hit prime time TV in 1982. But Saturday morning cartoons eluded him until 1988. His creator, Jim Davis, a Marion, Indiana, man, received Emmy Awards for outstanding animated program for "Garfield in the Rough" (1984), "Garfield's Halloween Adventure" (1985), and "Garfield: Babes and Bullets" (1988).

Garfield is a Hoosier

❦ Frank "Kin" McKinney Hubbard, was a self-taught sketch artist who went to work for the *Indianapolis Journal* in 1891. While traveling through Indiana on a campaign train in 1904, he made several sketches that were published in the paper. The editor liked one of the sketches so well that he asked Kin to do a series. The *Abe Martin* series, starring Hubbard's country philosopher, was born. Will Rogers, his famous contemporary, said that "No man within our generation was within a mile of him." Hubbard's first published collection of sketches was *Abe Martin, Brown County, Indiana* (1906). *Abe Martin's Town Pump* (1929) was the last collection of sketches published.

Sketch artist creates Abe Martin

ON STAGE

Indianapolis theater's humble beginnings

The first theatrical performance in Indianapolis took place at Carter's Tavern on December 8, 1823. It was in taverns, old shops, and buildings that those who aspired to being actors could be found.

An old wagon shop on Washington Street in Indianapolis became the stage for William Lindsay's theatrical company during the winter of 1837-38. The make-shift stage with no floor. Hard two-inch planks for benches and tallow candles for lighting offered less than comfortable surroundings, but that didn't keep the audiences at home. They were hungry for entertainment. The most popular plays of that season were *Othello* and Robert Dale Owen's *Pocahontas*.

Thespians organize

The Thespians was the earliest organized amateur theatrical group in Indianapolis. They performed on a 15- by 20-foot stage in an old foundry at the corner of Market and Senate streets. In order to break down church opposition, the group frequently put on *Pocahontas,* a play of unquestionable morality. Jacob Cox, well-known Indiana artist, painted the scenery for the group's first performance. Lewis Wallace, later to be known as General Lew Wallace, the author of *Ben Hur,* played the heroine's sister, Nomony. His brother, William, later to become a well-known politician, played the heroine.

The Great Divide brings success

The Great Divide brought William Vaughn Moody recognition in 1906. The prose play dealt with conflict rather than the nobility of the poetic works of his earlier writings. His new approach to writing, cut short by his death at age 41, labeled him as a promising young writer of his day.

Pop ballets are trademark

At the age of 23, Portland native Twyla Tharp founded her own ballet troupe. From early on in her career she was an innovator. Far from conventional, she worked with a bare stage, no music, and simple costumes. The focus was on exploring movement. As she grew in her profession, the choreographer presented "pop ballets," a combination of modern dance, pop music, and ballet, to the public.

Ruth Page creates Chicago Ballet

The beauty of her choreography of operas and operettas gave international recognition to Ruth Page, born in Indianapolis. Among her accomplishments was the founding of the Chicago Ballet in 1955. It was disbanded in 1969 and reorganized in 1974. Page performed on stage with Anna Pavlova when she was 15.

A singing steelworker

The son of a Gary fireman, James McCracken turned from a life as a steelworker to that of leading tenor at the Metropolitan Opera. His 1959 performance of Verdi's *Otello* in Europe brought international acclaim. He has the distinction of being the first American to perform *Otello* at the Metropolitan Opera in New York.

Pining on the piano

Mary Wright was the daughter of an aristocratic English family who came to the Vevay area in 1817. They were impoverished at the time and Mary, heartbroken by the loss of her English fiancé, lived a hermit's life in the cabin with one exception—her family had brought with them a beautiful Muzio Clementi piano and she was an accomplished musician.

Once a week she gave concerts for the settlers. It was said that she descended a ladder in the rough log cabin in full "court dress," complete with jewelry and bows. There in front of the simple settlers, Mary would play an entire concert. After her final piece, she would step away from her beloved piano and climb up the ladder to her room never having spoken a word. These concerts continued for 40 years in exactly the same manner. It was said that she left the house only to wander in the moonlight. Mary died at age 82 in 1874 in her room at the top of the ladder.

TOP DESIGNERS

From a Midwestern life to Fifth Avenue, Bill Blass has made it to the top as a high-fashion designer and a most sought after high-society escort. His father, who owned a hardware store in Fort Wayne, committed suicide during the early part of the Depression, leaving his mother to raise Blass and his sister. Once out of high school, Blass headed for the bright lights of New York. There he took a job as sketch artist for a sportswear firm. World War II called him away from his budding profession. Returning as Corporal Blass, he began designing men's clothes in Manhattan. By 1961 he was vice-president of Maurice Renter, Ltd., and soon formed his own company, Bill Blass, Inc. His signature is on menswear and other products, including sheets and cars.

Bill Blass: High in demand

Remember the 1960s culotte skirt? It was all the rage. Women had spent decades wearing dresses. Then came the culotte. It was the next best thing to wearing the pants in the family. A Hoosier from Noblesville, Norman Norell, was responsible for turning the female population away from following in the footsteps of Mrs. Cleaver from TV's "Leave It to Beaver." (You would never catch her in culottes.) His plan for the culotte and other designs always focused on allowing women to move freely. Commissioned by Paramount Studios, Norell designed costumes for such leading silent screen stars as Valentino and Gloria Swanson. He also introduced the chemise, the Empire-styled dress, and the sequined sheath dress. Norell died in 1972, never having seen today's resurrection of the culotte, now known as the split skirt.

Oh . . . Where have all the culottes gone?

WITH BRUSH AND CANVAS

From stoves to sketches of fancy

When Jacob Cox arrived in Indianapolis, he planned on selling stoves and tinware. Instead, his portraits, landscapes, and "sketches of fancy" drew the publics attention. During the 1860s, his popularity grew, as well as his prominence as a local artist. He shared his good fortune with other artists who came to town by helping them get started. Among his more prominent protegés were Joseph O. Eaton and Thomas W. Whittredge. Both became popular artists in the East.

Monet, Matisse, and Warhol

Indiana University's Art Museum, designed by I.M. Pei, was dedicated in 1982. Pei masterfully designed a 110-foot atrium with a skylight in the concrete building. The museum houses artwork from such greats as Monet, Matisse, Rodin, and Warhol.

Art within art

The Indianapolis Museum of Art is a object of art itself. The 154 acres it is located on displays gardens, forests, greenhouses, and wildlife. Four art pavilions overlook the White River. The Lilly Pavilion of Decorative Arts houses the largest collection in the U.S. of J. M. W. Turner watercolors. The Lilly Pavilion is the original house of the Oldfields estate of J. K. Lilly, Jr., of Eli Lilly and Company.

Gilbert Wilson murals

Gilbert Wilson wanted to do something special for his hometown of Terre Haute in 1934. One of Indiana's more modern artists and a social activist of the time, he chose to create murals in pastel chalk around the city. One of the few murals remaining is located in Woodrow Wilson Junior High School. The murals include many prominent citizens of Terre Haute, and occasionally Wilson added himself to the story they told on the school walls. Today, the murals look as if they were recently completed. Their excellent condition is due to the school's art teacher, Don Hadley, who spent a year and a half working after-hours to refurbish the magnificent murals.

INDIANA ENCORE

How do Hoosiers live? Some have quiet lives, others more dramatic. Indiana, like most states in the nation, is a cross section of humanity. It is a melting pot. Indiana began as a cross-roads for the early settlers. Some settlers stayed and some moved on. Those that stayed have enriched the lives of Hoosiers and others in the nation and world by establishing excellent universities and colleges.

Many individuals, such as AIDS victim Ryan White, have made their mark on the whole world. Dr. George Dick and his wife, Gladys, saved countless lives, then and now, with their discovery of an immunization for scarlet fever.

Others, like John Dillinger, left death and destruction behind them and represent the dark side of Indiana.

On a lighter note, 15-year-old John Sain of South Bend was able to build a 68-story, freestanding house of standard playing cards. The 1984 feat placed him in the Guinness Book of World Records for the greatest number of stories in a house of cards. Putting the last card on at a height of 12 feet 10 inches must have been one tense moment. (Warning! No sneezing in the construction zone!)

Come and discover the lifestyles of the Hoosier.

- Famous Hoosiers
- Nobel Recipients
- Infamous Hoosiers
- Indiana's Higher Education
- Lifestyles

FAMOUS HOOSIERS

Trapped in Apollo

◆ An Air Force veteran of the Korean War, Virgil I. Grissom was the second man in space, July 21, 1961. Gus, as he was called, grew up in Mitchell, Indiana, where he spent much of his boyhood playing in nearby Spring Mill State Park. His astronautical life was not as carefree as romping in the park. His first trip into space ended with mishap. His Mercury capsule sank into the Atlantic. Valuable film was lost and Grissom had to be plucked from the sea. Then on January 27, 1967, tragedy struck. Grissom and two other astronauts, Edward H. White and Roger B. Chaffee, were killed in a flash fire during a simulation of the upcoming Apollo 1 spacecraft flight. Trapped in Apollo 1, the last words spoken by the astronauts were, "Get us out of here!" The Apollo craft was totally redesinged after the fire.

Grissom is remembered by the Virgil I. Grissom State Memorial in his old stomping ground, Spring Mill State Park. His spacesuit and Gemini 3 capsule are on display there.

First manned flight around the moon

◆ A boy from Gary, Indiana, became one of three men to be the first to go to the moon. Frank Borman teamed up with James A. Lovell and William A. Anders to make history in December 1968 as they sped toward the moon in Apollo 8. Borman had already spent 330 hours and 35 minutes three years earlier in Gemini 7 as an endurance test for the future moon flights. A West Point graduate and Air Force fighter-bomber instructor, Borman became the deputy director of flight-crew operations for NASA. He resigned in 1970 to join Eastern Airlines; however, even as president, Borman was unable to hold the ill-fated airline together. When Eastern was bought out by Texas Air in Houston, Borman became vice chairman. Eastern is now defunct.

The rest of Indiana's astronauts

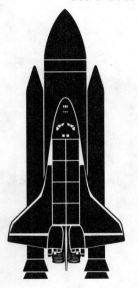

◆ The following are the rest of Indiana's astronauts who have made their voyage into space or are waiting for their debut:

• Crawfordsville's Joseph P. Allen was chosen in 1967. He flew on two shuttle missions, one in November 1982 and one in November 1984. After leaving NASA, Allen became president and chief executive officer, Space Industries International Inc., Houston, Texas.

• Donald E. Williams, born in Lafayette was chosen in 1966. He flew one mission, Apollo 15 in July 1971. After his space stint, Williams became senior systems engineer at Science Applications Internatioinal Corporation.

• Jerry L. Ross, born in Crown Point. Chosen in 1980, he has served as a mission specialist on three missions, one in November. 1985, one in December 1988, and one in June 1991.

• Mark N. Brown from Valparaiso. He was chosen in 1984 to join the elite team of space explorers. Brown has flown two shuttle missions as a mission specialist, one in August 1989 and one in September 1991.

• Janice E. Voss of South Bend was chosen in 1990 and is a mission specialist who had not flown any missions yet.

• Indianapolis-native David A. Wolf was chosen in 1990. He is a mission specialist waiting for his first mission.

❖ Ryan White's quest to educate people, especially other children, about AIDS continues even after his death. His message lives on in his book, *Ryan White: My Own Story*, published by Dial Books for Young Readers. During the last few months of his life, he received countless letters from children. He spent that time writing back to the children and working on his book. The book looks back on the final five years of his life.

**Ryan White:
A young hero**

Ryan became infected with the AIDS virus at age 13 through a blood transfusion for his hemophilia. The young boy became a nationwide "personality" when he was banned from attending school in Russiaville, Indiana, because authorities and parents still believed that AIDS could be transmitted through casual contact.

Ryan and his parents subsequently spoke out about the illness and helped educate people about AIDS. Eventually, Ryan won a court case which would have allowed him to return to school in Russiaville, but his parents chose to move to Cicero, Indiana, where he was welcomed with support and friendship. Ryan's plight came to the attention of singers Elton John and Michael Jackson, both of whom, befriended him.

Ryan testified in front of the U. S. AIDS Commission in 1988, and his life was portrayed in a TV movie, "The Ryan White Story," in 1989. Because of his youth, optimistic personality, and his ability to dispel previously believed myths about AIDS, his death at age 18 brought a huge outpouring of grief. Ryan White's funeral took place at the Second Presbyterian Church in Indianapolis on April 11, 1990. Singer Elton John had stayed in Indianapolis since April 2 to be with Ryan until his death and to help with funeral arrangements.

❖ Dr. George Frederick Dick, born in Fort Wayne, and his wife, Gladys Henry Dick, discovered a test for scarlet fever. In 1923, he and his wife were able to isolate the hemolytic streptococci which cause scarlet fever. They developed the Dick test to see if a person is susceptible to the disease, the Dick toxin for immunization, and the Dick method of prevention.

**Discoverers of
scarlet fever toxin**

❖ Good Indiana home cooking has not gone unnoticed. For years, Indiana cooks have been honored for their delectable creations in the Pillsbury Bake-Off contest. Linda Wood of Indianapolis was a winner for her chick-n-broccoli pot pies in the 1978 refrigerated catagory. In 1975, Fort Wayne resident Barbara Gibson won in the same category as Wood for her easy crescent Danish. Apple pie made Mrs. Erwin J. Smogor of South Bend a Pillsbury winner in 1962.

A taste of winning

❖ Bernard Vonnegut became a modern-day rain maker when he discovered that crystals of silver iodide can make it rain. His experiments proved that if he seeded clouds with the fine crystals they were more effective than dry ice. It is estimated that two pounds of silver iodide would be enough to seed clouds over the entire United States. Vonneguts brother is the famed science fiction novelist, Kurt.

The rain man cometh

Sleepless nights and days

Anderson farmer David Jones was quite a novelty to the medical world when he went 131 days in 1894 without sleep. The insomniac blamed his abnormality on ". . . the use of tobacco while very young."

NOBEL RECIPIENTS

Conqueror of the flu

❖ Stanley Wendell Meredith was born in Ridgeville on August 16, 1904. After playing football at Earlham College, his plans to be a football coach were changed by a visit to the University of Illinois where a chemistry professor got him interested in a different world. He is best known for his work with viruses. He was able to crystallize tobacco mosaic viruses in 1935. He worked on the influenza virus and developed vaccines against it. He shared the 1946 Nobel Prize in chemistry with James Sumner and John Northrup. Ironically, he died while attending a virus conference in Salamanca, Spain, in 1971.

Scholar on the effects of radiation

❖ Hermann Joseph Muller was a pioneer geneticist who studied the effects of radiation and mutations. He was awarded the 1946 Nobel Prize in medicine and physiology. Born in New York in 1890, Muller died in Indianapolis in 1967. As a result of his work in radiation and mutations, he warned against the overuse of X-rays for therapy and diagnosis, and worked for the outlawing of nuclear bombs. He also supported the establishment of sperm banks, to which "gifted" men could donate so their intelligence could spread throughout the human species.

Other Nobel winners

❖ American economist and journalist Paul Anthony Samuelson received the Nobel Prize for economics in 1970. He was born in 1915, in Gary.

Phillip Warren Anderson, born in Indianapolis, worked mainly with the properties of semiconductors and superconductivity. He shared the Nobel Prize for physics in 1977 with Sir Francis Nevill Mott and John H. Van Vleck.

INFAMOUS HOOSIERS

First train robbery in United States

❖ The first train robbery in the United States was committed by the Reno Brothers. In 1866, they hopped the Ohio and Minnesota train as it pulled out of the Seymour depot in Indiana. Their take was $15,000 from the first safe pushed out of the moving train. They never cracked the second safe, which contained $30,000.

So much for motherly love

❖ Gertrude Wright Baniszewski was an Indianapolis single mother of three. To complicate matters, she took in additional children during the summer in 1965. Baniszewski agreed to board the two teenage daughters (the younger one crippled) of a circus couple for $20 a week. Every bit of Baniszewski's anger at life manifested itself that summer and was directed toward Sylvia Likens, the oldest girl, whom Baniszewski decided was a whore. She began by starving both children, and then tortured Sylvia, encouraging her own children to join in. Not satisfied with the torture imposed on Sylvia, Baniszewski crushed her head against a stone wall, killing her. Baniszewski called the police with a fake story, blaming the death on a gang of boys, but Jennie, the younger sister, managed to whisper enough of the truth to make the police investigate further. Gertrude Baniszewski was sent to prison for life.

The Dillinger reign of terror

Motherless at three, an avid reader of Wild West stories, a killer-instinct in athletics . . . could these have been the tell-tale signs of a future bank robber and murderer? Who knows? But they are a part of John Dillinger's youth. His father was a hard-working grocer in

Indianapolis who later moved the family out of the city to Mooresville. By then, Dillinger was already showing signs of delinquency. Early on he dabbled in auto theft. Even a stint in the Navy ended in desertion. Not exactly what you would call a promising future.

Dillinger's life took a turn for the worse after he attempted to rob a Mooresville grocer. His part in the robbery earned him 2-14 years for robbery and 10-20 years for assault (the grocer was beaten in the robbery). Paroled after nine years in Indiana State Prison, he took his anger out on society. He robbed eight banks in the next four months. His rampage was halted by Ohio police. The Midwest countryside had only a short respite. Sprung from jail, Dillinger and his gang continued to rob, wound, and kill.

He prided himself on the March 3, 1934, Crown Point jailbreak. A gun whittled out of wood was enough to scare the jail guards. Or was it his reputation? Whatever it was, they complied with his demands. Once free, Dillinger headed for the Illinois border in the sheriff's car. But this time the Feds were on his case. He had crossed a state line with a stolen car. His reign of terror continued through Illinois, Iowa, Minnesota, and Wisconsin.

It ended in a shoot-out on the streets of Chicago at the Biograph Theater, July 22, 1934. Dillinger lay dead in a pool of blood, fingered by Anna Sage, the "Lady in Red." Dillinger was buried in Crown Hill Cemetery near many of Indiana's famous Hoosiers.

That is to say, the FBI announced Dillinger dead. At the time of the shoot-out and subsequent death of Dillinger, there were many unanswered questions. Why were prescription glasses found on the body, when Dillinger had 20/20 vision? How could the dead man, who the FBI claimed to be Dillinger, have brown eyes? Dillinger had blue or blue-gray eyes, according to all his records. And the list of inconsistencies go on and on. Who knows? Dillinger could still be out there leading an average American life. After all, the statute of limitations does not run out on the capital offense of murder.

Lost and found

A 43-year-old Indianapolis teacher, Miss Carrie T. Selvage, disappeared on March 11, 1900. Her students may have been guilty of driving Miss Selvage to a nervous breakdown, but the reasons for her vanishing act from a hospital has never been determined. Her body was found 20 years later by workmen remodeling the hospital building. The strung-out teacher was found in an attic. (A little *Psycho* music here, please.) Her skeleton was sitting on a rocking chair still clothed in a flannelette wrapper and house slippers.

Doing time in Indiana

◆ Songwriter/singer Chuck Berry spent two years in the Federal Penitentiary at Terre Haute from 1962 to 1964 after he was found guilty of having violated the Mann Act (transporting a minor across state lines for immoral purposes) in 1959, even though the jury accepted the fact that the girl (a hat-check girl he had fired from his St. Louis club) had willingly come with him. Berry's career was never the same after his release, but his songs lived on through other performers.

Always a labor leader

◆ Jimmy Hoffa organized his first strike against management at the age of 16. The managers of a Kroger store gave in to the strikers' demands in four minutes rather than see their perishable foods perish. Finding his niche in life, Hoffa quit his job at the store to become a labor leader. He even found romance on the picket line—it's where he met his wife.

His climb to supremacy in the unions was a rocky one. In 1957, he was indicted by a federal grand jury for bribery, conspiracy, and obstruction of justice in his attempt to obtain information from a U.S. Senate committee's files concerning improper activities in labor and management. Hoffa was acquitted and in that same year made head of the Teamsters union. Again he was indicted for accepting $1 million from a Detroit trucking firm. The case was dismissed as a mistrial after the jury couldn't reach a verdict. Finally, in 1964, he was sentenced to eight years in prison for jury tampering on that case. In 1972, President Nixon commuted Hoffa's sentence. A changed man, Hoffa sought to go to Hanoi on a peace-seeking mission; however, the U. S. would not allow him to go.

Hoffa's colorful life ended in mystery. On July 30, 1975, Hoffa went to lunch at Machus Red Fox restaurant in Birmingham, Michigan. He never returned. He is presumed dead, but his body has never been found. A New Jersey wetland, the Pine Barrens Nature Preserve, is thought to be his resting place. Others believe he is in the concrete surface under the playing field of the Meadowlands Sports Complex in East Rutherford, New Jersey.

Indiana's round jail

The only round jail in operating condition of six remaining in the nation is Montgomery County Jail in Crawfordsville. It was built in 1882 for about $26,000. A description from the patent application, submitted by William H. Brown and Benjamin F. Haugh, of Indianapolis, best describes why a round jail was such a good idea:

"The object of our invention is to produce a jail in which prisoners can be controlled without the necessity of personal contact between them and the jailer . . . it consists of a circular cell structure of considerable size divided into several cells capable of being rotated, surrounded by a grating which has only one opening for the handling of prisoners . . ." The jail remained in use until June of 1973. It later became a museum in 1975.

❖ His life began in Lynn, but Reverend Jim Jones's death in Guyana made horrifying healines the world over because he encouraged hundreds of his followers to drink cyanide-laced Kool-Aid. Where did this path of destruction begin?

Jonestown Massacre

Jim Jones was an Indiana University dropout who started a Methodist mssion with his wife, Marceline Baldwin (a high school sweetheart). Jones and his church fathers didn't quite have the same vision; he was expelled in 1954. He then raised $50,000 to buy an Indianapolis neighborhood synagogue and founded the People's Temple in 1957. Recognized for his contributions to a poor neighborhood, Jones was appointed director of the Human Rights Commission by the Indiana governor. Jones's disappointment in people's attitude toward racial rights and a fear of impending nuclear holocaust led him to South America where he thought it would be safe.

He returned to Indianapolis when he learned his People's Temple was in trouble. By 1964, Jones became a minister of the Disciples of Christ. He led 100 followers from Indiana to California where he founded another synagogue. His ministry looked to be a positive one as it started food kitchens and day-care centers. The number of his followers grew, as did his psychopathic religious fanaticism. In his mind, suicide was the only escape from an oppressive world.

After purchasing 27,000 acres in Guyana, he led 1,000 of his followers to the retreat. A U.S. congressional investigation into Jones's activities ended in an ambush in Guyana. Five persons were dead including California congressman Leo Ryan. Jones could not be stopped. On November 19, 1978, he returned to the task at hand. Within five minutes, 913 adults and children, including Jones, were dead.

INDIANA'S HIGHER EDUCATION

Indiana University

❖ Indiana University began as a state seminary in Bloomington, opening in 1820 with one professor and ten male students. In 1883, after a fire, the university was moved to its present site, which has a 2,000-acre main campus. Over 30,000 students attend from all over the nation and the world.

The university's Lilly Library contains a number of rare books and manuscripts. It has a copy of the Gutenberg Bible, a first printing of the Declaration of Independence, and one of the five major Lincoln collections. The library also has a collection of 800 film scripts including *Citizen Kane, Gone With the Wind*, and *The Godfather*. A movie was even filmed in Bloomington featuring the university's Little 500 Bicycle Race (see p. 65).

Former students include Wendell Willkie, Republican presidential candidate in 1940, and Theodore Dreiser, who wrote about the university in his book *Dawn*.

Hoagy Carmichael

❖ Indiana University was the inspiration for the musical talents of Hoagland "Hoagy" Carmichael. Born in Bloomington, he first became aware of his talents at age 12 after hearing the tune "Indiana Frangipani" from the university's belltower. He sat down and played it on the piano. The family moved to Indianapolis in 1915. Carmichael, already hooked on jazz, returned to Bloomington four years later to complete his high school education and then go on to college to study law. It wasn't exactly in the Indiana University library or student union that he began writing songs. Instead it was at a Bloomington bar, the Book Nook. "Free Wheeling" and "Washboard Blues" were products of his talent, a broken-down piano, and the Book Nook.

After graduation the young composer joined a law firm in West Palm Beach, Florida. Deciding he was a piano player rather than a legal eagle, he returned to Bloomington. and it was there that he created "Stardust." The melody first came to him while sitting on the "spooning wall," a place for lovers, at Indiana University. He completed it at his favorite spot, the Book Nook.

The Kinsey Report

❖ *Sexual Behavior in the Human Male* (1948) and *Sexual Behavior in the Human Female* (1953) brought researcher Alfred Kinsey international attention. The two books represented his scientific approach to the study of sex. They were based on personal interviews of 18,500 people. The reports caused much controversy at a time when sex was not a household word and not commonly discussed. Some parents of students at Indiana University, at that time, threatened to take their sons and daughters out of the school. He was the director of Indiana University's Institute for Sex Research beginning in 1942. Kinsey died August 25, 1956, in Bloomington, before the "sexual revolution" got underway.

◆ Valparaiso University, under the management of Henry Baker Brown, became nationally known as "the poor man's Harvard." In 1914-15, its student body was 6,000—second in size only to Harvard. After Brown's death and the beginning of World War I, enrollment plummeted. The 1939-40 enrollment was 513. Purchased in 1925 by the Lutheran Church and opened to all faiths, Valparaiso University is now the largest Lutheran university in the nation. The writer Lowell Thomas is among its more noteworthy alumni.

Poor man's Harvard

A student's scorn

Heidi Gerdts, a freshman at Indiana University in 1992, is believed to have gotten even with fellow high school students at Greenwood before moving on to the university. One of the school's yearbook editors, she was accused of defacing the yearbook some time between the last proofreading and before printing. Five hundred copies of the yearbook went to eager students containing blackened teeth, penciled-in underarm hair, and an obscenity under the photo of certain students. The recipients of Heidi's scorn said she defaced their pictures out of jeolousy over boyfriends. Heidi's parents sent an apology to the families of the girls involved and the school recalled the 500 yearbooks.

LIFESTYLES

◆ Elkhart County was a magnet to many members of the Amish and Mennonite Christian denominations. With farming as their trade, they were attracted to the fertile soil of this area. The Amish first arrived in 1841. Two years later the Mennonites established settlements in the Goshen area. Today the Amish-Mennonite settlement in Indiana is among the largest settlements, including those in Ohio, Pennsylvania, Iowa, Illinois, and Kansas. The Amish influence is found in such communities as Shipsewana, Nappanee, Goshen, Bristol, Middlebury, Benten, Millersburg, New Paris, and Wakarusa. Nappanee, the heart of northeastern Indiana's Amish settlements, is listed on the National Register of Historic Places. It is also one of 16 pilot communities participating in the National Trust for Historic Preservation Tourism Initiative.

The Amish

All sorts of stuff found in museum

Located in the heart of Orange County's Amish County, the Museum of All Sorts of Stuff is an odd collection of memorabilia. Opened as Punkin Center General Store on October 31, 1922, with $327.28 worth of groceries purchased from a New Orleans wholesaler, the store is now a museum. Artifacts range from an old-fashioned soda fountain, a collection of Indiana license plates (with the only plate in Indiana ever made with the number 1,000,000) to Colorado sagebrush and all kinds of stuff from all kinds of places. The proprietor, Add Gray, hasn't thrown anything away since 1917.

Quakers

◆ The Quakers built a settlement near Richmond shortly after the town was platted in 1816. Many of them were strong abolitionists. When Henry Clay addressed a gathering of 20,000 Whigs in Richmond, he was handed a petition by Quaker leader Hiram Mendenhall, signed by 2,000 Quakers, demanding that the slaves be freed. Clay told the crowd that while slavery was an evil, indiscriminate emancipation was also a bad idea. He stated that he owned 50 slaves worth about $15,000. He asked the Quaker hecklers if any of them would be willing to supply $15,000 for their benefit if he were to free them. Clay then told the Quaker group to go home and mind their own business. This event probably contributed to Clay's defeat in the 1844 presidential election.

Lost collie goes home

The *Guinness Book of World Records* reports that the longest distance known to have been traveled by a dog trying to follow its family was about 2,000 miles, accomplished in 1923 by a collie who was lost in Wolcott, Indiana, by a family passing through. Unable to find him, the sad family returned home to Silverton, Oregon. However, six months later, including a bitter winter, the dog showed up in Silverton, having crossed mountains, valleys, and incredibly long distances of open plains.

Harmonie

◆ Father George Rapp was among the first settlers of Harmonie. The leader of the Harmony Society, known as the Rappites, shared with his members the belief that the Second Coming of Christ was imminent. The Rappites moved from Beaver County, Pennsylvania, to Harmonie in Posey County, Indiana, in 1814, where they prospered on 30,000 acres of land along the Wabash River. They developed a variety of industries, from producing fine silk cloth to distilling whiskey. Among their more creative ideas was prefabricated houses with tunnels dug under them for air conditioning in the summer. Oranges were grown all year in greenhouses. Afraid that the worldly success of their community would not be acceptable in the eyes of Christ when he came to earth again, the Rappites sold Harmonie in 1824 to Robert Owen.

The building of New Harmony

◆ Robert Owen, a wealthy Scottish industrialist, had quite a lasting impact on U.S. history and its institutions. When he purchased Harmonie, Indiana, he wanted to create a new type of utopia—one based on intellectual pursuits and innovative education. He lured scientists, writers, educators, social reformers, and artists to New Harmony. Among his first settlers were 40 highly educated and respected individuals. They had taken a keelboat from Pittsburgh down the Ohio and up the Wabash to New Harmony. The group was given the name "Boatload of Knowledge." Among its members were a wealthy geologist and mineralogist, a naturalist, a Quaker doctor, and an educator.

Many of America's firsts came out of New Harmony, including the first free library, the first free public school system and kindergarten, a day-care center, a woman's club, and a civic dramatic club. Under the leadership of William Maclure and Robert Owen, New Harmony became a center for innovative education. The School of Industry—the first vocational school in Indiana—taught drawing, painting, music, lithography, printing, and bookbinding.

The community faded in 1827 because its people didn't possess the necessary farming or husbandry skills to support its intellectual life. However, it was never totally deserted, and New Harmony became a more typical Indiana town. After Jane Owen, wife of a direct descendant of Robert Owen, visited New Harmony in the 1940s, she spearheaded a restoration project to preserve its history.

The New Harmony Atheneum Center, which opened in 1980, is a glossy white porcelain building designed by Richard Meier. In the Atheneum auditorium visitors learn the 165-year history of New Harmony.

Workingmen's Insitute in New Harmony is Indiana's oldest continuously open public lending library, founded in 1838 by William Maclure.

Frances Wright fights for women's rights

♦ After seeing the success of New Harmony in 1825, Frances Wright tried to found her own community in Tennessee. Three years later it was a bust and she headed back to New Harmony. Wright worked with Robert Dale Owen, son New Harmony's founder, by helping to edit his newspaper, the New Harmony *Gazette*. When New Harmony failed, she moved to New York, and eventually became a controversial lecturer. Many of her lectures dealt with freedom of thought, free education for children from the age of two, and the right of women to have control of their property and children.

The first women's club

❖ The first women's club ever to have a constitution and by-laws was formed in New Harmony, Indiana, in 1858. The Minerva Club even had quarters in a five-room house donated by the founder of the club, Constance Owen Fauntleroy. The quarters are now a "shrine" belonging to the Indiana Federation of Women's Clubs.

ROBERT OWEN'S CHILDREN

The Owen legacy

❖ Although the utopian community failed, Robert Owen's children went on to play major roles in the development of Indiana. Only William, due to his early death in 1842, was unable to achieve greatness like his brothers.

Robert Dale Owen

Indiana owes much to Robert Dale. He served in Congress from 1842 to 1846. He originated and introduced a bill which founded the Smithsonian Institution. As a member of the State Convention of 1851, he was largely responsible for a free tax-supported school system. He was a supporter of equal rights for women. In 1852 he improved divorce laws and income rights for married women in Indiana. His greatest achievement may be his influence in the emancipation movement. A letter he wrote to President Lincoln in 1862 is credited with having more influence than anything or anyone else on Lincoln's decision to free the slaves. Owen died in New York in 1877, but his bones were re-interred in New Harmony in 1937.

David Dale Owen

David Dale made the first geological study of Indiana in 1837 and became head of the U.S. Geological Survey in 1839 and ran the organization for 17 years from New Harmony. He also made the first government survey of new government lands in the West.

Richard Owen

Richard was a professor of natural history at the University of Indiana and was the first president of Purdue University.

A message from Gabriel

In the yard of the Rapp-Maclure Home in New Harmony is Gabriel's Rock. The impression of two large human feet appears on the stone, and popular folklore says that the Angel Gabriel stood on the rock while he brought Father George Rapp a message from heaven. The truth is that the rock was purchased in St. Louis by Rapp's son.

The following calendar items are events that occurred in Indiana on the different days of the year. Check the index to see if more information can be found on the event in this AWESOME ALMANAC.

JANUARY

1   Evansville's Mesker Park Zoo acquired a white-throated capuchin monkey 1935

Indianapolis Unigov plan put in motion 1970

First female Episcopal priest, Jacqueline Means, ordained in Indianapolis 1977

2   First woman to be employed in the office of the U.S. president 1890

Explosion at packing plant kills 16 Terre Haute 1963

5   Baseball player Ron Kittle born in Gary 1958

7   Baseball player Mack Mattingly born in Anderson 1931

8   The great steel strike couldn't hold up against U.S. Steel, called off 1920

11 Actor Monte Blue born in Indianapolis 1890 appeared in 200 films playing romantic leads

Hall of Fame baseball player Max George Carey born in Terre Haute 1890

12 Tommy Pruett of TV's "Life Goes On," born 1971 in Gary

13 Journalist-radio performer Elmer Davis born Aurora 1890

Pulitzer winning novelist of the Old West, A. B., Guthrie Jr., born in Bedford 1901

15 Basketball player Cliff Barker born in Yorktown 1921

16 Journalist Carl William Ackerman born in Richmond 1890

18 Engineer James Weir Graydon born in Indianapolis 1848

20 Actor Leon Ames born 1903 in Portland

Astronaut Jerry L. Ross born in Crown Point 1948

21 William A. Wirt, inventor of the "Gary system" of school, born in Markle 1874

22 Jazz musician J.J. Johnson born in 1924 in Indianapolis

Senator Birch Bayh born in 1928 in Terre Haute

25 Bass player and songwriter Rick Finch born in Indianapolis 1954

26 Science fiction writer Philip Jose Farmer (winner of Hugo Award) born in Terre Haute 1918

27 The Ohio River causes disastrous flood in 1937

FEBRUARY

2   Jack Dillon light-heavyweight champion in the 1900s born in 1891 in Frankfurt

3   Actor Robert Terrel Haines born in 1870 in Muncie

Miami Dolphins quarterback Hall of Famer Bob Griese born in Evansville 1945

Indiana University honors its swimming coach, Doc Counsilman, 1990

5   Architect for the Sears Tower Nathaniel Alexander Owings, born in Indianapolis 1903

8   Tony-winning (for *South Pacific*) actor Myron McCormick born in Albany 1908

James Dean, film actor and cult hero, born in Marion 1931

9   Humorist and columnist George Ade born in Kentland 1866

11 Longtime Indianapolis Speedway president Tony Hulman, Jr., born in Terre Haute 1901

12 Actor Forrest Meredith Tucker born in 1919 in Plainfield

13 Astronaut Donald E. Williams born in Lafayette 1942

14 Labor leader Jimmy Hoffa born in Brazil 1913

Singer and Brady Bunch mom Florence Henderson born in Dale 1934

Lebanon high school basketball player Rick Mount on *Sports Illustrated* cover 1966

15 Indiana included in blizzard which kills 500 over two days 1958

17 "Tossin' and Turnin' " singer Bobby Lewis born in Indianapolis 1933

18 Presidential candidate Wendell L. Willkie born in Elwood 1892

19 Lincoln Boyhood National Monument was authorized in Lincoln City 1962

20 Baseball's Edgar "Sam" Rice born in Morocco 1892

22 Basketball players Dick and Tom Van Arsdale born in Indianapolis 1943

26 Governor Otis Bowen born in Rochester 1918

27 Trains collide at Porter killing 37 people 1921

28 Immunologist Herald Rea Cox, developer of oral polio vaccine, born in Rosedale 1907

MARCH

1 Ball Brothers began glass production in Muncie 1888

3 John Dillinger escaped from Lake County Jail 1934

5 Right fielder Sam Thompson born in Danville 1860

Football player, announcer/actor Fred Williamson born in Gary 1938

Actor Michael Warren born in South Bend 1946

6 Jazz musician Wes Montgomery born in 1925 in Indianapolis

7 Owner-publisher of *Kansas City Star* William Rockhill Nelson born in Fort Wayne 1841

8 Edmund B. Ball, canning jar manufacturer, died in Muncie 1925

9 Actor Will Geer born in 1902 in Frankfort

Sculptor David Smith born in 1906 in Decatur

12 Jackson 5 family member Marlon Jackson born in Gary 1957

13 Author of *An American in Paris,* Janet Flanner was born in Indianapolis in 1892

Winamac court found Ford innocent in case of Ford Pinto deaths 1980

14 U.S. vice president Thomas Riley Marshall born in 1854 in North Manchester.

Astronaut Frank Borman born in Gary 1928

17 Chinese Theatre founder Sid Grauman born in Indianapolis 1879

W.R. Clifford Wells, co-founder of Indiana High School Coaches Association, born in Indianapolis 1896

Northwest Airlines Electra drops from sky near Tell City, killing 63 aboard 1960

18 Real life Johnny Appleseed, John Chapman, dies in Fort Wayne 1845

Political cartoonist William Hulfish Crawford born in 1913 in Hammond

Indiana among victims of the Great Tornado killing 689 people 1925

19 Short story writer Joe L. Hensley born in Bloomington 1926

21 St. Meinrad became the location of the first abbey in the New World 1854

22 Journalist Kent Cooper born in Columbus 1880, established Associated Press in several countries

Dancer Ruth Page, founded Chicago Ballet, born in 1899 in Indianapolis

Actor Karl Malden born in 1913 in Gary

23 Famous miniature painter Amalia Kussner Coudert born in Terre Haute 1873

24 Landscape artist John Rogers Cox born in Terre Haute 1915

Actor Steve McQueen born in 1930 in Indianapolis

25 Detroit Tigers owner John Earl Fetzer born in 1901 in Decatur

26 Strother Martin, actor in *Cool Hand Luke* and *True Grit,* born in 1919 in Kokomo

28 Series of deadly tornadoes strike Indiana and Ohio killing 71 in 1920

Albert Von Tilzer, songwriter, born in Indianapolis 1878

Artist and sculptor Eugene Francis Savage born in Covington 1883

29 Olympic gymnast Kurt Thomas born in Terre Haute 1956

Wabash becomes first city to use public electric lighting 1880

Author Jeannette Covert Nolan born in Evansville 1896

31 Knute Rockne killed in airplane crash 1931

APRIL

1 Author of *Ben Hur,* Lew Wallace born in 1827 in Brookville

3 Astronaut Gus Grissom born in Mitchell 1926

4 William Henry Harrison inaugurated 1841, died 31 days later

Journalist Steve Hannagan born in Lafayette 1899

First batsman Gil Hodges born in Princeton 1924

Senator Richard G. Lugar (R/Indiana) born in Indianapolis 1932

5 Bell Aircraft founder Lawrence Dale Bell born in Mentone 1894

Nobel winner Hermann Muller research on radiation and mutation dies in Indianapolis 1967

6 Sports store explosion kills 43 in Richmond 1968

7 Chief executive of the New York Public Library Vartan Gregorian born in Tabriz 1935

8 Rose McConnell Long, congresswoman, widow of Huey, born in Greensburg 1892

8 Football player Mark Clayton born in Indianapolis 1961

9 Baseball player Kyle Robert Macy born in Fort Wayne 1957

10 Longtime Gimbel's president Bernard F. Gimbel born in Vincennes 1885

A member of the Basketball Hall of Fame, Charles "Stretch" Murphy born in Marion 1907

11 Thirty-five tornadoes hit Midwest April 11, 1965, Indiana hit the hardest

12 Comedian/talk-show host David Letterman born in 1947 in Indianapolis

16 Wilbur Wright, aviation pioneer, was born in near Newcastle 1867

17 Screenwriter of *The Country Girl* George Seaton born in 1911 in South Bend

18 First laundromat opened in Fort Wayne by J. F. Cantrell 1934

Tenor George Shirley, over 20 leading roles at the Met, was born in Indianapolis 1934

19 Michigan center and All-American "Germany" Schulz born in Fort Wayne 1883

20 Norman Norell, creator of the 1960 culotte, born in Noblesville 1900

Baseball player Don Mattingly born in Evansville 1961

21 Songwriter Paul Dresser, creator of Indiana's state song, born in Terre Haute 1858

24 TV documentary, "Middletown," features Muncie, a typically American town 1982

25 Author Ross Lockridge born in Bloomington 1914

Mayor William Hudnut, III opens lower canal revitalization 1989

26 Jules Stein, founder of MCA (Music Corporation of America), born in South Bend 1896

27 CBS Capitol Hill correspondent Phil Jones born in Marion 1937

29 Nobel Prize-winning chemist Harold Clayton Urey born in Walkerton 1893

MAY

1 Seat of Indiana territorial government moved from Vincennes to Corydon 1813

3 Writer called the "Sage of Potato Hill," Edgar Watson Howe born in Treaty 1853

4 Jackie Jackson of Jackson 5 born in Gary 1951

6 Pulitzer Prize winning cartoonist John Tinney McCutcheon born in South Raub 1870

Football coach Weeb Ewbank born in Richmond 1907

7 Oscar-winning actress Anne Baxter born in Michigan City 1923

8 Baseball Hall of Fame member Edd J. Roush born in Oakland City 1893

12 Sociologist James Coleman born in Bedford 1926

Science fiction writer Robert (Buck) Coulson born in Sullivan 1928

15 Annie Fellows Johnston of *The Little Colonel* fame born in Evansville 1863

American economist and journalist Paul Anthony Samuelson born in Gary 1915

Astronaut Anthony W. England born in Indianapolis 1942

16 Singer-actress Janet Damita Jackson born in 1966 in Gary

17 Greenback Party organized in Indianapolis 1874

19 Steel manufacturer Tom Mercer Girdler born in Clark County 1877

21 Actor (and father of Joan and Constance) Richard Bennett born in Deacon's Mills 1873

Singer/actress Lola Lane born in 1906 in Macy

Author Dan Wakefield born in 1932 in Indianapolis

22 Baseball player Tommy John born in Terre Haute 1943

23 Bridge engineer James Buchanan Eads born in Lawrenceburg 1820

Civil War General Ambrose Everett Burnside born in Liberty 1924

Actor/singer Scatman Crothers born in 1910 in Terre Haute

26 Two days of tornadoes killing 249 includes Indiana in 293 mile path 1917

28 First Indianapolis 500 automobile race held at Indianapolis 1911. Ray Harroun wins inaugural Indianapolis 500

29 Oldest child of singing Jackson family, Rebbie, born in Gary 1950

Civil rights activist Vernon E. Jordan, Jr., wounded in Fort Wayne 1980.

30 Baseball pitcher Amos Rusie born in Mooresville 1871

Film director Howard Hawks born in Goshen in 1896

31 Senator Vance Hartke, among men behind the Great Debates, born in Stendal 1919

JUNE

2 The first night baseball game was played in Fort Wayne 1883

3 Singer Deniece Williams born in Gary 1951

5 Writer Harry Mark Petrakis born in St. Louis 1923

6 Senator Homer Capehart born in Algiers 1897

Sculptor George Warren Rickey born in 1907 in South Bend

Cartoonist Tom Kreusch Ryan born in 1926 in Anderson

Opera singer Peter Glossop born in Indianapolis 1928

7 Indianapolis chosen state capital 1820

9 Composer-lyricist Cole Porter born in 1891 in Peru

Basketball player and coach Branch McCracken born in Monrovia 1908

10 Arthur Trester, secretary of the Indiana HSAA in 1913 born in Pecksburg 1878

11 Actor John Bromfield born in South Bend 1922

Actor Chad Everett of "Medical Center" born in South Bend 1937

16 Writer George Paul Elliott born in Knightstown 1918

17 Mack Sennett comedy actress Louise Fazenda born in Lafayette 1899

18 Cartoonist Dave Gerard born in 1909 in Crawfordsville

22 Troop and circus trains collide killing 53 performers in Ivanhoe 1918

Menswear designer Bill Blass born in Fort Wayne 1922

24 Chuck Taylor, who perfected the Converse All-Star basketball shoe, born in Brown County 1901

Comedian/band leader Phil Harris born in Linton 1906

26 Prohibition party convention met at Winona Lake 1947

Elvis Presley appeared in last concert in Indianapolis 1977

27 Sen. Jesse Bright introduced amendment to extend the Missouri Compromise line 1848

Astronaut Joseph P. Allen born in Crawfordsville 1937

29 Baseball player "Dizzy" Trout born in Sandcut 1915

JULY

1 Bandleader/lyricist Noble Sissle born in 1889 in Indianapolis.

Political leader Richard Gordon Hatcher born in 1933 in Michigan City.

Oscar winning movie director Sydney Pollack born in 1934 in Lafayette

"Pop ballet" choreographer Twyla Tharp born in Portland 1941

3 Secretary of Agriculture Earl Lauer Butz born in Noble County 1909

USS *Vincennes* shoots down Iranian airliner, killing 290 civilians 1988

4 First newspaper plant in Indiana opened in Vincennes 1804

First railroad completed on nation's birthday 1834

Elwood Haynes of Kokomo demonstrated the first clutch-driven car in 1894

The Indiana Territory Sesquicentennial celebrated in Vincennes 1950

5 Prohibition party convention was held at Indianapolis in 1932

7 Hall of Fame baseball player Billy Herman born in New Albany 1909

8 *The Great Divide* author William Vaughn Moody born in Spencer 1869

9 Corydon was the scene of the only Civil War battle fought on Indiana ground 1863

Architect Michael Graves born in Indianapolis 1934

Oil-recycling facility opened 1991 in East Chicago

10 Actor Ron Glass born in 1945 in Evansville

11 Vernon is only Indiana town Col. John Morgan couldn't take during Civil War raid 1863

Actor and radio announcer Harry Von Zell born in 1906 in Indianapolis

12 Janet Gray Hayes, first woman mayor of a major city (San Jose), born in Rushville 1926

13 Northwest Ordinance passed 1787

14 Collegeville recorded one of the hottest spots in the U.S., 116 degrees in 1936

15 Scientist Thomas Francis, Jr., born in Gas City 1900

Football player and film producer Alex Karras born in Gary 1935

Actor Ken Kercheval of TV's "Dallas" born in Wolcottville 1935

Elephants topple a barricade injuring nine people in Lafayette 1992

16 Popcorn popper Orville Redenbacher born in Brazil 1907

18 Governor Paul V. McNutt born in Franklin 1891

Golfer Charles Evans, Jr., born in Indianapolis 1893

Novelist Jessamyn West tells life of early Quakers born in near North Vernon 1902

Emmy-winning comedian Red Skelton born in Vincennes 1913

Guitarist Lonnie Mack (1962 "Memphis" hit) born in Aurora 1941

21 Train robber Sam Bass, born in Mitchell 1851, killed in 1878 Texas bank robbery

Founder of scarlet fever immunization Dr. George F. Dick born in Fort Wayne 1881

Cowboy actor known for riding stunts Ken Maynard born in 1895 in Vevey

22 First coal mining strike east of Rockies involved nearly 26,000 workers 1935

Emmy-winning director John Korty born in Lafayette 1936

23 George Rogers Clark National Historical Park was authorized in Vincennes 1966

26 Author-editor George Barr McCutcheon born in 1866 in South Raub

Actor Charles Butterworth born in South Bend 1897

Aircraft trainer inventor Edwin Link born in Huntington 1904

28 Vaudeville performer and actor Richard "Skeets" Gallagher born in Terre Haute 1891

Lovable Garfield's creator Jim Davis born in Marion 1945

29 *The Magnificent Ambersons* author Booth Tarkington born in 1869 in Indianapolis

30 U.S.S. *Indianapolis* sunk on return trip from carrying uranium for A-bomb 1945

AUGUST

1 George Croghan, an English agent, makes peace with the Indiana Indians 1765

2 Actress Lurene Tuttle born in 1906 in Pleasant Lake

Tony-winning playwright and novelist Joseph Hayes born in Indianapolis 1918.

3 Pulitzer Prize-winning journalist Ernie Pyle born in 1900 in Dana

4 Political leader Oliver Perry Morton born in 1823 in Salisbury.

Unofficial poet laureate of the Hoosier State, Sarah Bolton died in Indianapolis 1893

5 Historian Mary Ritter Beard born in Indianapolis 1876

6 Indiana Congressman Adam Benjamin, Jr., born in Gary 1935

7 New York Yankee Don Larsen born in Michigan City 1929

9 Allegheny Airlines DC-9 flight crashes outside Shelbyville, killing all 83 in 1969

10 Jockey Todd Sloan, who revolutionized riding, was born in Kokomo 1874

Baseball player Don Buse born in Holland 1950

12 Writer of Greek and Roman mythology, Edith Hamilton born in Fort Wayne 1867

Teacher Zerna A. Sharp, originator of the "Dick and Jane" readers, born in Hillisburg 1889

Basketball player George McGinnis born in Indianapolis 1950

14 Country singer Connie Smith born in Elkhart 1941

15 Christmas rock & roller Bobby Helms born in Bloomington 1934

16 Nobel prize-winning biochemist Stanley W. Meredith born in Ridgeville 1904

Caldecott recipient Beatrice S. DeRegniers, children's writer, born in 1914 in Lafayette

17 A balloon carrying the first airmail in United States takes off from Lafayette 1859

19 W. Stewart Woodfill, owner of the Grand Hotel on Mackinac Island, born in Greensburg 1896

Actor William Marshall born in 1924 in Gary

20 Benjamin Harrison, known as an Indiana president, born in Ohio 1833

21 Sports journalist Chris Schenkel born in Bippus 1923

22 Violinist Maud Powell born in 1867 in Peru

Leader of the House of Representatives, Charles Halleck born in Demotte 1900

23 Humor writer Will Cuppy born in Auburn 1884

Literary critic Newton Arvin born in Valparaiso 1900

Emmy-winning actress Shelley Long of "Cheers" born in Fort Wayne 1949

Astronaut David A. Wolf born in Indianapolis 1956

24 Singer Fred Rose born in 1897 in Evansville

25 Emmy-winning actor David Canary born in 1939 in Elwood

Sex researcher Alfred Kinsey dies in Bloomington 1956

27 Realist author Theodore Dreiser born in Terre Haute 1871

Author of *Magnificent Obsession,* Lloyd C. Douglas born in 1877 in Columbia City

Writer of *The Snake Pit,* Mary Jane Ward born in Fairmont 1905

28 James Daywalt, Indy 500 Rookie of the Year in 1953, born in Wabash 1924

29 Father of cloud seeding Bernard Vonnegut born in Indianapolis 1914

Superstar Michael Jackson born in 1958 in Gary

31 Grand Army of Republic held final meeting at Indianapolis 1949

SEPTEMBER

2 Jazz musician Wilbur DeParis born in 1900 in Crawfordsville

3 Final Peace of Paris with Great Britain 1783

4 Dramatist/screenwriter Paul Osborn born in 1901 in Evansville

Actor Dick York, who played Darin on "Bewitched," born in 1928 in Fort Wayne

6 Comedianne Jo Anne Worley born in Lowell 1937

9 Author of *Alice of Old Vincennes*, Maurice Thompson born in 1844 in Crawfordsville

Actor Raymond Walburn born in 1887 in Plymouth

KFC's Col. Sanders born in near Henryville 1890

10 Oscar-winning movie director Robert Wise born in 1914 in Winchester

12 Father of the Selective Service in WWII Gen. Lewis B. Hershey born in Steuben County 1893

13 Artist Robert Indiana born in 1928 in New Castle

14 *Closing of the American Mind* author Allan David Bloom born in Indianapolis 1930

20 Constance Fauntleroy founded the first women's club 1859

21 Physicist Lee Du Bridge, "Senior Statesman of Science," born in Terre Haute 1901

22 Baseball player George August "Hooks" Dauss born in Indianapolis 1889

23 Dillinger escapes from Indiana State prison in 1933

24 Bechtel Corporation's founder Stephen Bechtel born in Aurora 1900

25 Chemist Edgar Clay Britton born in Rockville 1891

26 Sociologist Robert Staughton Lynd born in New Albany 1892

29 Cartoonist Fred Neher born in 1903 in Nappanee

30 Little Turtle cedes three million acres on White and Wabash rivers to the U.S. 1809

OCTOBER

1 Steam boiler exhibit explosion in Indianapolis causes stampede, killing 27 people, 1869

Grammy-winning conductor Margaret Hillis born in Kokomo 1921

5 Actress Louise Dresser born in 1882 in Evansville

CIA director in the 1950s Walter Bedell Smith born in Indianapolis 1895

6 First train robbery in U.S. pulled by Reno brothers near Seymour 1866

Carole Lombard, actress and wife of Clark Gable, born in Fort Wayne 1909

7 Hoosier's poetic son, James Whitcomb Riley, born in Greenfield 1849

Baseball player Chuck Klein born in Indianapolis 1904

Singer and songwriter John Cougar Mellencamp, born in 1951 in Seymour

8 Lincoln's secretary and biographer John Milton Hay born in Salem 1838

TV personality Sarah Purcell was born in 1948 in Richmond

Astronaut Janice E. Voss born in South Bend 1956

10 Dr. Ravdin Isidor, who once operated on President Eisenhower, born 1894 in Evansville

Singer David Lee Roth of the Van Halen group born in Bloomington 1955

12 Hall of Fame baseball player Oscar McKinley Charleston born in Indianapolis 1896

14 UCLA basketball coach John Robert Wooden born in Martinsville 1910

15 Author Hubert L. Dreyfus born in 1929 in Terre Haute.

Singer-musician Tito of the Jackson 5 born in 1953 in Gary

17 Pathologist Ernest Goodpasture born in Montgomery County 1886

Playwright and actress Gretchen Cryer born in Indianapolis 1935

18 Chemist-reformer Harvey Washington Wiley born in 1844 in Kent

19 Hall of Fame pitcher Mordecai Peter Centennial Brown born in Nyesville 1876

Producer Jules Power born in 1921 in Hammond

Actor Lloyd Haynes born in 1935 in South Bend

20 Supreme Court Justice Sherman Minton born in Georgetown 1890

22 Downtown Ft. Wayne land was bought for $1.25/acre in 1823

23 Humor writer-lecturer Emily Kimbrough born in Muncie 1899

Betty Scott becomes first woman to fly an airplane 1910

Sgt. Alex Arch of South Bend commanded battery that fired first shot in WWI 1917

Composer Ned Rorem born in Richmond 1923 recipient of Pulitzer

Dillinger nets $75,346 in 5 minutes from the Greencastle Central National Bank 1933

25 Artist-art patron Marjorie Acker Phillips born in 1894 in Bourbon

29 Randy Jackson of the Jackson 5 born in Gary 1961

31 Race driver Wilbur Shaw born in Shelbyville 1902

TV news anchor Jane Pauley born in 1950 in Indianapolis

Explosion at State Fair Coliseum kills 73 in Indianapolis 1963

NOVEMBER

1 Still-life painter William Merritt Chase born in Williamsburg 1849

Education reformer Caleb Mills's programs adopted into state constitution 1851

Actress Betsy Palmer born in 1926 in East Chicago.

3 Automatic telephone inventor Almon Strowger born in LaPorte 1892

5 Labor leader Eugene V. Debs was born in Terre Haute 1855

Egyptologist George Andrew Reisner born in Indianapolis 1867

Movie czar and statesman Will Harrison Hays born in Sullivan 1879

Indiana Dunes National Lakeshore was authorized in Porter 1966

6 Indiana's first congresswoman, Virginia Ellis Jenckes, born in Terre Haute 1877

Comedian Ole Olsen of Olsen and Johnson born in Peru 1892

Blinding snowstorm causes fiery train collision near Woodville, killing 43, 1906

7 Battle of Tippecanoe takes place near Lafayette 1811

9 Journalist Bernard Kilgore born in Albany 1908

10 Joaquin Miller, called "Poet of the Sierras," was born in near Richmond in 1837

11 Vesto Slipher of Mulberry was the first person to successfully photo Mars born in 1875

Slaughterhouse Five Kurt Vonnegut, Jr., born in 1922 in Indianapolis

Golfer Fuzzy Zoeller born in New Albany 1951

12 Notre Dame football center turned mayor of Indianapolis Albert Feeny, born Indianapolis 1892

16 Bandleader/jazz musician Eddie Condon born in 1905 in Goodland

18 Journalist Ludwell Denny born in Boonville 1894

Author of *My Sister Eileen*, Ruth McKenney, born in Mishawaka 1911

Astronaut Mark N. Brown born in Valparaiso 1951

19 The "terribly British " Hoosier actor Clifton Webb born in 1891 in Indianapolis

Shortstop Everett "Deacon" Scott born in Bluffton 1892

Indiana-born in Jim Jones leads followers into Jonestown massacre in Guyana 1978

22 Songwriter Hoagy Carmichael born in 1899 in Bloomington

24 Founder of *The Little Review* Margaret Anderson born in Indianapolis 1886

Baseball player Bob Friend born in Lafayette 1930

29 Broadcast journalist Frank Reynolds born in 1923 in East Chicago

Indianapolis basketball great Oscar Robertson born in Tennessee 1938

"Breaking Away" makes debut on TV in 1980 but canceled soon after

31 David Graham Phillips, whose birthplace at Madison was basis of his greatest novel *Susan Lennox: Her Rise and Fall,* born 1867

DECEMBER

1 Mystery writer Rex Stout, creator of Nero Wolfe, born in Noblesville 1885

4 Two steamboats, *America* and *United States* collided on Ohio River near Indiana border, killing an estimated 72, 1868

"Rough Rider" hero Buck Jones born in 1891 in Vincennes

David Shoup, Marine Commander, Medal of Honor recipient, born in Battleground 1904

7 Basketball star Larry Bird born in French Lick 1956

8 Henry Clay and Humphrey Marshall are wounded in 1808 duel outside Clarksville

First theatrical performance in Indianapolis took place at Carter's Tavern 1823

Poet Jean Garrigue born in Evansville 1914

9 John Birch Society branch formed in Indianapolis 1958

10 Hoosier writer Edward Eggleston born in Vevay 1837

11 Singer-musician Jermaine La Jaune Jackson of the Jackson 5 born 1954 in Gary

13 Director Norman Foster of "Davy Crockett" fame born 1903 in Richmond

Nobel Prize-winning physicist Philip Warren Anderson born in Indianapolis 1923

U.S. DC-3 crashes after takeoff in Evansville killing 29, including University of Evansville basketball players, 1977

14 Congressman Louis Ludlow proposes war amendment 1937

16 One of the Metropolitan Opera's leading tenors, James McCracken born in Gary 1926

AIDS victim Ryan White born in Kokomo 1971

TV sitcom, "One Day at a Time, " portraying an Indianapolis single-parent family, first televised 1975

18 Leader in "corporate identity" Walter D. Teague, designer, born in Decatur 1883

Country singer-musician Janie Fricke born in 1950 in Whitney.

19 Ford Christopher Frick, baseball's third commissioner, born in Wawaka 1894

Butler University basketball coach Paul Hinkle born in Logansport 1899

20 John Livingston Lowes, scholar who wrote *The Road to Xanadu* born in Decatur 1867

22 Poet Kenneth Rexroth born in 1982 in South Bend

23 Scientist Harold Masurksy born in Fort Wayne 1923

Bowling Hall of Fame member in 1977 Dick Weber was born in Indianapolis 1929

25 Gilbert C. Van Camp, packing company magnate, born in Brookline 1817

27 New law regulating out-of-state trash ruled unconstitutional 1991

28 Actor Andrew Duggan born in 1923 in Franklin

29 Hot-water heating engineer Mark Charles Honeywell born in Wabash 1874

A

A.L. Shotwell 82
Aaron, Hank 84
Abrell, Cpl. Charles G. 47
Ackerman, Carl William 131
Adams County 12
Adams, John Quincey 12
Adams, Neile 62
Ade, George 115, 131
Albany 131, 138
Albion 13
Alexandria 79
Alexandria's Mud Creek 79
Algiers 134
Alka Seltzer 83
All American Girls Professional
    Baseball League 100
Allen County 12
Allen, Col. John 12
Allen, Joseph P. 120, 135
American Basketball League 93
American Basketball Association
    93
American Beauty Rose 78
American United Life building 51
Ames, Leon 131
Amish 127
Anders, William A. 120
Anderson 9, 13, 30, 90, 131, 134
Anderson Democrat 109
Anderson Duffy Packers 93
Anderson, James 67
Anderson, Margaret 113, 139
Anderson, Philip Warren 122, 139
Anderson River 36
Anderson, Sherwood 111
Angel Mounds State Memorial
    Park 30
Angola 13
Antrim, Lt. Richard 47
Arch, Sgt. Alex 46, 138
Arden, Elizabeth 85
Armstrong Glade 25
Arrowhead Arch 24
Art Hammer Wetlands 25
Arvin, Newton 136
Auburn 74, 75, 136
Auburn Automobile Company 74
Auburn-Cord-Duesenberg Festival
    75

Aurora 131, 135, 137
Avanti 76

B

Baillytown 16
Bainbridge 26
Ball Brothers, The 84, 132
Ball canning jar 84
Ball, Edmund B. 132
Ball State University 68
Baniszewski, Gertrude 122, 123
Banneker, Benjamin 114
Banta 54
Barker, Cliff 131
Barr, John W. 37
Bartholomew County 12
Bartholomew, Gen. Joseph 12
Bartmess, Ann 44
Bass, Sam 135
Battle of Tippecanoe 13, 44, 138
Battleground 47, 139
Baxter, Anne 64, 133
Bayh, Birch, Jr. 41, 131
Bayh, Gov. Birch Evans III 8
Beard, Mary Ritter 136
Beardsley, A.H. 83
Beatty, Clyde 67
Beaver Bend 27
Beaver Dam 89
Bechtel Corporation 82
Bechtel, Stephen Davison 82, 137
Bedford 13, 16, 83, 131, 133
Beech Grove 62
Bell Aircraft Corporation 78
Bell, Lawrence Dale 78, 133
Bench, Johnny 84
Benjamin, Adam Jr. 136
Bennett, Constance 134
Bennett, Joan 134
Bennett, Richard 134
Benten 127
Benton County 12
Benton, Sen. Thomas H. 12
Berry, Chuck 124
Beveridge, Albert J. 52
Beverly Shores 55
Biddle, Nicholas 46
Biddle, Pfc. Melvin 47

Bierce, Ambrose 110
Big Clifty Falls 25
Big Walnut Valley Natural Area
    26
Billingsley, Peter 65
Biograph Theater 123
Bippus 136
Bird, Larry 5, 87, 92, 139
Bird's Eye View Museum 54
Black, Charles H. 74
Blackford County 12
Blackford, Isaac 12, 39
Blackwell, Mr. 64
Blass, Bill 117, 134
Bloom, Allan David 137
Bloomfield 13, 50, 89
Bloomingdale Glen 24
Bloomington 9, 13, 16, 23, 60, 65,
    68, 78, 95, 105, 126, 132,
    133, 136, 137, 138
Blue River 21, 108
Blue, Monte 131
Bluffton 13, 138
Bobo 27
Bolton, Sarah 108, 136
Booger Hollow 5, 11
Boone County 6, 12
Boone, Daniel 12, 18
Boone, Squire 18
Boonville 13, 138
Boris III, king of Bulgaria 54
Borman, Frank 120, 132
Boston Lyric Opera Company 61
Bourbon 138
Bowen, Otis R. 37, 132
Bowles, William 56
Bowman, Charles 81
Bowser, Sylvanus F. 53
Bradsby, Frank W. 84
Brady, Diamond Jim 57
Brazil 53, 81, 131, 135
Bright, Jesse 135
Bristol 127
Britton, Edgar Clay 137
Broad Axe of Freedom 85
Bromfield, John 134
Brookline 139
Brookville 39, 133
Brown County 11, 12, 115, 134
Brown County State Park 11, 26
Brown, Henry Baker 127

Brown, Gen. Jacob 12
Brown, Mark N. 120, 138
Brown, Mordecai Peter Centennial 100, 138
Brown, William H. 125
Browning, Pete "The Old Gladiator" 84
Brownstown 13
Bruce, Pfc. Daniel 47
Buena Vista 57
Burnside, General Ambrose Everett 134
Burns Harbor 10
Burton, Richard 113
Buse, Don 136
Butler University 88
Butlerville High School 88
Butterworth, Charles 135
Butz, Earl Lauer 37, 52, 135

C

C.G. Conn Band Instrument Company 80
Cafaro, J.J. 76
Camp Chesterfield 54
Canaan 79
Canary, David 65, 136
Cannelton 13
Canton, Ray 62
Cantrell, J.F. 133
Capehart, Homer 134
Capone, Al 57
Carmichael, Hoagy 126, 138
Carter, Atty. General Pam 8
Carter's Tavern 116
Carrol County 12
Carrol, Charles 12
Caruso, Enrico 113
Carver, George Washington 114
Cary, Max George 102, 131
Case, Everett N. 95
Cass County 12
Cass, Louis 12
Cassidy, Shawn 65
Centerville 35
Century of Progress Exposition, Chicago 55
Chamberlain, Neville 54

Chapman, John "Johnny Appleseed" 132
Chapman, Joseph 39
Charles McClue Nature Preserve 25
Charleston, Oscar McKinley 99, 102, 137
Chase, William Merritt 138
Chesterfield 54
Chicago Ballet 116, 132
Chicago's Tribune Tower 83
Chippewa Indians 6
Christopher, Dennis 65
Choctaw Indians 18
Cicero 89, 121
Civil War 85
Clark County 12, 27, 134
Clark, George Rogers 12, 33, 60
Clark Maritime 10
Clarksville 16, 139
Clay County 12
Clay, Henry 12, 128, 139
Claypool 23
Clayton, Mark 133
Clevenger, Zora 104
Clifty Canyon State Nature Preserve 25
Cline, Elmer 82
Clinton County 12
Clinton, Dewitt 12
Cobb, Ty 84
Coe, Isaac 50
Coffin, Levi & Katherine 48
Coleman, James 133
Colfax, Schuyler 38
College Life Insurance 50
Collegeville 28, 135
Columbia City 13, 23, 113, 136
Columbian Enameling and Stamping 81
Columbus 23, 50, 79, 95, 96, 132
Commercial Solvents Company 83
Condon, Eddie 138
Conn, Charles G. 53, 80
Conner Prairie Pioneer Settlement 55
Connersville 86
Continental Baking Company 82
Converse All-Star Basketball shoe 96
Coon-Skinner 85

Cooper, Gary 112
Cooper, Kent 132
Cooper, Peter 39
Cord, Errett Lobban 74
Corydon 8, 13, 18, 34, 86, 133, 135
Costigan, Francis 51
Coudert, Amalia Kussner 132
Coulson, Robert "Buck" 134
Council Oak 33
Counsilman, Doc 105, 131
Covington 44, 132
Cox, Herald Rea 132
Cox, Jacob 116, 118
Cox, John Rogers 132
Cox, Joseph 24
Crawford County 11, 12, 19, 21
Crawford, William Harris 12
Crawford, William Hulfish 132
Crawfordsville 13, 88, 89, 110, 112, 113, 120, 125, 134, 135
Crispus Attucks High School 92
Croghan, George 136
Crosley, Powell , Jr 75
"Crossroads of America" 6
Crothers, Scatman 134
Crown Hill Cemetery 52, 123
Crown Point 13, 120, 123, 131
Cryer, Gretchen 138
Crystal Chemical Works 79
Cummins, Clessie 79
Cummins Engine Company 50, 79
Cuppy, Will 136
Curtiss, Glenn 78

D

Dale 62, 131
Dana 85, 136
Danville 13, 102, 132
Dark Hollow Quarry Company 83
Dauss, George August "Hooks" 137
Daviess County 12, 57
Daviess, Joseph Hamilton 12
Davis, Elmer 131
Davis, Jim 115, 136
Davis, Peter 72
Daywalt, James 136

De La Garza, Jr., Lance Cpl
  Emilio 47
Deacon's Mills 134
Dean, Everett 95
Dean, James 61, 63, 131
Dearborn County 12
Dearborn, Major Gen. Henry
Debs, Eugene V. 40, 138
Decatur 132, 139
Decatur County 12
Decatur, Steven 12
Declaration of Independence 126
De Kalb County 12
De Kalb, Gen. Johann
Delaware County 12
Delaware Indians 31
Delta Air Lines 78
Democratic Party 39
Demotte 136
Denny, Ludwell 138
DeRegniers, Beatrice S. 136
Devine, Dan 104
Devore, Ann G. 8
Dick, Dr. George F. 119, 121, 135
Dick, Gladys Henry 119, 121
Dillinger, John 52, 119, 123, 132,
  137, 138
Dillon, Jack 131
DiMaggio, Joe 66
Dischinger, Terry 89
Dog-Fennel Gazette 85
Dorsey, Azel 36
Dos Passo, John 111
Doubleday 111
Douglas, Lloyd C. 113, 136
Douglas, Michael 64
Dowell, Joe 68
Dr. Miles Laboratories 83
Dreiser, Theodore 70, 111, 126, 136
Dresser, Louise 137
Dresser, Paul 6, 70, 133
Dreyfus, Hubert L. 137
Drysdale, Don 93
Du Bridge, Lee 137
Dublin 42
Dubois County 12
Dubois High School Jeeps 91
Dubois, Toussaint 12
DuBois, W.E.B. 114
Duesenberg, Fred 75
Duesenberg Model J 75

Duesenberg Motors Company 74
Duffy, Hugh 84
Duggan, Andrew 139
Dugger 89
Dunlap 28
Dunlap County 28

E

Eads, James Buchanan 46, 134
Eagle Creek Park 18
Eagles Crest Addition Nature
  Preserve 25
Earhart, Amelia 78
Earlham College 55
East Chicago 22, 23, 66, 135, 138,
  139
East Chicago Harbor 10
Eaton, Joseph O. 118
Eckhart, Frank and Morris 74
Eclipse 82
Eden 89
Eggleston, Edward 110, 112, 139
Eisenhower, President Dwight D.
  137
Eiteljorg, Harrison 59
Eiteljorg Museum of American
  Indian and Western Ar 59
Elkhart 23, 28, 53, 58, 73, 80,
  110, 136
Elkhart County 12, 28, 127
Elkhart Indians 12
Elliott, George Paul 134
Ellsworth, Ann 41
Elwood 37, 132, 136
Empire State Building 83
Endangered species 19
England, Anthony W. 134
Evans, Charles Jr. 135
Evansville 9, 13, 27, 28, 30, 46,
  50, 60, 61, 65, 99, 106, 112,
  115, 131, 132, 133, 134, 135,
  136, 137, 139
Evansville, University of 106
Everett, Chad 62, 134
Ewbank, Weeb 133
Ewry, Ray 106
Ewing, George 32

F

Fairbanks, Charles W. 38, 52
Fairmount 63, 136
Fairview 57
Faith, Jr., Lt. Col. Don 47
Falls of the Ohio State Park and
  National Wildlife 16
Farmer, Philip Jose 131
Fauntleroy, Constance Owen 42,
  130, 137
Fayette County 12
Fawn River Fen 25
Fazenda, Louise 134
Feeny, Albert 138
Ferris, Gale 79
Fetzer, John Earl 132
Fields, Absolom 18
Finch, Rick 131
Firsts in Indiana 24, 26, 41, 42, 43,
  46, 74, 78, 86, 129, 130
Firsts in the United States 24, 41,
  42, 43, 46, 63, 78, 80, 85, 89,
  93, 96, 98, 99, 105, 116, 122,
  128, 130
Flanner, Janet 112, 132
Floyd County 12
Floyd, John 12
Foellinger-Freimann Botanical
  Conservatory 53
Fontaine, Major James 12
Foot-Eazer 81
Foote, Dr. William 83
Ford's Theater 76
Fort Wayne 9, 28, 30, 34, 50, 53,
  58, 64, 78, 93, 99, 117, 121,
  132, 133, 134, 135, 136, 137,
  139
Fort Wayne County 28
Fort Wayne Knights 93
Fort Wayne Pistons 93
Fort Wayne Zollners 93
Foster, John W. 37
Foster, Norman 139
Fountain County 12
Fountain City 48
Francis, Thomas Jr. 135
Frankfort 62, 90, 132
Frankfort Hot Dogs 90
Frankfurt 131
Franklin 13, 135, 139

Franklin County 12
Franklin, Benjamin 12
Franklin, Bonnie 72
Franklin Township 6
French Lick 56, 92, 139
Frick, Ford C. 101, 139
Fricke, Janie 69, 139
Friend, Bob 139
Ft. Wayne 138
Fudge Mound 30
Fulton County 11, 12
Fulton, Robert 12
Funny Forum 72

G

Gable, Clark 63, 137
Gabriel's Rock 130
Gallagher, Richard "Skeets" 136
Galloway, Rebecca 31
Garrigue, Jean 139
Gary 9, 23, 42, 44, 60, 64, 65, 77,
    89, 116, 120, 122, 131, 132,
    133, 134, 135, 136, 137, 138,
    139
Gary, Elbert H. 77
Gary Land Company 77
Gas City 135
Gateway to the Northern Indiana
    Lake Region 58
Gazzara, Ben 62
Geer, Will 62, 132
Gene Stratton Porter State
    Memorial 111
Gentry, Conrad 80
Georgetown 57, 138
Gerard, Dave 134
Gerdts, Heidi 127
German Methodist Cemetery
    Prairie 27
Gibson, Barbara 121
Gibson County 12, 14
Gibson, Gen. John 12
Gimbel, Bernard F. 133
Girdler, Tom Mercer 134
Glass, Ron 135
Glossop, Peter 134
Gnaw Bone 5, 11, 49, 58
Goodheart, Billy Jr. 70

Goodland 138
Goodpasture, Ernest 137
Goshen 28, 66, 127, 134
Goshen County 28
Graham, Shirley 114
Grand Army of the Republic 46
Grand Master of the Mystery
    Writers of America 112
Grange, Red 66
Grant County 12
Grant, Moses and Samuel 12
Grant, Ulysses S. 76
Grassyfork Fisheries, Inc., 79
Grauman, Sid 132
Graves, Michael 135
Gray, Add 127
Gray, Annie 109
Graydon, James Weir 131
Great Depression 75
Greenback Party 39, 134
Greencastle 13, 138
Greendale 83
Greene County 13, 14
Greene, Gen. Nathaneal 13
Greenfield 13, 109, 137
Greensburg 43, 54, 133, 136
Gregorian, Vartan 133
Gresham, James B. 46
Gresham, Walter 37
Griese, Bob 104, 131
Griffey Woods 25
Griffith 23
Grissom, Virgil I. "Gus" 120, 133
Grouseland 35
Grubbing Hoe of Truth 85
Gruelle, John 109, 115
Gruelle, R.B. 115
Guns N' Roses 69
Gustav V, king of Sweden 54
Gutenberg Bible 126
Guthrie, A.B. Jr. 131
Guthrie, Janet 98

H

Hackman, Gene 65
Hadley, Don 118
Hagenbach-Wallace Circus 57,
    67, 68

Hagerstown 50
Haines, Robert Terrel 131
Haley, Jackie Earle 65
Hall, Katie Beatrice 44
Halleck, Charles 136
Hamilton, Alexander 13
Hamilton County 13
Hamilton, Edith 136
Hammond 9, 77, 132, 138
Hammond Technical High School
    88
Hancock County 13, 23
Hancock County Courthouse 109
Hancock, John 13
Hannagan, Steve 133
Hannah, Robert 39
Harden, Cecil Murray 44
Hardin, Clifford 37
Harmonie 128
Harmony 53
Harper, Jesse C. 104
Harris, Eliza 48
Harris, Phil 70, 134
Harrison, Benjamin 37, 52, 60,
    76, 136
Harrison County 13
Harrison, Davis 83
Harrison, William Henry 8, 13,
    34, 35, 37, 44, 133
Harroun, Ray 96, 97, 134
Hart, Leon 103
Hartke, Vance 134
Hatcher, Richard G. 42, 135
Haugh, Benjamin 125
Hawks, Howard 66, 86, 134
Hay, John Milton 137
Hayes, Janet Gray 135
Hayes, Joseph 136
Haynes, Elwood 74, 80, 135
Haynes, Lloyd 138
Hays, Will Harrison 66, 138
Hazelton 89
Helms, Bobby 136
Hemlock Cliffs 24
Henderson, Florence 62, 131
Hendricks County 13
Hendricks, Thomas A. 38
Hendricks, William 13
Henry County 13, 25
Henry, Patrick 13
Henryville 80

Hensley, Joe L. 132
Herman, Billy 101, 135
Herschell, William 108
Hershey, Gen. Lewis B. 46, 137
Heston, Charleton 113
Heth, Henry 8
Hill, Charles C. 79
Hill, E. Gurney 78
Hill Floral Products, Inc 78
Hillerich & Bradsby Company 84
Hillerich, John "Bud" 84
Hillis, Margaret 137
Hillisburg 136
Hinkle, Paul 95, 139
Hitler, Adolf 54
Hodges, Gil 99, 133
Hoffa, Jimmy 124, 131
Hoffman, Dustin 66
Holiday World 58
Holland 136
Hollenbeck, Webb Parmallee 64
Holmes, Oliver Wendell 108
Hopper, Dennis 65
Holtz, Lou 103
Honeywell, Mark Charles 139
Hoosier Hysteria 87, 88, 89
Hoosier National Forest 11, 24
Hoosier Prairie 28
Hoosier, Sam 5
Hornbeam Addition 25
Hornung, Paul 87, 103
Horse Thief Detective Association
    40
Hovey Lake State Fish and
    Wildlife Area 17
Howard, Charles W. 58
Howard County 13
Howard, Tilghman Ashurst 13
Howe 39
Howe, Edgar Watson 133
Huarte, John 104
Hubbard, Frank "Kin" McKinney
    52, 115
Hubbard, Kin 52
Hudnut, William III 51, 133
Hudson, Rock 113
Huerta, Victoriano 110
Huff Daland Dusters 78
Hulman, Tony Jr. 96, 131
Hunt-Wesson Foods 81
Huntington 13, 32, 54, 89, 135

Huntington County 13
Huntington, Samuel 13
Hymera 58

I

Illinois Central Railroad 14
Illinois, Elgin 22
Illinois Medical College 81
Indiana Central Canal 51
Indiana Dunes National Lakeshore
    17, 138
Indiana Dunes State Park 17
Indiana Heritage Trust 26
Indiana High School Athletic
    Association 89, 96
Indiana High School Coaches
    Association 95
Indiana Non-game and
    Endangered Wildlife Program
    19
Indiana Pacers 87, 93, 94
Indiana Pioneer Mothers'
    Association 24
Indiana Planting Zones 7
Indiana, Robert 137
Indiana State Song 6, 70
Indiana University 87, 91, 104,
    126
Indianapolis 8, 9, 13, 18, 21, 23,
    24, 37, 46, 51, 52, 54, 56, 59,
    60, 68, 74, 72, 80, 85, 86, 89,
    92, 96, 102, 105, 106, 112,
    116, 118, 120, 121, 122, 123,
    125, 131, 132, 133, 134, 135,
    136, 137, 138, 139
Indianapolis Canal Walk 51
Indianapolis Children's Museum
    52
Indianapolis 500 96
Indianapolis 500 champs 98
Indianapolis Colts..87, 105
Indianapolis Hoosier Dome 94
Indianapolis Jets 93, 94
Indianapolis Journal 61
Indianapolis Olympians 94
Indianapolis Motor Speedway 96,
    131
Indianapolis Star 112

Indianapolis State Fair 60
Indianapolis Times 85
Indianapolis, USS 47
Indianapolis Zoo 26
Inland Steel 10, 77
Institute for Sex Research 126
International Friendship Gardens
    54
ironclads 46
Irwin, W.G. 79
Isbell, Cecil 104
Isidor, Dr. Ravdin 137
Ivanhoe 67, 134

J

Jackson County 13
Jackson 5 71, 132, 133, 137, 138,
    139
Jackson, Jackie 71, 133
Jackson, Janet Damita 71, 134
Jackson, Jermaine La Jaune 71,
    139
Jackson, Joseph 71
Jackson, Katherine 71
Jackson, Margaret Weymouth 112
Jackson, Marlon 71, 132
Jackson, Michael 61, 71, 121, 137
Jackson, Randy 71, 138
Jackson, Rebbie 71, 134
Jackson, Tito 71, 137
Jamestown 57
Jasper County 13, 14, 25
Jasper Pulaski State Fish and
    Wildlife Area 26
Jasper, William 13
Jay, Chief Justice John 13
Jay County 13
Jefferson County 13
Jefferson, Thomas 13
Jeffersonville 10, 84
Jenckes, Virginia Ellis 43, 138
Jennings County 13, 27
Jennings, Jonathan 8, 13
John Birch Society 139
John, Elton 121
John, Tommy 134
Johns-Manville Corporation 79
Johnson , J.J. 131

Johnson County 13
Johnson, John 13
Johnson, Sarah Bush 36
Johnston, Annie Fellows 112, 134
Jones, Buck 139
Jones, David 122
Jones, Phil 133
Jones, Rev. Jim 125, 138
Jonestown, Guyana 138
Jordan, Vernon E., Jr. 134
Joseph 13
Joyce, James 113
Jug Rock 27

K

Karras, Alex 87, 135
Keeler, Willie 84
Kekionga 30
Kelly, Emmett 67
Kent 138
Kentland 13, 115, 131
Kentucky Fried Chicken 80
Kenworthy, Don 80
Kercheval, Ken 62, 135
Keyes, Leroy 104
Kickapoo Indians 6, 31
Kilgore, Bernard 138
Kimbrough, Emily 138
Kinsey, Alfred 126, 136
Kiskakon 30
Kisters, Sgt. Gerry 47
Kittle, Ron 131
Klein, Chuck 102, 137
Klondike 57
Knight, Bobby 87, 89
Knightstown 108, 134
Knobstone Trail 27
Knobstone Trailblazers 27
Knox 13
Knox County 13
Knox, Henry 13
Kokomo 13, 23, 28, 74, 109, 132, 135, 136, 137, 139
Korty, John 66, 135
Kosciusko County 6, 13
Kosciusko, Thadeus 13
Ku Klux Klan 40

L

La Salle, Robert Cavelier, Sieur de 32, 33
Lafayette 13, 23, 25, 42, 50, 60, 66, 67, 68, 106, 115, 131, 133, 134, 135, 136, 138, 139
Lafayette *Daily Courier* 110
LaFontaine, Chief 32
Lagrange 13
Lagrange County 13, 25
Lake County 13, 14, 22, 27, 28, 48, 66, 132
Lake Forest 22
Lake Michigan 13, 17, 77
Lake Michigan Land Company 77
Lake Monroe 19
Lake Wawasee 6, 21
Landgrebe, Rep. Earl 41
Lane, John 56
Lane, Lola 134
LaPorte 13, 23, 80, 101, 138
LaPorte County 13, 14, 48, 81
LaPorte Herald 85
Larsen, Don 99, 136
Lawrence 13
Lawrence, Capt. James 13
Lawrence County 13
Lawrenceburg 46, 50, 53, 83, 134
Leavenworth 28
Lebanon 23, 89, 131
Lennon, John 75
Leonard, Bob 93
Letterman, David 61, 68, 133
Lewis, Bobby 68, 132
Liberty 13, 134
Lieber, Col. Richard 24
Lilly, Eli 85
Lilly, J.K., Jr 118
Lilly Library 126
Limberlost 111
Limestone Belt 16
Lincoln, Abraham 5, 36, 41
Lincoln Boyhood National Memorial 36
Lincoln City 36, 132
Lincoln Ferry Landing State Wayside Park 36
Lincoln, Nancy Hanks 36
Lindsay, William 116

Link, Edwin 135
Linton 134
Lipscomb, George 114
Little 500 Bicycle Race 126
Little Turtle, Chief 30, 34, 137
Lockheed Electra 78
Lockridge, Ross 113, 133
Logansport 50, 57, 95, 139
Lombard, Carole 61, 63, 137
Long, Huey 43, 133
Long, Lynnette Jill 44
Long, Rep. Rose McConnell 43, 133
Long, Shelley 64, 136
Loogootee 59
Louisville, New Albany & Corydon Railroad 86
Louisville Slugger 84
Lovell, James A. 120
Lovellette, Clyde E. 95
Lowell 68
Lowes, John Livingston 139
Ludlow, Louis 139
Lugar, Richard, G. 51, 133
Lynd, Robert and Helen Merrel 49
Lynd, Robert Staughton 137

M

Mac-con-a-qua 32
Mack, Lonnie 135
Mackinac Island 136
Maclure, William 128, 129
Macy 134
Macy, Kyle Robert 133
Madame C.J. Walker Manufacturing Company 82
Madison 13, 49, 51, 61, 139
Madison County 13
Madison, James 13
Mahican Indians 31
Major Taylor Velodrome 106
Malden, Karl 64, 132
Manhattan, NY 117
Mansfield 43
Mansfield, Arabella 43
Mantle, Mickey 84
Mapes, Arthur Franklin 7

Marengo Cave 18
Marion 23, 28, 63, 75, 115, 131, 133, 136
Marion County 13, 22, 25, 28, 51
Marion, Gen. Francis 13
Markle 131
Marriage Tree 16
Marshall County 13
Marshall, Humphrey 139
Marshall, John 13
Marshall, Thomas R. 38, 52, 132
Marshall, William 136
Martin County 13, 14
Martin, Jim 58
Martin, John P. 13
Martin, Strother 132
Martinsville 13, 79, 95, 137
Mary Maid 82
Masurksy, Harold 139
Matisse 118
Mattingly, Don 99, 133
Mattingly, Mack 131
Mayflower Transit 80
Maynard, Ken 135
McBride's Bluffs 18
McCall, S Sgt. Thomas 47
McCormick, Myron 131
McCormick's Creek 24
McCoy, Isaac 58
McCracken, Branch 95, 134
McCracken, James 116, 139
McCulloch, Hugh 37
McCutchan, Arad A. 95
McCutcheon, George Barr 110, 135
McCutcheon, John Tinney 114, 133
McGee, Pvt. William D. 47
McGinnis, George 136
McGraw, Ali 62
McKay, Rev. Nicholas 88
McKenney, Ruth 138
McKinney, James 39
McNutt, Paul V. 34, 135
McQueen, Steve 62, 132
Means, Jacqueline 131
Mechanicsburg 57
Mellencamp, John Cougar 68, 137
Mendenhall, Hiram 128
Mengerson Nature Preserve 25
Mennonites 127

Mentone 78, 89, 133
Meredith, Stanley W. 122, 136
Mesker Park Zoo 27
Metamora 86
Metropolitan Opera 116
Meyers, Ann 93
Miami County 13, 67
Miami Dolphins 131
Miami Indians 6, 13, 30, 31
Michael, 2nd Lt. Harry J. 47
Michigan Central's Canadian 86
Michigan City 23, 54, 64, 99, 133, 135, 136
Middlebury 127
Milan 89
Milan High School 88
Miller, Hulings 108
Miller, J. Irwin 50
Miller, Joaquin 138
Miller, William H.H. 37
Millersburg 57, 127
Mills, Caleb 138
Milltown 11
Minerva Club 130
Minton, Sherman 138
Minty, Barbara 62
Mishawaka 23, 138
Mitchell 120, 133, 135
Mix, Tom 66, 67
Mollenkopf, Ken 104
Monet 118
Monroe County 13, 17, 25
Monroe, James 13
Monroe Reservoir 6
Monrovia 95, 134
Montgomery County 13, 25, 125, 137
Montgomery, Gen. Richard 13
Montgomery, Wes 132
Monticello 13
Moody, William Vaughn 116, 135
Mooresville 102, 123, 134
Morgan, Col. John 135
Morgan County 13, 29
Morgan, Daniel 13
Morocco 102, 132
Morse, Samuel 41
Morton, Oliver Perry 35, 52, 136
Moses, Horace A. 60
Mott, Sir Francis Neville 122
Mounds State Park 30

Mount Baldy 17
Mount Pleasant 57
Mount, Rick 89, 131
Mount Tom 17
Mount Vernon 10, 13
Mulberry 138
Mulford, Ralph 97
Muller, Herman Joseph 122, 133
Muncie 9, 49, 65, 68, 84, 89, 131, 132, 133, 138
Muncie Central High School 88
Munsee Indians 31
Murphy, Charles "Stretch" 95, 133
Muscatatuck National Wildlife Refuge 26
Museum of All Sorts of Stuff 127
Musgrave, Boyd and Madonna 54
Music Corporation of America 70
Mussolini, Benito 54
Myers, Theodore "Pop" 97

N

Nader, Ralph 83
Naismith, Dr. James 88
Nanticoke Indians 31
Nappanee 54, 127, 137
Nashville 11, 55
National Football Foundations's College Hall of Fame 104
National Guardsmen 81
National Road 38
Neal Foundries 51
Needmore 57
Neher, Fred 137
Nelson, William Rockhill 132
Newman, Paul 66
New Albany 161, 01, 135, 137, 138
New Albany & Salem Railroad 83
New Castle 13, 137
New Harmony 43, 128, 129, 130
New Harmony Atheneum Center 129
New Madison 25
New Paris 127
New, Sen. Harry Stewart 42
New York Central's Interstate Express 86

New York City 115, 117
Newcastle 133
Newman, Leo 76
Newport 13
Newton County 13, 14
Newton, Sgt. John 13
Nicholson, Meredith 110, 112
Nippon Steel of Japan 77
Nobel, James 39
Nobel, Noah 39
Nobel Prize 122
Noble County 13, 25, 135
Noble, Sen. James 13
Noblesville 13, 55, 117, 133, 139
Nolan, Jeannette Covert 132
Norell, Norman 117, 133
North Manchester 113, 132
North Vernon 135
Northrup, John 122
Northwood Institute 57
Notre Dame University 60, 87,
  102, 103, 104
Nyesville 100, 138

O

Oak Hill Cemetery 113
Oakland City 101, 133
O'Bannon, Lt. Gov. Frank 8
Oberholtzer, Madge 40
Ohio County 13
Ohio River 17, 131, 139
Old Flat Belly 21
O'Laughlin, Marjorie H. 8
Old National Road 7
Oliver Chilled Plow Works 79
Oliver, James 79
Olsen and Johnson 138
Olsen, Ole 138
Omee Town 30
Orange County 13
Orangeville 21
Orangeville Rise of the Lost River
  21
Osborn, Paul 65, 115
Osceola 23
Ossian 89
Ottawa Indians 6
Owen, Col. Abraham 13

Owen County 13
Owen, David Dale 130
Owen, Jane 129
Owen, Richard 130
Owen, Robert 128
Owen, Robert Dale 116, 130
Owensville 89
Owings, Nathaniel Alexander 131

P

Packard Motor Car Company 76
Page, Ruth 116, 132
Palmer, Betsy 138
Pan Am Games 87, 105
Paoli 13
Paramount Studios 63, 117
Park Cemetery 63
Parke, Benjamin 13
Parke County 13,14, 25, 57
Parseghian, Ara 104
Pauley, Jane 72, 138
Pavlova, Anna 116
Peasley, Judge W. J. 86
Pecksburg 96, 134
Pei, I.M. 50, 118
Pelli, Cesar 50
People's Temple 125
Perry County 13, 25
Perry, Oliver H. 13
Pershing, Gen. John J. 57
Peru 13, 60, 67, 134, 136
Peter, John 76
Petersburg 13, 53
Petrakis, Harry Mark 134
Phillips, David Graham 139
Phillips, Marjorie Acker 138
Piankashaw Indians 6
Pigeon Creek 36
Pihos, Peter 104
Pike County 13
Pike, Zebulon 13
Pillsbury Bake-Off 121
Pine Hills State Nature Preserve 24
Pioneer Mothers' Memorial Forest
  24
Pittsburg 58
Plainfield 38, 131
Plainville 89

Pleasant Lake 136
Plump, Bobby 88, 89
Plymouth 13
Poe, Edgar Allan 109
Pollack, Sydney 66, 135
Portage 10
Porter 86, 132, 138
Porter, Cole 60, 70, 134
Porter, Comm. David 13
Porter County 13, 14, 48
Porter, Gene Stratton 111, 112
Portland 13, 131, 135
Posey, Brig. Gen. Thomas 13
Posey County 6, 13, 14, 22, 128
Potawatomi Indians 31
Powell, Maud 136
Power, Jules 138
Presley, Elvis 134
Princeton 27, 99, 133
Prophet, The 44
Prophet's Town 44
Prophetstown State Park 25
Pruett, Tommy 131
Pulaski, Casimir 13
Pulaski County 13
Pulitzer Prize 85
Pulpit Rock 18
Pumpkin Center 49, 57
Punkin Center 127
Purcell, Sarah 137
Purdue University 78, 81
Putnam County 13, 14
Putnam, Israel 13
Pyle, Ernie Taylor 85, 136

Q

Quakers 128
Quayle, J. Danforth 38

R

Raiche, Bessica 78
Ralston, Albert 8
Ralston, Gov. Samuel 24
Randolph County 13
Randolph, Thomas 13

Rapp, Father George 128, 130
Ray, James Brown 39
Rear Adm. Norman Scott 47
Reagan, Ronald 66
Redenbacher, Orville 52, 81, 135
Rees, Raymond 88
Reisner, George Andrew 138
"Remembering James Dean" 63
Reno Brothers 122, 137
Rensselaer 13
Republic Steel 77
Rexroth, Kenneth 139
Reynolds, Frank 72, 139
Reynolds, Myra 24
Rice, Edgar "Sam" 102, 132
Richie, Lionel 71
Richmond 13, 55, 75, 128, 131,
    133, 137, 138, 139
Richmond Rose 78
Rickenbacker, Eddie 96
Rickey, George Warren 134
Ridgeville 122, 136
Riley, James Whitcomb 52, 109,
    112, 114, 115, 137
Ripley County 13
Ripley, Eleazar Wheelock 13
Rising Sun 13
Roachdale 99
Robertson, Oscar 87, 89, 92, 93,
    139
Roche and Dinkeloo 50
Roche, Kevin 50
Rochester 132
Rocherster Zebras 90
Rockne, Knute 60, 87, 102, 104,
    132
Rockport 13, 36, 48
Rockville 13, 24, 137
Rocky Hollow Nature Preserve
    25
Rodin 118
Rogers III, Capt. William C. 48
Rogers, Will 115
Rome City 111
Roosevelt, President 63
Rorem, Ned 114, 138
Rose, Axle 69
Rose, DeVon 54
Rose, Fred 136
Rosedale 132
Roselawn 57

Ross, Jerry 120, 131
Roth, David Lee 137
Roush, Edd J. 101, 133
Roussillon, Alice 33, 110
Roussillon, Gaspard 33
Rudolph, Wilma 105
Rush County 13
Rush, Dr. Benjamin 13
Rushville 13, 85, 135
Rusie, Amos 102, 134
Russiaville 121
Ruth, Babe 84
Ryan, Cong. Leo 125
Ryan, Tom Kreusch 134

S

Saarinen, Eero 50
Saarinen, Eliel 50
Safety-Kleen Corporation 22
Sain, John 119
Salem 13, 57, 59, 137
Salisbury 136
Samuelson, Paul Anthony 122,
    134
Sandcut 135
Sanders, Colonel Harland 80
Sandusky 89
Sanger, Alice B. 43
Santa Claus 49, 58, 60
Santa's Country 58
Sargent, Å.K. 67
Savage, Eugene Francis 132
Schenkel, Chris 136
Schmitz, Bruno 46
Scholl, William "Billy" 81
School of Industry 129
Schreiber, Ken 101
Schulz, "Germany" 133
Scott, Blanche (Betty) Stuart 60,
    78, 138
Scott County 13, 27
Scott, Everett "Deacon" 138
Scott, Gov. Charles 13
Scottish Rite Cathedral 52
Scottsburg 13
Seagram, Joseph. E. 83
Sears Tower 131
Seaton, George 65, 133

Selective Service Program 46
Selvage, Carrie T. 123
Sennett, Mack 63, 134
Seymour 23, 26, 122, 137
Shades State Park 24
Sharp, Zerna A. 136
Shaw, Wilbur 97, 138
Shawnee Indians 6, 31
Shelby County 13
Shelby, Gov. Isaac 13
Shelbyville 13, 60, 97, 136, 138
Shepherd Jean 65
Shipsewana 127
Shirley, George 133
Shoals 13, 18, 27
Shoals Jug Rox 90
Shortridge High School 112
Shoup, Col David 47, 139
Shrewsbury Home 51
Sissle, Noble 69, 135
Skelton, Red 68, 135
Skylab 84
Slipher, Vesto 138
Sloan, Todd 136
Slocum, Frances 32
Smith, Andrew 104
Smith, Caleb B. 37
Smith, Connie 136
Smith, David 132
Smith, Walter Bedell 137
Smithsonian Institute 74
Smogor, Mrs. Erwin J. 121
Socialist Party of the United States
    40
Soldiers and Sailors Monument
    46
Sonotabac Indian Mound 30
Sousa, John Philip 53, 61
South Bend 9, 13, 23, 33, 46, 60,
    62, 65, 75, 76, 79, 119, 121,
    132, 133, 134, 135, 137, 138,
    139
South Raub 133, 135
South Side High 88
South Wind Maritime 10
Spencer 13, 16, 23, 135
Spencer, Capt. Spear 13
Spencer County 13, 14
Spring Creek Seeps 25
Spring Mill State Park 120
Squire Boone Caverns 18

St. Clair, Gen. Arthur 34
St. John the Divine Cathedral 83
St. Joseph County 13
St. Louis 134
St. Meinrad 132
Standard Oil Company 77
Stark, Gen. John 13
Starke County 13, 14
Stein, Jules 70, 133
Steinbeck, John 111
Stendal 134
Stephens, Stephen 39
Stephenson, D.C. 40
Stern, Daniel 65
Steuben County 13, 25, 46, 137
Steuber, Robert 104
Stinesville 28
Stokely-Van Camp 80
Stout, Rex Todhunter 112, 139
Stoutsburg Savanna 25
Strauss, Juliet 24
Strowger, Almon 80, 138
Studebaker, Clement and Henry 75
Studebaker Corporation 76
Studebaker, J.M. 57
Studebaker National Museum 76
Studebaker, P.E. 36
Sugar Creek 24
Sukilovich, Malden 64
Sullivan 13, 66, 134, 138
Sullivan County 13
Sullivan, Daniel 13
Sumner, James 122
Swanson, Gloria 117
Swarthout, Merlin 88
Switzerland 13
Switzerland County 13
Sylvan Lake 111

T

Tabriz 133
Taggart Baking Company 82
Taggart, Thomas 52, 56
Taliaferro, George 104
Tarkington, Booth 114, 136
Tarzan Zerbini International
    Circus 67

Tavener, John 104
Taylor, Chuck 96, 134
Taylor, Elizabeth 113
Taylor, Marshall "Major" 106
Teague, Walter D. 139
Tecumseh, Chief 31, 35, 44
Tell City 59, 73, 132
Tell City Pretzel Company 73
Terre Haute 9, 13, 23, 43, 50, 81,
    102, 118, 124, 131, 132, 133,
    134, 136, 137, 138
Terre Haute County 81
Tesich, Steve 65, 66
Tharp, Twyla 116, 135
The Aeronautical Society of
    America 78
The Elkhart Truth 83
The Johns-Manville Corporation
    79
Thomas, Jesse Brooks 39
Thomas, Kurt 132
Thomas, Lowell 127
Thompson, James Maurice 33, 91,
    110
Thompson, Richard W. 37
Thompson, Sam 102, 132
Tinder, Judge John D. 21
Tinguely, Jean 50
Tippecanoe Battlefield Monument
    25
Tippecanoe County 13, 26
Tippecanoe River 13
Tipton 13
Tipton County 13
Tipton, Sen. John 13
Toran, Stacey 89
Tornado Alley 28
Treaty 133
Tree City Fall Festival 54
Trester, Arthur 96, 134
Trout, "Dizzy" 135
Troy 36
Tucker, Forrest Meredith 131
Turkey Run 24
Turkey Trot Festival 57
Tuttle, Lurene 136
Tyson, Mike 106

U

Underground Railroad 29, 48
Unified Government Bill 51
Unigov 51
Union County 13, 25
Union Station 86
United Nations of the Poultry
    World 79
United States Steel Corporation
    77
Urey, Harold Clayton 133
Usher, John P. 37

V

Valentino 117
Valentino, Rudolph 66
Valparaiso 13, 120, 136, 138
Valparaiso University 127
Van Arsdale, Dick 132
Van Arsdale, Tom 132
Van Buren Elm 38
Van Camp, Gilbert 80, 139
Van Camp Packing Company 80
Van Halen 137
Van Vleck, John 122
Vanderburgh County 13
Vanderburgh, Judge Henry 13
Vandivier, Robert 95
Verdi 116
Vermillion County 13
Vermillion River 13
Vernon 13, 135
Versailles 13
Vevay 13, 110, 135, 139
Vigo County 13
Vigo, Francis 13
Villa, Pancho 110
Vincennes 13, 23, 30, 32, 34, 41,
    60, 68, 133, 135, 139
Vincennes Alices 90
Vincennes, Sieur de 33
Vincennes University 110
Virgil I. Grissom State Memorial
    120
von Steuben, Baron Freidrich 13
Von Tilzer, Albert 72, 132
Von Zell, Harry 135

Vonnegut, Bernard 121, 136
Vonnegut, Kurt , Jr. 112, 138
Voss, Janice 120, 137

W

Wabash 13, 53, 132, 136, 139
Wabash & Erie Canal 50, 51, 58
Wabash County 13
Wabash River 13, 25, 137
Wagner, Honus 84
Wakarusa 127
Wakefield, Dan 134
Walk of Legends 52
Walker, C. J. 82
Walkerton 133
Wallace, Ben 67
Wallace, David 39
Wallace, Lew 110, 112, 113, 116, 133
Walnut Cathedral 24
"Wanted—Dead or Alive" 62
Ward, Mary Jane 136
Warhol 118
Warner Bros. 63
Warren County 13
Warren, Dr. Joseph 13
Warren, Michael 132
Warrick, Capt. Jacob 13
Warrick County 13, 14
Warsaw 13, 44, 89
Washington County 13, 27, 59
Washington, George 13
Watson, Glenda 54
Waveland 24
Wawaka 101, 139
Way, Amanda 42
Wayne County 6, 13
Wayne, Gen. "Mad Anthony" 13, 34
Wea 6, 31

Webb, Clifton 64, 138
Weber, Dick 139
Wells County 13
Wells, W.R. Clifford 95, 132
Wells, William 13
West Baden 56
West Baden Hotel 56
West Franklin 48
West, Jessamyn 112, 135
West Lafayette 78
West Point 58
Westfield 48
Whig Rifle 85
White, Col. Isaac 13
White County 13
White River 27, 137
White, Ryan 119, 121, 139
Whitewater Canal 51, 86
Whitewater Valley Railroad 86
Whiting 22, 77
Whitley County 13
Whitley, William 13
Whitney 139
Whittredge, Thomas W. 118
Wickard, Claude R. 37
Wiley, Harvey Washington 138
William Conner Estate 55
William IV of Orange, Prince 13
Williams, Deniece 69, 134
Williams, Donald E. 120, 131
Williams, James D. 35
Williams v. Smith 42
Williamsburg 138
Williamson, Fred 132
Williamsport 13, 50
Willkie, Wendell 37, 126, 132
Willson, Byron Forceythe 108
Wilson, Gilbert 118
Winamac 13, 89
Winchester 13, 30, 64
Wingate 89
Winona Lake 134
Wirt, William A. 131

Wise, Robert 64
Wolcott 128
Wolcottville 62, 135
Wolf, David A. 120, 136
Wolf Park 26
Wolfe, Nero 139
Women's Rights Society 42
Wonder Bread 82
Wood, Linda 121
Wooden, John Robert 95, 137
Woodfill, 1st Lt. Samuel 47
Woodfill, W. Stewart 136
Woodville 138
Woolman, C. E. 78
Workingmen's Insitute 129
Worley, Jo Anne 68
Worst-Dressed Women 64
Wright, Frances 129
Wright, Frank Lloyd 64
Wright, Mary 117
Wright, Wilbur 133
Wyandot Indians 6, 31
Wyandotte Cave 19

Y

Yaeger, Chuck 78
Yellowwood State Forest 11
Yorktown 131

Z

Ziegler Woods 25
Zion Evangelical Lutheran Church 113
Zionsville 23
Zoeller, Fuzzy 138

PHOTO CREDITS

Auburn-Cord-Duesenberg Museum: 75

Chuck Berry Music, Inc.: 124

©James Dean Foundation under license authorized by Curtis Management Group, Indianapolis, Indiana, USA: 63

Detroit Free Press: 71

Falls of the Ohio State Park: 16

Richard Fields/Indiana Department of Natural Resources: 19, 25

Hillerich & Bradsby Co./Lin Caufield: 84

Historic New Harmony, Inc: 129

Courtesy Historic Landmarks Foundation of Indiana/Piero Madar: 125

IMS Photo by Ron McQueeney: 97

Indiana Division of Tourism: 17, 21

Indiana High School Basketball Hall of Fame: 90

Indiana Historical Society Library (Negative No. LP3-Madison-Shrewsbury House): 51

Indiana State Library: 10, 35, 38, 41, 42, 44, 50, 56, 77, 83, 86. 102, 109, 111, 123, 126

Indiana State University, Sports Information: 92

Indiana University, Sports Information: 91

The Indianapolis Project/Delores Wright: 8, 46, 52, 59, 94, 106

Lincoln Boyhood National Memorial: 36

McCaffrey & McCall/David Stanton: 127

National Baseball Library, Cooperstown, N.Y.: 100, 101

National Park Service/Indiana Dunes National Lakeshore: 55

NBC Television Network: 68, 72

Northern Indiana Historical Society: 33

Parke County Convention and Visitors Bureau: 14

Orville Redenbacher: 81

The Ryan White Foundation: 121

Woodrow Wilson Junior High School/Linda Hill: 118